MASSACRE AT TOBRUK

Massacre at Tobruk

The story of Operation Agreement

PETER C. SMITH

With a Foreword by
Lieutenant-Colonel E. H. W. Unwin,
Royal Marines

WILLIAM KIMBER · LONDON

First published in 1987 by
WILLIAM KIMBER & CO. LIMITED
100 Jermyn Street, London, SW1Y 6EE

© Peter C. Smith, 1987

ISBN 0 – 7183 – 0664 – 3

Typeset by Grove Graphics, Tring
and printed in Great Britain by
Redwood Burn Limited
Trowbridge, Wiltshire

For

Dawn Tracey

*My beautiful and talented daughter —
and also the best author in the family!*

Contents

List of Illustrations

List of Illustrations

MAPS IN THE TEXT

Foreword

by Lieutenant-Colonel E. H. M. Unwin, Royal Marines

My memories of Operation Agreement are not exactly happy ones. What was supposed to have been a night operation had, due to circumstances, to be conducted during daylight. When the destroyer *Sikh* was sunk I spent twelve hours in the water before being taken by the Germans, who had to protect us from the enraged Italians. I then spent three-and-half grim years as a POW. It seemed to me that plans for our operation were already in the hands of the Axis because during my interrogation the Germans asked me why my force had arrived late!

I was what was known as a 'Blue' Marine. That is to say, when I joined the Corps it was as a Royal Marine Artillery officer as distinct from the Royal Marine Light Infantry, the 'Red' Marines. It was not until the economies in the aftermath of World War I that the two were combined as simply Royal Marines. In any event I first saw service aboard the monitor *Lord Clive* and I fired the first salvoes from two 12-inch guns in the twin turret.

Later I went out to the Middle East in another monitor and served at the bombardment of Gaza during the Palestine Campaign bombarding the Turkish army ashore.

I witnessed my second war in the same area, the Greek–Turkish Anatolian conflict, this time from the decks of the battleship *Marlborough*, including the burning of Smyrna in September 1922. Operation Agreement seemed to me to be yet another British battle planned from Shepheards Hotel in Cairo!

When I first took command of the 11th Battalion they were at Arborfield in Berkshire awaiting embarkation for the Middle East. We went to Portsmouth and sailed from there for the Mediterranean. Half the unit was lost at Crete but we never got there. Instead, after a stay in Egypt, we did a lot of training in the Lebanon prior to the actual operation. I remember the dummy run for the landing, which took place on a small islet off Cyprus. Coming in from the sea things went amiss and I ended up being shot

11

at by our own forces. Nobody had told the local defence and they
started banging off at us! This certainly gave me a taste of what we
were in for. Unfortunately there proved no time for further practice
to take place so there was no opportunity to test the real landing
barges we were to use; they were still being built.

I can remember a Scottish officer approaching me at Cairo and
asking me to take him on the operation as he was an expert folbotist
and was just what I needed to make the operation a success. He was
grandly attired in full kilt and so on, but I recalled the old Royal
Marine saying that the two worse things to take in a boat were an
umbrella and a naval officer, so I declined his services! On the other
hand I lost my driver in the landing, a splendid fellow. A short time
before we sailed he said please could he come with us. I told him
there was no need for him to do so but he particularly wanted to
come, so he did and never returned.

The plan was to hold the docks at Tobruk for twenty-four hours,
but we felt we were expected to win the war that night! We only had
small arms of course, but we *could* have done a great deal. We had
a battalion of Marines and a battalion of soldiers, SAS and people
like that, who had a splendid chap commanding them called
Haselden. He was killed in action that night.

I know we had bad luck but I think we would have got away with
the bad luck if the enemy had not been alerted before we landed. I
remember saying to the RAF at the Cairo briefings, if you want to
help me with your bombing then kill all the Germans; but if you
want to give me the *most* help of all then stay in your perishing beds
and don't make a sound! But they didn't so the Germans were all
up and dressed and ready for us when we arrived.

The guns that actually sank *Sikh* were the German 88's. Their
shells went through her hull like butter. We were picked up by
searchlights long before we hit the beach. I had to make a decision
then whether to go with the landing or withdraw. We decided to go
on.

I was something of a yachtsman and in my opinion the landing
craft that were constructed for our use in this operation were a
disgrace, badly designed and poorly built. They did not stand up to
the conditions of sea and weather that night and contributed much
to our failure to get all the Royal Marines ashore. I don't recall the
swell being particularly heavy however; at any rate it was not so
great as to put me off. They did not have hinged bow ramps like
later landing craft, we were just supposed to clamber over the side.

We hit the shore in daylight, another time when I thought about cancelling the operation but it was rather too late by then. It had been planned as a night operation. And on top of that we found we had been landed in the wrong place. They talk about cliffs but they were only small cliffs, rocky but not very high.

I had managed to get a set of long khaki trousers for all the men on that night instead of our more normal shorts. They were warmer at night and you didn't get bitten by mosquitoes, scorpions and the like, but I lost most of my clothes before I was picked up.

We didn't see much of the Italians during the battle but afterwards they went through my pockets and stole everything that I had. The Germans were very correct, absurdly so really. And in fact we were eventually moved by the Germans from the Italians and driven into a German prison camp. Eventually I walked the length of Italy and up into Germany, from camp to camp. The food was very poor but considering that we were doing everything we could to stop food getting through that is not surprising and I don't blame them for it. But in some ways they were daft people, we couldn't understand how they acted, blind obedience. Once the POW's were playing volleyball and one of the prisoners strayed over the single ankle-high warning wire strand inside the main perimeter. The guard shot at him, missed, then quite deliberately re-loaded, took aim and shot the man dead for this simple offence. Just because their orders were to stop anyone from crossing this line. Most of the Army people were fine but they were all scared stiff of the SS of course.

By the last days of the war things changed abruptly and all our personal belongings were suddenly returned to us, including my fountain pen which had been 'lost' some considerable time before!

It all seems a very long time ago now, but many of my splendid battalion fought like lions that night. Their memory fully deserves preserving for posterity. Peter Smith's book does that very well indeed.

Amesbury Abbey, Wiltshire. March, 1987.

Acknowledgements

The completion of a book of this nature owes much to the kindness of former participants in the battle who were generous enough to share their recollections and memoirs of that fateful night with me. Their kindness in allowing me to use their stories to illuminate my researches into half-forgotten documents makes the story of Operation Agreement complete and shows how the human spirit can overcome even the darkest despair and the deepest tragedies. For their help and graciousness I would therefore like to offer sincere thanks to the following. (Their connections with the night of 13th/14th September 1942 are given in brackets after their names for convenience only.)

The late Hans-Otto Behrendt (Afrika Korps Intelligence Officer); Major Con Mahoney (Royal Marines); J. J. Fallon (Royal Marines); W. Fraser (Long Range Desert Group); E. A. Graham (Army Film Unit); Ronald Hill (Long Range Desert Group); D. Hutchins (Long Range Desert Group); F. Gordon Harrison (Long Range Desert Group); Jim Patch (Long Range Desert Group and Secretary of the thriving LRDG Association); Leslie Stevenson (HMS *Coventry*); Rev Donald L. Peyton Jones (HMS *Coventry*); Claude Nice (HMS *Coventry*); Fred Foyle (HMS *Zulu*); W. Wright (HMS *Sikh*); Nigel West (author on British Intelligence); 'Tug' Wilson (HMS *Sikh*); Gerd Stamp (Pilot LG.1); F. McCall, for making available the contemporary notes of Lieutenant-Commander A. H. L. Harvey, DSC (HMS *Croome*).

I would also like to thank the following historians and organisations for their help in tracking down obscure sources and thin leads and helping me discover rare details before they vanished for ever. My old friend Edwin R. Walker, as always a mine of information and wisdom; the ever helpful and willing staff of Bedford Central Library, exceptional and outstanding in their co-operation; Colonel Arnaldo Ceccato, Stato Maggiore Dell'Aeronautica, Ufficio Storico, Rome, for Italian War Diaries; M. McAloon, Naval Historical Section, MOD; Herr Baldes and

Herr Meyer of the Bundesarchiv-Militararchiv at Aachen and Freiburg, for German War Diaries, Maps and documents; H. Dodsworth of the *Sikh* Survivors' Group.

Peter C. Smith

Riseley, Bedford. March, 1987.

CHAPTER ONE

Giving up Tobruk

Fortress Tobruk! How different becomes the name of any town given the emotive prefix 'Fortress', deserved or not. Down through the long history of warfare sieges and impregnable strongholds have been the very essence of battle and bloody conflict. From Troy to Stalingrad, from grand custom-built warrior-towns like Sebastopol to strange and unheard-of little smudges on obscure maps, Kut, Mafeking and, for the British population in the Second World War, a small, drab little port in the desert-girted Italian colony of Cyrenaica, Tobruk.

The bombastic and vainglorious Benito Mussolini, Duce of the unwarlike Italian nation and leader of its dictatorship, finally had to make good his years of boasting and bragging and declared that his country was at war with Great Britain. He did this, certain in his own mind that Italy would not have to fight very hard. The time was June 1940, and Britain seemed to be already on her knees. His Axis partner, Adolf Hitler, had in a few short years forged the German nation into a military machine of unprecedented power and strength. Using a combination of the natural German flair for warfare, a good industrial base and the supra-nationalistic fervour of the nation whipped up by relentless propaganda, the Nazi armies had relied also on fresh ideas and innovation to overcome every one of its enemies. It did this by conducting lightning campaigns, Blitzkrieg, that lasted weeks instead of years, and which brought proud old nations crashing to their knees in surrender almost before they realised they were at war.

Mobility was the key to these early German victories, the combination of tank and dive-bomber giving their armies hitherto undreamt of versatility in which the ability to stun and numb the opposition played as large a part as the ability to both outmanoeuvre and then develop their slow-moving or static defences. Thus they quickly defeated Poland, Norway, the Netherlands, Belgium and France and the British were driven into the sea.

In such fluid warfare sieges appeared to be a thing of the past but the English Channel proved too wide for the Panzers and Stukas to bridge in one quick movement and so the siege of England began with U-boat and long-range bomber. Initially, however, in the crash and wreck of a continent, it was not expected that such a long war would be required. Britain, witnessing the ruthless efficiency of the German armed forces and the destruction of all her allies, was expected to sue for peace while she was still able.

Invasion, thought Hitler, was both unnecessary and, for him, distasteful. The whole conquest of western Europe was but a prelude, a necessary chore, to his main and burning ambition, the destruction of the Soviet Union. He freely admitted that he had no wish to smash the British Empire as long as he had a free hand in the East. But to his brittle fellow dictator in the south, who had seen his own pale star totally eclipsed by the German upstart, the imminent defeat of Britain seemed to give him a fleeting opportunity to grab his share of the world stage and further his own cause of Mediterranean expansion by hitting Britain while she was down. He reckoned without two things, the will of the new British prime minister, Winston Churchill, and the Royal Navy. Mussolini quickly found that he was blocked by one and thwarted, and then frequently humiliated, by the other.

At sea in the Mediterranean Italy's larger fleet was put to flight so frequently by small British naval squadrons operating from the two extremities of Gibraltar and Alexandria in Egypt, that it became almost a laughing stock. On land the Duce's grand advance from Libya into Egypt was turned into a rout, with tens of thousands of Italian prisoners and very few Italian dead, as his much-vaunted legions raised their hands and voted with their feet. It was not until the Germans took a grip early in 1941, with the arrival of the Luftwaffe in Sicily and a small mobile force under a dynamic and ambitious young general, Erwin Rommel, that things changed. At sea the Stuka dive bombers did in a few days what the whole Italian fleet had failed to do for six months; close the Sicilian Channel to heavy warships and make each supply convoy to the only centrally-placed British base, Malta, a hazardous business. On land the Blitzkrieg tactics in miniature were applied by one of its masters with a rare and wily skill and proved just as efficient. Thus it was the British army's turn to be bundled out and along the North African coast.

Logistics now dominated the war in Libya for the next eighteen months. Could the Axis land forces, poised to make the final spring to the Suez Canal and Cairo, be supplied across the narrow central Mediterranean sea routes faster than the numerically superior British forces using the long sea routes via the Cape of Good Hope? Each side built up its forces to a level which its commander felt might prove decisive and then attacked. Meanwhile its opponent husbanded its strength between battles and prepared to make a counter-strike. Thus a ding-dong struggle raged constantly up and down the coastal strip. When the Germans went through the Balkans with the same speed and efficiency that they had moved through France, their northern flank was secured with the conquest of Yugoslavia, Greece and Crete. The Aegean islands were already Italian. The British retained only their toe-holds in Egypt and Malta.

Thus mobile warfare took on a new meaning, for the desert was a strictly neutral and very harsh environment across which the two armies fought and circled and sparred and frequently clashed. Away from the coastal zone and the solitary roadway, the grandly named Via Balbia which ran the length of Italian Libya, the interior was stark desert and rock with great sand seas that were impassable to most vehicles and which formed great barriers for armies. Only small clandestine units could pass hidden through it from oasis to oasis on secret missions against the enemy rear areas.

Hemmed in by the Mediterranean to the north and the sand seas to the south the variations on a theme that could be adopted by the contesting armies were limited. He who held the most supply ports could build up stocks of vital petrol, food, water and ammunition at a greater rate than his opponent. Therefore the control of these hitherto unremarkable and almost unknown harbours became the crucial link-pin of the land campaigns. Malta was *the* thorn in the side of the Axis and strikes by submarines, naval and RAF torpedo bombers and, from time-to-time, naval surface striking forces, kept up a constant cull of the vital mercantile oil-tankers that kept Rommel's tanks mobile.

The Germans and Italians had two choices here: they could try and keep Malta subdued by continual bombing or they could invade and put an end to its intervention once and for all. The trouble was that with over ninety per cent of the German army and most of the Luftwaffe busy in Russia little could be spared to do either chore completely efficiently. For Britain the North African war was the *main* battle front to continue their limited role in the war. For Hitler and his legions it was but an irritating side-show of little significance other than to keep his bumbling ally in the war. For Mussolini it was the final front from which he might yet salvage some vestige of his shattered pride, because the rest of his African Empire had already fallen. The difference in each nation's attitude should be realised when assessing the desert struggle.

When the Luftwaffe was switched from the Eastern Front to Malta it quickly subdued that island, although it never vanquished it totally, but when the Stukas returned to the Crimea and the Volga fronts fresh British convoys fought their way through, fresh fighter aircraft were flown in and Malta revived. The plans for the parachute landing to occupy the island, Operation Hercules, were discussed, abandoned, dusted down, abandoned again and again and finally never took place.

During the long period of German ascendancy in North Africa, however, one port held out, although surrounded by the sweep of the Axis advance, and this was Tobruk. It dug itself in behind barbed wire, trenches and minefields and was supplied by sea for many long months. As it was the only land battle they were engaged in, it was a natural focal point for the British people (and also for the Australians whose soldiers contributed the major part of the defence) to identify with. Tobruk quickly became firstly a newspaper lead story and then a legend, and the longer it held out the greater the legend grew.

The British premier had an almost mystic faith in fortresses, even when they were not fortresses in the accepted sense of the word, and he was for ever urging commanders to stand firm, and fight to the last man to defend towns or areas which were largely indefensible. In this mania he was almost identical in thought, word and deed to his opposite number in Berlin. Churchill's obsession with 'Fortress' Singapore led to the greatest disaster to British arms in the whole war while Hitler's similar myopic view of the need to take Stalingrad had an equally traumatic effect on Germany's war.

Thus the volatile British premier became identified with Tobruk's heroic defence. When it was finally relieved, after 242 days, there was great rejoicing. (The British tradition for such events is a long one going back through Ladysmith in the Boer War, Kabul and Kandahar on the North-West Frontier and even more remote sieges.) Rommel renewed his offensive in the spring of 1942, once again outthinking and outfighting his numerically superior opponent and sending the Eighth Army streaming back down the coast road towards the frontier.

In Whitehall it was confidently expected that the British garrison at Tobruk would once more retreat into itself, batten down the hatches and again carry on against the odds until the tide turned. It was all the more of a shock, to both nation and indignant Prime Minister, when this 'invincible' fortress fell to a combined Stuka/Panzer thrust of the old type in a matter of a few short days. Having just survived a Motion of Censure in the House of Commons on the Government's conduct (or misconduct) of the war, Churchill was in no mood to passively accept the easy surrender of yet another token of British pride! His obvious anguish and anger came through, both at the time and also retrospectively in his memoirs.

On 14th June he had telegraphed General Sir Claude Auchinleck, then British C-in-C, Middle East: 'Presume there is no question in any case of giving up Tobruk.'

The general's response was not to the premier's liking, being merely a general assurance that although he had no intention of allowing the Eighth Army to become besieged there he was not surrendering Tobruk. Churchill wanted a firmer commitment than that and, on 15th June, he sent another cable winging on its way: 'War Cabinet interpret your telegram to mean that, if the need arises, General Ritchie would have as many troops in Tobruk as are necessary to hold the place for certain.'

When, on 20th June, Rommel's attack went in from the east and the fortress fell while its 50,000-strong garrison surrendered, Churchill was bitterly dismayed. He described the surrender in his memoirs as a 'shattering and grievous loss'.

Once the fortress so dear to his heart had been lost he was full of resolve to somehow get it back, or, failing that, ensure that the Axis had no use and no joy of it. Neither the German and Italian defenders, nor the Allied commanders back at Cairo, were to get any peace on the issue until such a blow had been struck.

*

The Axis themselves knew full well what a prize the port was to their cause. For a start they captured huge stocks of Allied stores completely intact, '. . . supplies for 30,000 men for three months . . .', which in themselves were worth several convoys to their armies. The German General Westphal, Chief of Staff, German Armies in the West, was frank about such an unexpected windfall:

Without this booty adequate rations and clothing for the armoured divisions would not have been possible in the coming months. Stores arriving by sea had only on one occasion – in April 1942 – been enough to supply the army for one month.

As well as stores the Germans also took possession (despite Churchill's claims that *all* petrol stocks had been destroyed) of 10,000 cubic metres of petrol, which was the very life-blood of a highly mechanised army like Erwin Rommel's Afrika Korps. The Führer too realised the immense importance possession of Tobruk had in bringing the Axis advance in North Africa to a swift and successful conclusion. He wrote to Mussolini that:

> In Tobruk the port installations are almost intact. You now possess, Duce, an auxiliary base whose significance is all the greater because the English themselves have built from there a railway leading almost into Egypt.

Mussolini needed no convincing. He had already ordered a suitable white horse be found to enable him to take the victory salute in Cairo! So Operation Hercules was cancelled and Rommel rushed on to cross the Egyptian frontier on 24th June and three days later smashed the next British defence line at Mersa Matruh. The British now high-tailed it back to the El Alamein position, only forty miles from Alexandria itself. This was the final sticking point. Cairo, the Suez Canal and indeed the whole British position in the Middle East now rested on this final line.

Having seen Rommel, at the end of his strength, dash himself in vain against this final obstacle and then reeling back themselves in the failure to reverse the position in the abortive counter-attack of 18th and 26th July, the British, as did Rommel, prepared for another final blow. Rommel's final throw came a month later and, at the bloody battle of Alam el Halfa, this gamble also failed. Both sides had poured in reinforcements at an unprecedented rate in readiness for their respective offensives. It was a race which the British, with the vast power-house of American industry behind them, were to win hands down. In addition there came the penalties for failure, and this period also saw the appointment of a new overall Army Commander, General Alexander taking over from Auchinleck on 15th August and, two days earlier, a new commander of the Eighth Army, General Bernard Montgomery, was appointed.

It can be said that the desperate days between the fall of Tobruk and the first battle at El Alamein, when between 1st and 5th July Rommel's last gasp rush was held, marked the absolute nadir of the British position in North Africa and the Middle East. And not only on land; at sea Admiral Sir Henry Harwood, the naval C-in-C who had taken over from the ever-victorious Cunningham, had seen his fleet decimated in a series of disastrous attempts to relieve Malta. Operation Vigorous in June had been a ghastly failure: the ships had been forced to turn back after days of heavy bombing when the Italian fleet sailed to interpose itself between the convoy and Malta. This was owing to the fact that the Royal Navy had no battleships left on the station to contest matters. Had they had, the Italians would not have been so bold. Nor did Harwood have any aircraft-carriers to help redress the loss of heavy ships while the RAF striking forces proved ineffective in deterring the enemy fleet. Failures, whether beyond his control or not, were marked up against the unfortunate admiral and Churchill's earlier championship of him had by now turned sour. We shall examine this further, but meanwhile at sea the need to strike decisive blows to negate the Axis build-up became the predominant issue for the remnants of the Mediterranean Fleet, which had by now been reduced to a few cruisers and two under-strength destroyer flotillas.

Not surprisingly then, a string of prodding signals began to emanate from the Admiralty, signed by the First Sea Lord but, as all knew, instigated by the premier himself. They urged 'Action This Day' and a series of wild and desperate measures to be taken both to sever the enemy convoy routes, even though there was no prospect of Allied air cover to the ships involved, and to block the Axis ports of disembarkation, Tripoli, Benghazi, Derna and, closest to the front line, Tobruk.

The blocking of the enemy ports had always been a favourite idea with Churchill and his advisors, although not with the Navy, either in Whitehall or Alexandria. This theme had constantly raised its head in the past and continued to fascinate the premier eager for a spectacular operation. He was quite prepared to sacrifice both ships and crews if he felt the result was worthwhile and the blocking of Benghazi or Tripoli was worth one of Britain's few battleships in his mind.

When Admiral Andrew Cunningham had been C-in-C Mediterranean Fleet in 1940 and 1941 he had stoutly resisted such schemes, and this had not earned him any points with Churchill, despite his outstanding leadership and a string of positive victories at sea. Thus on 15th April 1941 Cunningham received a long message from the Admiralty telling him that 'drastic measures' were necessary and that it was vital that Axis communications with North Africa had to be disrupted for a considerable period. They therefore told him that 'an attempt must be made to carry out a combined blocking and bombardment, the latter being carried out by the blocking ships at point-blank range.' He was told that the sacrificial lambs were to be one of his only three battleships, *Barham*, and an old 6-inch light cruiser *Caledon*.

The message concluded: 'Rather than damage several ships in a bombardment of doubtful value, the deliberate sacrifice of a ship to achieve something really worth while is considered preferable, although doubtless you will regret this use of *Barham*.' The whole thing, said Cunningham in his memoirs, was 'apparently dictated by somebody who appeared to know little of Tripoli, or to have any true realization of our circumstances in the Mediterranean.'

Cunningham fought this mad scheme from first to last, pointing out the hazards, the loss of a first-class fighting ship, the fillip this would give to Italian morale, the possible loss of over 1,000 highly skilled officers and men, the unlikelihood of a complete block being achieved, the difficulties of even approaching and positioning such a force through the shallow waters off the harbour, the minefields and the continual air attacks from nearby airfields. In vain! On 27th April, after a successful bombardment of the port by the whole Mediterranean Fleet, the prime minister himself directly intervened and wrote a personal letter to Cunningham haranguing him on his duty and responsibilities. Cunningham sensibly ignored it!

But the concept of hopeless sacrifice did not die in Whitehall. With the British retreat in the summer of 1942 it was hauled out again and resulted, on 21st July, in Harwood receiving the following signal (originated at 0209 which indicated Churchill's presence behind it) from Admiral Sir Dudley Pound.

Have you considered sending one destroyer to shoot up anything in Tobruk Harbour with HE at dawn when it is known that a convoy has just arrived there? Admittedly this is a desperate measure but the destruction of a convoy at the present time would in my opinion justify the possible loss of a destroyer.

This message is even more incredible in view of what had happened to a British destroyer flotilla a scant two months earlier in an abortive attempt to intercept the Axis convoys. This had come badly to grief in May, with the destruction of the destroyers *Jackal*, *Kipling* and *Lively*, which had been caught and quickly sunk in the eastern basin by the Junkers Ju88 bombers of LG1 based in Crete during a futile and pointless attempt to attack a convoy that did not exist! Everyone felt badly about this waste of valuable modern destroyers and their crews, especially Admiral Pound, but the lesson was seemingly not really digested, nor did it ultimately stop the sacrifice of two more such vessels plus a cruiser, which were to be sacrificed in the self-same manner just to show that something, however useless, was being done.

The hysteria was by no means confined to London. In Cairo a similar nervous expectancy prevailed at this time for to many it was only a matter of time before Afrika Korps tanks were expected in the city streets! Fitzroy Maclean gave the picture as he saw it:

> In Cairo the staff at GHQ Middle East were burning their files and the Italian colony were getting out their black shirts and Fascist badges in preparation for Mussolini's triumphant entry.

It was with the background of 'Ash Wednesday' and the prevalent mood of near panic that Operation Agreement first began to take shape.

*

The initial roots of the scheme are claimed to have originated with Captain David Stirling, leader of the small nucleus of what was to grow into that renowned fighting force, the Special Air Service. At that time it consisted of half-a-dozen officers and twenty other ranks, mainly from the disbanded 62 Commando and the Small Scale Raiding Force, and known as 'L' detachment. All the men were parachute-trained but in fact they only ever made one airborne attack. Normally they utilised specially modified jeeps, heavily armed with Browning machine guns, Lewis guns or Vickers K-guns. Stirling himself believed that small bands of dedicated men operating behind enemy lines could achieve much more than larger parties. Thus, despite their small numbers and independent working, they were a completely professional unit, as Stirling himself later made plain in a post-war newsletter to those who served under him:

When I gained permission to raise the SAS Unit I was
determined that we would be the best trained, smartest and most
highly disciplined soldiers in the Army. I insisted on this and as
the unit began so has the Regiment continued. Far from being
café gangsters, the men of the SAS exercised high standards of
security realising that their lives depended upon their keeping
their own counsel.

He added:

The desert SAS was not a collection of amateurs on 'safari', out
of sight of the orthodox army; every hour spent in action was
preceded by careful preparations. Each man had to be highly
trained in many trades and skills and there was no place for any
but individuals of high potential. There was not the time to spend
months in training men to the right point of efficiency and
competence as is possible with the peacetime Regular Army. We
had to make our initiating course exceedingly tough to eliminate
all but the very best material. If a man survived our full training
he was good and right for the purpose. By these same means we
exerted the very highest standards of discipline, of smartness and
of unit pride.

According to one version, given by Virginia Cowles in her history
of the regiment, the whole concept of the Operation Agreement
(which she, like the majority of other post-war writers, mistakenly
calls Operation Daffodil) started with David Stirling.

In July he had suggested taking a small party into Benghazi to
destroy shipping, on the same lines as his previous three attempts.
As an added fillip he had proposed that a small naval unit should
accompany him and try to block the mouth of the harbour with
a sunken ship. This last suggestion apparently had fired the
imagination of the planners and now the scheme had swollen
beyond recognition.

As we have seen, the concept of blocking Axis ports had 'fired the
imagination' of more senior persons than the Cairo staff officers and
for a much longer period than David Stirling's scheme. However his
idea may well have reintroduced the concept at local level and may
thus have been the essential kernel from which all else stemmed as

she suggests. Be that as it may, Stirling himself was quite perturbed by the scheme as rehashed and represented to him later.

Fitzroy Maclean relates how much enthusiasm there was at GHQ for a raid on Benghazi.

Much of the enthusiasm had been generated by Colonel John E. Haselden whom Cowles described as 'an Arab expert who for some time had been acting as a British agent behind the enemy lines.'

In fact John Haselden was the Egyptian-born son of mixed English-Greek parentage. He became a British Intelligence officer and, as a captain, he had guided in the special raiding force commanded by Lieutenant-Colonel R. E. Laycock, which had landed by submarine off Hanna in November 1941 in an abortive attempt to kill General Rommel at what was mistakenly thought to be his headquarters at Beda Littoria. The failure of this raid had not dampened Haselden's enthusiasm for behind-the-line attacks. He had gathered around him a little troop of specialists with particular skills: Captain Herbert Bray, for example, was a fluent German speaker and former Oxford University man, Lieutenant David Lanark, who was reputed to have been fluent in six German dialects and shadowy characters recruited from Palestine, former German nationals and anti-Nazis, who formed the SIG (Special Identification Group).

Another ex-Varsity man, this time Cambridge, was of Russian parentage although Belgian-born. This was Lieutenant-Colonel Vladimir Peniakoff (known as 'Popski'). Multi-lingual and a resident sugar-manufacturer in Egypt and with many contacts in the Arab world, he was commissioned into the Libyan Arab Force and he had a roving commission in the great wastes behind the fronts. He recorded his impression of the scheming and planning going on at this time at G (Plans) and MO4 Rooms, Middle Eastern GHQ thus: 'My sense of propriety was shocked at the light-hearted manner in which the problems were tackled: ten per cent planning, ninety per cent wishful thinking.'

The organisation that Peniakoff was enthusiastic about was the Long Range Desert Group. This had its origins in the reconnaissance work done by armoured car patrols during the First World War when vast areas of the desert were explored properly for the first time and mapped. This work was forgotten between the wars but some of the old skills were renewed by small parties of army and political officers based in Egypt who undertook their own surveys largely at their own initiative and own expense. When war with Italy broke out one of these officers, Ralph Bagnold, was serving at HQ in Cairo and volunteered his services and that of his former companions, William B. Kennedy Shaw, of the Palestine Civil Service, Pat Clayton of the Egyptian Survey Department, Teddy Mitford from the Royal Tank Regiment and Guy Prendergast. The enlightened commander of 7th Armoured Division, General P. Hobart, backed him and he became the first leader of this group.

These officers recruited men from the New Zealand Division and commandeered ten 30 cwt trucks from the Chevrolet Company in Alexandria and completed them to their own specifications. Then they formed three patrols, each of two officers and twenty-five NCOs and men. They had to be versatile to survive in the desert and the ability to navigate was as important as the skill to drive and fire a Lewis gun. They had to obtain theodolites and Nautical Almanacs, they had to be self-sufficient in stores and water, they had to familiarise themselves with the enemy so that they could report accurately what they found. Between August 1940 and April 1943 they roamed freely through those barren wastes and proved themselves invaluable, time and time again.

Gradually the group was expanded with fresh patrols formed from the Coldstream and Scots Guards under Michael Crichton-Stuart, a Yeomanry patrol under Pat McCraith and a Rhodesian patrol commanded by Gus Hilliman. A base was established at the oasis of Kufra with a forward base at Siwa oasis, both in the Libyan desert beyond the Great Sand Sea. From here they struck time and time again at the Italian rear areas and later they harassed the German forces as well. When Pat McCraith was wounded in one operation his place was taken by Lieutenant-Colonel David Lloyd Owen.

These were some of the special forces, and special men, around whom the land attack side of the attack on Tobruk was built, but the plan also included two seaborne assaults as well. Before describing the units assigned to take part in that part of the grand design let us follow the progression of thought from Stirling's original idea through its growth in scope and widening complexity.

Another plan that formed part of the origins of Operation Agreement had been proposed by Directorate of Combined Operations (Middle East) around this time. This involved yet another specialist force, the Special Boat Section. This had been formed as 101 Troop which was originated by Lieutenant Roger Courtney in Scotland in 1940 from 6 Commando. They were two-man teams of canoeists equipped with ten folbots. The lightweight canoes had buoyant bags fore and aft and a rubberised canvas skin stretched over a frame some 16ft overall and 2½ft at its widest. The plan was for each commando to have a team of thirty men so equipped, but Courtney had arrived in the Middle East in February 1941 with half that number and operated independently for the most part, conducting some daring and successful raids, including ones against airfields at Kastelli on 9/10th June 1942, and Heraklion on 13/14th June.

The DCO plan was for five or six teams of these SBS men and their canoes to be carried in three submarines to the approaches to Tobruk and there be launched. It was hoped their low silhouette would in itself evade detection and that these canoes would be able to penetrate into the harbour itself and attach limpet mines to any ships they found there. Once they had planted the mines they were to make good their escape and hug the coast back towards Alexandria, hiding up by day and proceeding at night until picked up by a force of fast MTBs from the coast south of Bardia. This scheme showed promise but was dropped due to lack of spare submarines. Many parts of it were to show up in the subsequent ramifications that led to Agreement however.

But by far the great-grandaddy of all the schemes for raiding Tobruk go back much further than either the original Stirling concept, Haselden's modifications of it or even the earlier DCO scheme with the folbots. This plan originated at the beginning of October 1940, and was to have been implemented the following spring. Not much mention is made of the existence of this plan; in fact it is mentioned by very few historians and seems to have been generally forgotten, probably because it never got further than planning stage.

At that early date the Planning Staff had only Italians to contend with, of course, but they estimated for the need for much greater British strength in order to carry it out than was budgeted for, or indeed possible, for Agreement two years later. The plan, although never put into effect, was very comprehensive and fully worked out. The objective was much the same, the destruction of the Italian oil and petrol reserves as well as the harbour facilities in order to cause maximum interference to the working of the port.

The known targets at that time were itemised as four large sunk oil tanks on the harbour front to the east of the Naval barracks which had a 32,000 ton capacity, four large benzine tanks 450 yards due north of the northern boundary of the aerodrome (there was only one at that time), petrol stores 300 yards north of the Arab village and a petrol dump at the junction of the El Adem road seven miles south of Tobruk. There was also a magazine 200 yards north of the centre of the aerodrome and explosives stored in a cage two miles WSW of the town. Other targets included the electric power station, wireless station and the distilling plant, all located centrally.

The Italian gun batteries in those days consisted of five of Coast Defence guns situated astride the harbour and one battery of two 5.9-inch guns 1,000 yards north of the Arab village. Two booms protected the harbour entrance, one running from Marsa Agaisa to the blockhouse on the northern shore and another from a point on the south shore 400 yards west of the Marsa Sciarafa to the coaling pier. There was also a local minefield at the harbour entrance. The Italian garrison was estimated at just over 17,000 men, with HQ Tenth Army (1,000 officers and men), HQ 22 Corps (200), the 4th Blackshirt Division (10,000) and 6,000 Frontier Guards.

The 1940 planners considered two alternative methods of attack: a lightning raid carried out under cover of darkness or a larger scale raid which might spill over into daylight hours. They reasoned that whichever method was chosen it would depend on achieving surprise. 'This might be achieved if the raiding party were conveyed in destroyers. If a transport or MT ships were included surprise would be difficult to achieve.' It was the lack of enough spare destroyers, even then when the Mediterranean Fleet was at a relatively high strength compared with its sorry state in 1942, that limited the scope of the operation.

They also concluded that, 'Without local fighter cover it would be difficult to maintain our position in Tobruk and the re-embarkation would be hazardous.' Two years later there was equally no chance of fighter cover being available to cover the ships and men by day and yet the risks, which seemed to rule such a scheme impracticable in 1940, were blithely accepted as worth taking in 1942!

This plan envisaged a striking force organised in four parties. Party 'A' would be one Special Service Company with a Detachment of Royal Engineers. They would land on the coast 1,600 yards west of Mengar el Merkah and destroy the petrol tanks north of the airfield, with the magazine and signal station as their secondary objectives. Party 'B' would be made up of an identical force and land at the same place, their job being the destruction of the oil fuel installations east of the Naval barracks with the airfield and aircraft parked there as their secondary targets. Party 'C' was again of the same composition but were to land at either Mersa Abd-Rabba or the Mersa Mrara area and take out the Coastal Defence battery north of the Arab village or the petrol store in the same area. Finally Party 'D' would be the 'Alarm and Despondency Squad' whose job was to cause the maximum havoc in the centre of town and keep the defenders busy while the others got on with their jobs. For this just one Special Service Company on their own would land at Mersa Mrara with carte blanche to destroy the power house, W/T station, telephone exchange, commandant's house and married quarters. All these groups were to be put ashore simultaneously and were to be lightly equipped; 'rubber-soled shoes, tommy guns, no packs'.

To put these four parties ashore a small naval squadron consisting of four destroyers, one submarine and four MTBs serving as smoke-laying vessels was necessary but as a major diversion the whole Mediterranean Fleet was to sail as if protecting a normal Malta convoy. When some 80 miles north of Bomba, one hour after dark, the raiding force would be detached from the fleet's escort and make for the Libyan coast about five miles west of Tobruk itself. Meanwhile, the submarine would have plotted an exact landfall and surface to mark the entry point for the destroyers. Each would rendezvous with the submarine then proceed independently to its landing area and under cover of the MTBs' smoke screen to disembark the troops in the landing boats. The MTBs were to have sailed as an independent group from either Egypt or Crete (which at that time was being used by British forces as Italy had declared war on her on 28th October 1940). Once the landing boats were rehoisted the destroyers were to stand out to sea until it was time to re-embark the raiders and depart.

It should be noted that two methods of getting the raiding parties ashore from the destroyers were considered. Firstly by service boats, ordinary ships' boats, extra numbers of which could be embarked by the destroyers selected and special davits fitted just for the one operation. The alternative was to use 'specially constructed punts which can be stacked on a destroyer's upper deck and paddled ashore.' It was this latter which was adopted. The planners stated quite specifically that a calm sea and a light northerly wind were a 'fundamental requirement for the success of the operation.' They estimated that a minimum of five hours would be required for the tasks to be completed with three and a half hours of complete darkness for the approach and landing. 'A period of seven days in each month between January and April meets the above requirement.'

Although surprise and stealth were the prime requisites at the start of the raid, once the cat was out of the bag both an air and a full naval bombardment was to be part of the withdrawal cover. It should be noted that the precision work was to be done *first*, and the air raid, which would bring up every Italian soldier for miles around, was not to be carried out until one full hour after the whole force had re-embarked and withdrawn, thus ensuring surprise. Quite the opposite was to apply in 1942 after two years of RAF propaganda had greatly over-estimated their own ability to hit or damage anything! The bombing was to be done an hour before sunrise, the naval bombardment another hour later (at 0630) when dawn would ensure precise targeting of the battleships' 15-inch guns.

Anyone who has studied the final plans of Operation Agreement will see at once how much more that plan owed to the 1940 scheme than any of the smaller-style raids put forward in the summer of 1942. In fact, if one was cynical, one could guess that all the various ideas were taken in, the old plan pulled out of a cubby-hole where it had lain since October 1940, and the whole lot was then thrown together. It would then be rejigged as a new plan, including everything from all the various ideas and omitting nothing other than the naval bombardment afterwards! Again, anyone studying both schemes would surely come to the conclusion that the 1940 plan stood far greater chance of success than the 1942 version ever did!

*

The original codename allocated to the plan was Operation Waylay. Let us here deal with one of the curious and confusing issues which a whole generation of writers has presented as 'historical fact' but which are totally false. When W. B. Kennedy Shaw wrote his book on the work of the Long Range Desert Group in 1943, the Allied armies had only just cleared Tripoli of the last of the enemy. The actual operation itself was only a year or so old and naturally the wartime censor was vigorous in his application of the blue pencil. Thus, the true codenames for the various parts of this operation were deleted and Kennedy Shaw had, perforce, to substitute fictitious ones in their place. He was quite open about this, writing these entirely fictitious names inside inverted commas and using

The Prize: Tobruk seen from the air. A dirty little desert port had suddenly become the most important port in the whole Mediterranean for two warring armies.

The Victor: Rommel – unpredictable, dynamic, headstrong. He outthought and outfought superior numbers of British troops and the fall of Tobruk in June 1942 marked the nadir of British fortune in the war.

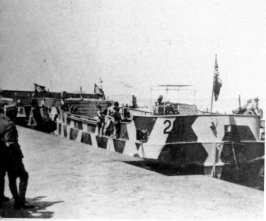

(*Top*) 'S.F.' (Siebel Ferry) – a heavy ferry of the 5/Bau Battalion. These were utilised extensively by the Germans at Tobruk, both to move stores and vehicles and as floating batteries to protect the harbour.

(*Above*) Landing craft of Pionier-Landungs-Kompanie 778 (Construction and Landing Company) who used them at Tobruk.

(*Right*) Indian and New Zealand POW's unloading a German MFP (F-lighter) at Tobruk 1942. This photo gives a good idea of the congestion at Tobruk harbour as the Afrika Korps unloaded the supplies to maintain its momentum.

flower names, as he did to illustrate a typical operation, 'Rosemary' earlier. Thus, in his book the attack on Tobruk was called 'Daffodil', the attack against Benghazi he called 'Snowdrop', the taking of the Gialo oasis he called 'Tulip' and the raid on Barce airfield was called 'Hyacinth.' All well so far; the only trouble was that succeeding batches of historians, from 1943 onwards took their information from Kennedy Shaw's book. Kennedy Shaw's falsely-named operations have therefore been perpetuated even up to the present day.

The attraction of striking at Tobruk, as well as Benghazi was that if it could be blocked then a huge transport problem would face the Germans and they would have to stretch their already over-burdened motor transport to the full to move the supplies all the way along the coast; this in turn would use up vital fuel. It was thought that by stopping the short cut through Tobruk a critical supply situation would arise very quickly and force Rommel to fall back to Agheila just to maintain himself. Also at Tobruk harbour were kept some forty-four landing ships which transhipped the cargoes from the big steamers to the shore. Destruction of these was also considered a worthy objective to the planners and so they were duly added to the list of targets.

The Joint Planning Staff issued a proposal (JPS Paper Nr 106) on attacking Benghazi and Tobruk on 3rd August 1942. The rationale for both was summed up this way: 'The enemy depends almost entirely on Tobruk and Benghazi for his supplies for the El Alamein area, with the exception of about 400 tons per day maximum at Matruh. If all shipping and port facilities at Tobruk and Benghazi can be destroyed, this may well lead to the rapid defeat of Rommel by land forces.'

So the objectives would be the destruction of shipping in the harbour and port facilities. Certain units were available to carry out such an operation without encroaching on the Eighth Army preparation at all. These were listed as follows:

Royal Navy
At Malta (for Benghazi): 2 destroyers (total carrying capacity 300 men)
At Haifa and Port Said (for Tobruk): 3 destroyers and about 15 MTBs (total carrying capacity 600 men)

Land Forces
(a) At Malta – 1 company of infantry and section field company as detailed by the land commander, Malta.
(b) In Egypt and Palestine –
11th Royal Marine Battalion
1 company infantry
1 field company
1 mountain battery
'L' Detachment SAS
LRDG
Buck (Captain Herbert A. Buck, Scots Guards, SIG)
AA Gunners (ex Tobruk now in Delta Force)
Personnel from
   Commando and Royal Engineers

It was considered that the best effects would be had if both ports were attacked at the same time, although it was far from certain if the forces available were strong enough to do this. If not, then Tobruk was to be the prime target. A landward approach to Benghazi was not considered to be capable of the same surprise effect as a seaborne landing. Such a landward approach 'would depend on the road being open somewhere between El Alamein and Siwa. At present the enemy does not appear to be occupying Qara, but there seems to be no reason why he should not do so shortly. In this case, it will be necessary either to fight a way through, which might forfeit surprise, or to approach from Kufra – the latter would be a long journey.'

In both cases the landward party were to take the coastal defence guns and AA batteries (turning them on the enemy if possible), while the seaborne troops should carry out the demolitions during the hours of daylight, re-embarking at dusk.

This was reviewed two days later by DMO, GHQ, MEF who issed a First Draft that was substantially as above. It was thought that the Eighth Army would not be ready to take the offensive until at least 30th September, although it could mount a counter-offensive before that date. Meanwhile the enemy was building up his resources. Current estimates were that within another five days there would be 200 German and 100 Italian tanks after which he would not receive any reinforcements for three weeks. The tanks were coming in through Benghazi and most of the fuel and some motor transport through Tobruk with a daily tonnage of

1200 – 2000 tons at the former port and 1200 at the latter, and the enemy was known to be short of fuel and facilities for storing it, including tanks and drums. Thus the most effective way of helping the main force defeat the enemy was to delay the Axis build-up by destroying oil stocks and storage facilities, ships in harbour, lighters and port facilities, means of transportation by land, including locomotives, rolling stock and MT. But while the former objectives could be achieved in less than twelve hours, the latter would mean prolonging the operation over a period of weeks and so rail links and the like were ruled out.

It was thought that the destruction of facilities at both Benghazi and Tobruk by the middle of August would delay Rommel's offensive by two to three weeks. If Tobruk only were dealt with then,

he might have to live on his reserves already accumulated for ten days. The deduction reached was that the destruction of oil, ships and port facilities at both ports should be accomplished simultaneously. A direct attack on the harbour by destroyers and landing parties would entail the use of too cumbersome a land force so the landing of parties some distance from the harbour had to be accepted.

They concluded:

The destruction of the petrol installations at both ports, more particularly in Tobruk, might seriously embarrass the enemy. The extent to which it would affect the enemy's operations would depend on our ability to sink tankers in the harbour. We must be prepared to accept the loss of some naval forces, together with many of the personnel taking part in the operation: ['some' was altered in pen to 'all' on the final draft!]

Time and space ruled out an August attack. Therefore the plan adopted was for attacks on both ports, both to be carried out from landward and seaward, with a target date of 6th September. Both operations were to be covered by an air raid at Tobruk and a land attack on the enemy landing ground at Benina. The forces to conduct the attack were now fleshed out more and were listed as below:

Tobruk – *Comd* Lt-Col Haselden

– *Tps. Land party* LRDG
Folbotists
60 Commandos
Det L
Det SAS
MTBs

Tps. Sea party – Three destroyers
MTBs
11 Royal Marines
Company Argyll and Sutherland Highlanders
Royal Engineers

Benghazi – *Comd* Major Stirling
Land Party L Det SAS
Folbotists
LRDG
RN Party for blocking operations

Sea Party – Two destroyers
One Coy. Infantry
Det. Royal Engineers

If the Joint Planners appeared somewhat less than overwhelmingly enthusiastic in their assessment of the operation's chances, then the violent reaction from C-in-C, Main Army, as spelled out in a Personal and Most Secret, 'Most Immediate-Clear the Line' Cipher Message which was sent to General Corbett, Mideast Command at 0905 on 8th August, soon jolted them out of it. It also made the launching of the operation, for good or ill, almost inevitable. It read:

I have just seen JPS Paper No 106, August 6th. Please inform other 3 members of Defence Committee that I was under impression that active preparations for operation proposed were already in progress. I am in NO rpt NO doubt that it is essential rpt essential that these operations take place in August and that probable losses must rpt must be accepted in view of advantages likely to result.

I urge Defence Committee to put preparations in hand at once for earliest execution projects. All possible aid will be given from here and plans already in hand for increased assistance. Request reply giving Defence Committee decision as early as possible today.

Consider JPS paper fails altogether to appreciate tremendous moral and psychological value of proposals and most unaccountably neglects to take into account enemy's present state of mind. Whole paper appears to me typical of JPS present defensive attitude which is in my opinion quite unjustified. I consider Defence Committee should enjoin JPS to adopt a more vigorous and offensive habit of thought.

Could it have been mere coincidence that the prime minister was in Cairo at this time? He had flown in on 4th August recording later that, 'Now for a short spell I became "the man on the spot". Instead of sitting at home waiting for news from the front I could send it myself. This was exhilarating.'

No doubt the Combined chiefs and other high-ranking officers found it so! In any event, memos and signals erupted from Middle East (changed by the premier to Near East) HQ at this period and the planning for the raids on Benghazi and Tobruk went into top gear once the premier got news of them.

Whether or not it was due to Churchill's intervention, this outburst evoked a very chastised response on the same day when the dog having been kicked by the farmer, it then turned on the cat. They agreed that the JPS paper failed to appreciate immense moral and psychological advantages of the proposed operation. They summarised the situation thus. It was not possible to carry out the operations in the dark moon period of August the 'essential repeat essential careful planning and move the necessary forces to the scene of action.' However, Admiral Harwood did not think the dark period was an indispensable condition and thus, subject to review, it might be possible to carry it out before the September dark period, 'obviously the sooner the better.'

They continued that, in view of enemy troop movements to the Qara area the overland parties would have to go via Kufra, but only if they dispensed 'with the rehearsal and accept the fact that some of Stirling's party will not be properly trained', could they execute the plan on 1st September. They stated that detailed planning was being carried out with the utmost urgency.

The operation should have been codenamed 'Topsy' because it continued to 'just grow'. Also on the 8th came the draft proposal for Operation Hoopoe which was revealed as the occupation of the Siwa oasis as a base for a raiding force there. A force of some armoured carriers, Honey tanks and a few infantry based there would, it was thought, play havoc with the enemy line of communications. Although he might temporarily shift his transport south of the main road, he would be unlikely to do so for long due to the state and scarceness of his motor vehicles. Such a move would also force the enemy to detach a force to deal with it; the larger the force the larger the detachment the enemy would have to make to deal with it. The enemy could, and almost certainly would, react by air attacks and thus a strong AA element was considered vital.

All in all then, with an Italian garrison of some 500 men with AFV's but no tanks and just four 37 mm AA guns it was expected that a surprise attack by a very small force of Stirling's troops and LRDG with possible a few AFV's in support would suffice. The main body of the holding force could then follow up behind. The possibility of backing them up with airborne troops was also considered. In fact the final order of battle was:

Comd.; Force HQ and Signals; one regiment Stuart tanks (4H/8H from 4th Light Armoured Brigade); two squadrons armed carriers; detachment of the LRDG; detachment of Stirling's force; one independent brigade in motor transport; one field regiment; one battery of 6-pdr anti-tank guns; one regiment of light AA (3 Batteries); one section Field Company; one Field Ambulance; Brigade RASC company, plus RAF personnel and general transport companies.

All this proved a little too rich for the army commander's taste however. It was placing too much at risk hundreds of miles behind enemy lines and in the middle of numerous air bases. But it showed how thinking was developing in the hot-house atmosphere of Cairo at this period. A memorandum dated 14th August put a temporary chain on the Hoopoe.

The Army commander has decided that the proposed operation for the capture of Siwa will not take place. He hopes, however, that preparations for the raids against Tobruk and Benghazi are going forward fast.

They were indeed. Again Peniakoff's memoirs give an exaggerated and none-too-flattering picture of the frantic activity at ME GHQ: 'friends joined in with suggestions picked from boyish books that they had poured over in earnest only a few years before, Drake and

Sir Walter Raleigh, Morgan and the Buccaneers were outbidden; new stratagems poured out in a stream of inventiveness . . .'

It was not quite as bad as that but the pressure was on for action and the ideas did keep flowing, each one more exotic than the last. Fortunately, there were men with cool heads to head off the wilder excesses, men like Stirling who changed crazy schemes back into practical propositions, men like Peniakoff who had the chance to use their own experience and side-step the more outrageous operations for those that looked more sensible. Meanwhile the detailing of the two main operations continued regardless of the discussions on the lesser sorties.

Lieutenant-Colonel Calthorpe of G1 (West) GHQ issued an appreciation summarising the work done on Waylay up to August. He re-iterated that the objective was to seize and hold such parts of the enemy defences as could interfere with the landing of demolition squads and covering parties from destroyers at both Benghazi and destroyers and MTBs combined at Tobruk. It repeated the 1940 consideration that surprise was the key factor but he now stated that 'It will also be necessary to provide cover in the form of an air raid for the approach march.' This, as we have seen, was the opposite viewpoint to that of the 1940 plan.

Another consideration was local knowledge of the area in which they were to operate:

> As the land attack must be carried out in darkness, it becomes an essential factor that the personnel taking part should be picked for their knowledge of the Tobruk and Benghazi areas, or at any rate a proportion must be conversant with the country and general layout. This ought to be easy in the case of Tobruk, but it will be difficult to find personnel who know both areas.

Suitable times for the operation to be carried out were dependent on moonrise and moonset and were whittled down to two main periods between 10th and 15th August or between 8th and 13th September. As for the troops available to carry out the attack these were listed as follows: 'L' Detachment, SAS (100 officers and men); LRDG (80); BUCK (20); AA and CD Gunners (20); 1 SS Regt. (60); RE (20), or a total of only 300 officers and men.

The JPS paper covering the plan in depth was studied and an appraisement issued from the point of view of detailed planning. Numerous conclusions were reached which resulted in considerable

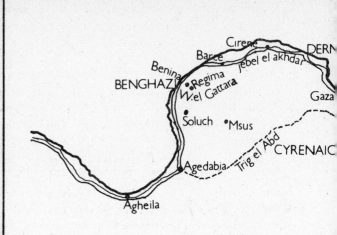

Cirene

DERN

Barce

Benina Jebel el akhdar

BENGHAZI Regima

W.el Gattara Gaza

Soluch Msus

Agedabia Trig el Abd CYRENAIC

Agheila

Aujila Gikherra

Gialo

LIBYA

KALANSH
SAND
SEA

TAZERBO

zighen
Bir Harash

REBIANA SAND SEA Kufra
oasis

© Dawn Smith

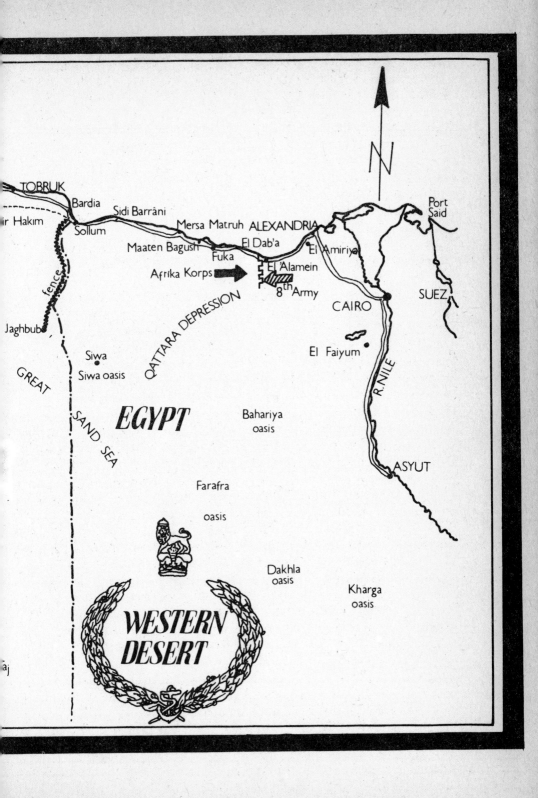

alterations. Although the Benghazi raid could not be prepared and carried out before 30th August, the Tobruk plan was feasible as early as the 17th or 18th of that month. However it was felt that *both* operations had to take place on the same night if one was not to prejudice the other. Thus the extra time could be utilised to ensure thorough preparation of both operations to ensure a good chance of success. Pressure to conduct the operation earlier, rather than later because of the uncertainty of the date of the main El Alamein offensive, was not allowed to cloud this judgement because destruction of the petrol tanks would be, 'equally valuable in August and September'.

A preliminary discussion had been held on the Tobruk operation alone and the broad outline was as follows. A land party was to seize the coastal defence guns at the SE entrance to the harbour shortly after dark. This done they were to advance to the west and also take the battery on the south side of the harbour. This accomplished, at around 0200 a force of MTBs carrying a total of 200 men was to enter the bay known as Mersa Umm Es Sciausc which would also have been secured by the land party. They would reinforce this party and the MTBs would remain within the cove. The combined force would deal with the guns on the southern shore and reach the head of the harbour just before dawn wiping out the petrol dumps, petrol tanks and pumping stations on their way.

In conjunction with this a party of Royal Marines was to land in assault boats from destroyers in Mersa Mreira to the north of Tobruk harbour one hour before dawn. By first light they were to reach the port area and deal with the gun batteries, oil tanks and the lighters on the north side of the harbour. This done the MTBs would leave their waiting positions, enter the harbour, torpedo any shipping found there, 'and then lie up among the wrecks until the RM Force had dealt with the guns on the north shore.' The MTBs would then assist in the demolition of the enemy lighters and barges moored there. They were then to be joined *in the harbour* by the destroyers who would, 'anchor or make fast to wrecks along the south shore where there is some protection from air attack', and from there command the approaches to the harbour and town from the west and north-west. Men of the landing forces would man any enemy AA guns that had survived to help the destroyers' air defence and then the whole force would re-embark and sail for home at dusk.

The idea that a destroyer force should also land men to help in the Benghazi attack was later dropped and it was proposed instead that 'L' Detachment (including small RN party) was to carry out the operation without any assistance by forces landed from HM ships'. Such a plan would obviate the need for 'L' Detachment to have to liquidate the coastal guns, lessen the time 'L' Detachment would have to hang around after doing their job, not expose valuable destroyers to day-long air attack from nearby air bases, and so on. One would have thought that the above objections could have been applied to the Tobruk half of the operation with equal validity, but they seem never to have been so applied. The same could be said of the final point made on the Benghazi operation, viz: 'L' Detachment has ample personnel to carry out the project and extra men brought by sea would be an embarrassment rather than a help.'

Thus, Stirling's sensible and patient reasoning had paid a dividend for the smallest group involved in the operation, although he still had grave reservations. In the meantime, the largest group concerned, the 11th Battalion, Royal Marines, had begun to brace itself for its long-awaited debut and the chance finally to show its mettle.

CHAPTER TWO

'Baggage go to the Fleet Club, you go to Tobruk'

The 11th Battalion, Royal Marines, owed its presence in the Mediterranean at this period to a long combination of circumstances. It had originally been assigned as the Land Defence Force for the Mobile Naval Base Defence Organisation [MNBDO(1)]. This had been projected pre-war to provide a temporary base for the Royal Navy to operate from in an emergency in whatever outlandish part of the world it might find itself fighting. The unit itself was finally initiated in January 1940, as a full Royal Marine Group but its establishment was a slow process. With the use of Suda Bay in Crete as an advanced naval base from October 1940 onward, it was decided to send MNBDO (1) there but it only arrived at Suez on 21st April 1941. About half the force had shipped to Crete before the Germans invaded and quickly captured the island, although Major-General Weston and his MNBDO units put up a spirited defence against overwhelming forces, mainly German paras. The 11th Battalion had shipped too late and was unable to get ashore to take part in the fighting. In the aftermath of the evacuation what remained of the MNBDO was left without a role until it was refitted and shipped east to the Indian Ocean but the 11th Battalion was left behind in Palestine and there it had kicked its heels impatiently as the war continued without any contribution by them. Instead it trained steadily and hard as a striking force for amphibious raids in true Royal Marines style.

Major Con J. Mahoney, RM, was second-in-command of a company at the landing and he recalled for me some of the battalion's background details, thus:

The officers were either recalled to service, Hostilities Only (HOs) or senior NCOs given temporary commissions. Other ranks were HO, CS or recalled from pension. The manning of the fleet had made heavy demands on the CS officers and men so very few were available for units not of high priority. A few

44

survivors from HM ships sunk in action came into the 11th Battalion when their ships, like, for example, the battleship *Royal Oak* sunk at Scapa Flow, went down.

The outward military style of the unit owed much to Major F. H. Nicholson, a former first drill instructor in pre-war Malta. He was one of the senior NCOs selected for commission in 1940 and gained unprecedented promotion with the infantry battalion embarked in 1941 for Suda Bay, Crete. The cadre formed up at Fort Cumberland in January, 1940, then went to Gosport and finally to front line responsibilities during the Battle of Britain holding a shallow coast sector from Kingsdown to Sandwich. The depot was evacuated as a training unit as shellfire prevailed but the battalion, until late in 1940, continued their commitment along the Kent coast and were housed there until embarkation in January 1941.

Although preoccupied with training on the Bitter Lakes as landing units, the remainder of 1941 was taken up with guard duties as garrison battalion in Morscar Barracks (evacuated earlier due to enemy bombing). 1942 brought a long period in Haifa on the refineries where precious fleet oil was available through the Anglo-Iranian Company. It was here where the Tribal destroyers, led by Captain Micklethwaite, RN, were based and used for rehearsing the Tobruk raid.

The first operation the 11th Battalion actually undertook did not take place until 15th April 1942. That night a raiding force of three officers and about 100 other ranks from 'B' Company, under the overall command of Lieutenant-Colonel E. H. M. Unwin, RM, embarked in the destroyer *Kelvin* and was landed by her boats on the tiny island of Kuphonisi off south-eastern Crete.

Here the Germans had established a wireless station and the Marines achieved complete surprise when they got ashore undetected and unopposed. A small group was left to guard the boats while the bulk of the force proceeded inland over rough terrain. As they approached they were eventually spotted by an alert sentry and machine-gun and rifle fire was encountered, but the Marines rushed the station and the defenders hastily fled. Having stormed and occupied the now empty building they duly destroyed all the radio equipment and detonated all the enemy munitions on the site for good measure. After packing every secret document they could lay their hands on into two suitcases, they then were forced to leave the way they had come due to a strict timetable. They also returned with a prize enemy porker they had made a POW (Pig of War). The cypher papers turned out to be in a code our own experts had already cracked and were avidly read, but now the enemy changed them and the de-coders had to start all over again, a real backfire and a good example of the right hand not knowing what the left was doing.

The next operation the battalion took part in was Agreement. Con Mahoney described some of the battalion's outstanding personalities.

Lieutenant-Colonel 'Mit' Unwin was taciturn but a good leader, bold in nature and concerned to turn 11 RM into an aggressive commando force. A recalled officer from a Kentish brewer's family, he joined 11th Battalion just prior to embarkation in January 1941, after a succession of CO's in the preceding twelve month period.

Major F. H. Nicholson was a senior NCO given a temporary commission in 1940. He gained accelerated promotion to Major on embarkation in January 1941 as the battalion's Second-in-Command. He was subsequently Naval Provost Marshal NW Europe and retired a Lieutenant-Colonel but did not go on the Tobruk raid.

Major 'Jack' Hedley was an outstanding small-arms expert. A powerful leader who gained a DSO on the raid for exceptional qualities in destroying strongpoints and enemy defenders. He was also I think a King's Badgeman.

Lieutenant Powell DSO was one of the determined young leaders of 'A' Company. A long-standing member of the British Council abroad, he was a graduate wartime entry.

Major Bob Sankey DSO was an ex pre-war Marine of short duration and a King's Badgeman. He was a temporary officer reaching the rank of lieutenant-colonel. He became CO of Lympstone and a wartime Commando battalion. He represented 'muscular dash' in the 11th Battalion and was a powerful character with strong leadership qualities. He was aboard *Zulu* but did not get ashore.

RSM Thompson, along with the second-in-command Nicholson, contributed to the acknowledged outward military style of the unit. He was a member of the 1935 battalion raised for London duties and he was almost evangelical in the gospel of the corps and his own commitment to it. He was promoted to commissioned rank during the war on a temporary basis.

Lieutenant Hugh Ryall was a temporary officer killed in the action. He was a strong platoon leader, 'Up Front' at all times and typical of the best to be found in a junior officer. He had been on the 'B' Company raid earlier in 1942.

Lieutenant W. J. Harris was the 'C' Company subaltern and was taken prisoner. He was exchanged early in 1943, the only RM officer exchanged.

Con Mahoney also gives this description of the build-up period for the raid:

It was no surprise with developments in the RM Brigade in the UK and the dispersal of MNBDO 1 units, for the 11th Battalion to be designated as Special Service troops and earmarked for commando duties in the Mediterranean. Sea training from Haifa and Alexandria was on a regular basis and boat work also took place in the Great Bitter Lakes on the Suez Canal. For training Tribal class destroyers were allocated, *Sikh* and *Zulu*, and, although large, they were well above reasonable capacity when two hundred marines and their boats were embarked. However, the Navy were at all times generous and enthusiastic to bring all their considerable resources to bear to ensure the success of the mission. Land training of an endurance nature took place in Palestine, Trans-Jordan and the western desert in Egypt.

The selected small craft were dumb lighters towed by small powered craft, and these small three-ply power boats with their dumb lighters were all the contemplated boats for the landing. They were pathetically slow and subjected mainly to fouled propellers in shallow waters during exercises.

'Tug' Wilson was serving aboard one of the destroyers at the time and he recalls these exercises very well indeed.

We first practised the landings at Cyprus with these special boats built in Lebanon and the *Sikh* could carry about half-a-dozen of these, I think. They were built with green Lebanon wood and were extremely fragile and far from handy. We started off making daylight landings then practised night landings. Depending on the state of the sea these makeshift landing boats were terrible to handle.

As far as I can remember they were not very long, about fifteen to sixteen feet and very lightly built of wood on steel frames. I was the bowman in one of these boats but I cannot recollect whether they had an inboard or outboard engine. I was normally a gunner rating at one of the twin 4.7s and I don't know why I was selected. I was suddenly there! But it was probably because I was one of the youngest and fittest at the time and knew the weapons. We were detailed off for the crews, three of us, coxswain, stoker and bowman, with sixteen or twenty Marines per boat.

Although their training continued at a high pitch nobody was really happy with these landing craft. But there were other worries too, not the least fears about the secrecy, or apparent lack of it, of the raid.

J. J. Fallon, then a Royal Marine serving in MNBDO(1), still has strong feelings after more than forty years, that the lack of security cost the lives of many of his friends in the 11th Battalion that fateful night.

Many of the 11th were friends of mine and we often met at Geneifa and Tobaq in Egypt, both places being Royal Marine Base Camps. I am firmly of the opinion the failure of the operation was due to the appalling level of security. It was common knowledge that the 11th were going to stage an event at Tobruk. The men in the battalion were put at a complete disadvantage by the way in which the news spread almost by bush telegraph.

I can personally recall friends telling me their destination, it was equally common knowledge in the cafes and bars together with the clubs frequented by servicemen in places like Ismailia. Another instance I recall is being in Haifa and purchasing an item in a shop and being served by an attractive shop-girl. Seeing my cap badge she asked if I was one of those going to Tobruk and did I know a chap in the unit who had apparently been courting her.

The strategic concept might well have been sound, but its execution was put at risk and ultimately resulted in failure due to the old war-time saying, 'Careless talk costs lives.'

That his memory was by no means faulty is confirmed by a report which was received from the Commandant, Combined Training Centre at Kabret and headed 'Serious Breach of Security'. It stated

(*Left*) Lieutenant-Colonel E.H.M. Unwin, Royal Marines. Under his leadership the 11th Battalion had become trained up to a peak of readiness for such an amphibious landing and had high hopes of a major achievement once ashore. (*Right*) Captain Richardson, Royal Marines, with his company sergeant major and 'B' Company's mascot, Major.

Major Sankey, Lieutenant Fagells and Captain Mahoney of 'C' Company, 11th Battalion, Royal Marines, waiting their turn.

Men of 'C' Company, 11th Battalion, Royal Marines, relaxing prior to the landing rehearsals at Cyprus when dummy landings were practised from the destroyers *Jaguar*, *Kelvin*, *Sikh* and *Zulu*. The practice was interrupted by a genuine submarine chase by the destroyers with the hapless Marines still embarked. Seen in the water from the left, Marine Duggie Moyle (captured at Tobruk and died as a POW), Marine Walker, Marine Cuthbert Hill, Marine Tinnion, Lieutenant Harris and Marine Walker.

Ready, aye, ready: 'C' Company at the Geneifa Base Camp, camp guard about to go on duty.

11th Battalion, Royal Marines, base camp at Geneifa in 1941. The stones and sand were laid by Italian POW's.

that on 2nd September, a corporal of the 11th Battalion had been
sent down from Haifa by Lieutenant-Colonel Unwin to the centre
to collect certain stores for a special operation. Later the same
evening, he was overheard by one of the CTC corporals holding
forth in the NAAFI that:

(a) He had passed a huge convoy en route from Palestine and
Syria to Kantara. He gave details of what he saw.

(b) He gave details of what he was collecting at the Combined
Training Centre and where it was going.

(c) He said some big operation must be on because two cruisers
and four destroyers and hundreds of Marines were in on it.

(d) He said that the operation was for Halfaya to get behind
the enemy.

(e) He said that a lot of people thought Ninth Army was in
Syria whereas it had moved to the Caucasus, etc., etc.

He was promptly placed under open arrest and sent back to
Lieutenant-Colonel Unwin with another corporal from the Royal
Marine Base Depot together with the charge and documentary
evidence of witnesses. The commandant of the CTC thought that
'this man has been spilling his mouth at every stop on his way down
from Haifa and that much damage may have been done.'

There were other examples that the raid had become common
knowledge in Egypt and Lebanon as we shall see. But whether
compromised or not the bulk of the 11th Battalion was training hard
and looking forward to at last being given the chance to show its true
mettle after such a long period of enforced idleness, which was so
contrary to the fighting instincts and traditions of the Royal
Marines.

*

Whether compromised or not the Royal Marines were now getting
down to detailed planning for their part in the attack. The
topography of the Tobruk area had to be fully understood for the
men would be working in darkness for most of the vital initial part
of the operation and under enemy fire. It was therefore vital that the
small parties could quickly make their way to the important target
areas and gun batteries, the neutralisation of which was crucial to
the whole mission.

Along the north shore of Tobruk harbour there were six main jetties, with depths of water at their outward extremities varying from 14 to 20 feet and there was also a slipway. In addition there was a coaling jetty and a boom jetty, both utilised as shoreward anchor points for the defensive boom strung across the harbour entrance and the principal hazard, other than the guns, to the entry of the MTBs to complete their task of destruction. The main quay was south of the town and was approached from the landward side by two roads running steeply downhill. If the raiders could effectively block these roads then enemy reinforcements rushing to the area could be effectively held off from the port area while demolition continued. Other suitable targets were the normal ones to be found in any such port; petrol and fuel installations naturally took priority. But there were motor transport repair workshops, good targets as the shortage of such trucks to the Axis was constantly emphasised due to the 260 mile road journey from Benghazi. There were also torpedo sheds, radio stations, the lighters themselves, which were to be captured and utilised rather than destroyed, and cranes.

The situation report available to the Royal Marines' planners one month in advance of the attack was that there might be the equivalent of one Italian infantry brigade as well as 1,000 German troops, but these were reported at a staging post some distance from the town. These figures were very inaccurate indeed but did much to ensure that estimates of success were almost all favourable. Nor was it thought that there was enough motor transport available to transport these reserves to the scene of the action quickly. Another mistake as it turned out! Air attack was of course a prime consideration; a great deal of risk was being taken by leaving the whole force exposed to the wrath of the Luftwaffe for a whole day, plus the withdrawal period. In view of the proven lethal qualities of the Stukas such risks appear very short-sighted but there seems very little objection at such exposure. Assessments of the likely Axis air opposition was, by contrast with the land force estimates, extremely accurate, indeed almost totally precise in the event. Only their capabilities were under-estimated, not their numbers!

'There are not likely to be any enemy bombers either at Tobruk or El Adem aerodromes,' read the 11th Battalion's Information sheet, 'but there are believed to be some 30 Macchi 200's.' These latter were single-engined monoplane fighter aircraft and presumably not considered a threat to the men or the ships, another costly error. 'At Derna there are a small number of Ju88's and some Me110's and 24 Italian torpedo bombers. One Gruppe of 30 Ju87's from Sidi Barrani could attack one hour after being called upon and a further Gruppe of dive bombers could be effective after three hours. Ju88's from Crete could operate within 1½ hours. It would appear, therefore, that within a few hours the enemy could attack British naval forces in harbour with some 130 aircraft but steps are being taken by the RAF to prevent or minimise this risk.' Unfortunately, as so often before, RAF attempts to neutralise the Luftwaffe proved to be almost totally ineffective.

The Royal Marine contingent to the attacking force was known as Force 'A' and consisted of the following participants:

HQ (including Signals).
3 infantry companies ('A', 'B' and 'C').
1 machine-gun platoon.
1 3-inch mortar platoon.
Detachment Royal Artillery (they were to man the captured enemy guns, and as many of them were AA weapons, not surprisingly mainly AA gunners were selected).
Detachment Field Company.
Detachment medical staff.

All were to be dressed in khaki shirts and shorts with commando boots, British pattern steel helmet and fighting order. This uniformity of dress was deliberate in order to avoid confusion among the many sub-units involved. The two destroyers were to embark 50,000 rounds of .303 Mk VII, 50,000 rounds of .303 Mk VIII, 100 3-inch high explosive mortar bombs, 200 lbs of gun-cotton slabs and 50 primers and this was to be landed ashore at No 4 jetty between 1100 and 1200 once the harbour was in British hands. All the forces involved were to land with 24 dry rations, an emergency ration and full water bottles. Captured enemy lighters were to be stocked with further rations and water for the voyage back.

Their objectives were spelled out in detail once more. They were to gain possession of the peninsula north of the harbour so that the naval vessels could enter and they were also to cover the destruction of all the fuel installations, repair shops and harbour facilities. The way the 11th Battalion and its attached units were to play their part in this were as follows:

The whole of Force 'A', under the command of Lieutenant-

Colonel E. H. M. Unwin himself, were to be landed at the small
inlet of Mersa Mreira from the destroyers *Sikh* and *Zulu* at 0330 and,
after assembling, were to move out to their objectives three-quarters
of an hour later.

'A' Company was to proceed direct to take up defensive positions
along the wall which ran from the hospital to the coast and form a
defensive perimeter. 'C' Company's job was to proceed directly to
Mengar Shansak to take and silence the Italian Coastal Defence
guns and the German AA batteries located there. This done they
were to push on westward taking over all the further batteries dug
in on the north shore one by one, up to the No IV jetty. The
attached detachment of Royal Engineers were then to carry out the
waterfront demolitions. The 3-inch mortar section was to march with
'C' Company for their protection but was to remain under
operational control of HQ, being used to break any strong enemy
resistance at the batteries. While these flanking operations were
taking place, 'B' Company was to move straight to the central area,
again taking over the AA batteries en route and then the Marines
themselves were to set about the destruction of the Motor Transport
workshops.

Stage two of the proceedings was then to begin with 'C'
Company; along with the mortar teams, it was to take over a sector
of the perimeter defence between 'A' Company and 'D' Company
of the Argyll and Sutherland Highlanders which were to be landed
from the MTBs of Force 'C' (of which more later) while 'B'
Company, moved out to a supporting position, also moved into
support behind the Highlanders. They were also to link up with
Force 'B' coming in from the desert at the head of the harbour and
until contact was made and inter-force boundary was laid down to
prevent friend firing on friend at the road running from the hospital to
the western end of the quays. Neither of the two British forces was to
operate or fire across this boundary until Lieutenant-Colonel Unwin
had assumed overall control and command of the combined force.

It was expected that the Royal Marines would be firmly
established by 0800. Both the Argylls and the Royal
Northumberland Fusiliers who were accompanying Force 'C', were
orthodox fighting sub-units and were to be used exclusively as
perimeter defence leaving the many specialised detachments to carry
out the demolitions and any mopping up of strong enemy bunkers,
under their, and the three Marine Companies' protection and under
their direction.

I have mentioned the importance attached to trying to capture as many as possible of the German self-propelled coastal transport barges, 'F' lighters as they were known. They were low-lying vessels, with a good accommodation for trucks, tanks and stores, and had light AA weapons for defence. They were a valuable asset to the Axis and they could be equally as useful for the British. It was thus hoped to take over a good number of these, as many as ten if possible, which had a good supply of fuel and were in good working order, and 'cut them out' in grand old naval style to bring them away with the withdrawal of the main naval forces. For this purpose Commander Nichol RN was to select the best of these vessels and despatch them eastward to a waiting position. Any that could not be got away, or were in too poor a state to sail away immediately, were to be destroyed along with any auxiliary barges and lighters.

Once all the demolitions had been completed then a Red/Green/White pyrotechnic signal was to be fired from No 3 jetty by Force 'B', around about 1000 that morning and the destroyers and MTBs waiting offshore were to be notified by radio.

Meanwhile, the medical team were to make contact with the Italian hospital and arrange for the treatment of any critical cases who would not be able to stand up to the voyage back. One of the captured 'F' lighters was to be earmarked to carry the less seriously wounded to safety. The evacuation of the whole force was to get underway by 1900 that night. So much for the Royal Marine force's duties in taking the port. But this was a closely knit operation and no one part could succeed without the other. Let us now examine the other two forces involved and what their role was to be.

*

Force 'C' was another seaborne force. Among its groups, as we have seen, was 'D' Company Argyll and Sutherland Highlanders. The rest of the force, under overall command of Captain A. N. Macfie, was to have been composed as follows:

One platoon of the 1st Royal Northumberland Fusiliers (less one machine-gun section).
Detachment of Royal Engineers.
Detachment of Royal Artillery.
Detachment of Royal Corps of Signals.
Detachment of Royal Army Medical Corps.

They were to be transported by MTBs from Alexandria taking an inshore route and were to land at the southern inlet of Mersa Umm Es Sciausc, the defences of which would be secured in advance by Force 'B'. Again the gunners were to man such captured enemy weapons as directed and the whole force was to merge with Force 'B' initially and then work their way west and then come under the overall command of 11th Battalion HQ. The MTB force were to lurk in the inlet until the bombing ended and then were to torpedo enemy shipping in the eastern end of the harbour.

But it was on one of the most fervent supporters of the idea that the crux of success or failure was initially to fall. Lieutenant-Colonel John Haselden was in command of Force 'B', the land-based part of the combined assault, and their part in the operation was by far the most daring and hazardous portion of the enterprise. Guided by a patrol of the LRDG by way of the Kufra Oasis to within striking distance of Tobruk, Force 'B' consisted of a total of 83 men embarked in eight 3-ton trucks; 'D' Squadron Special Service Regiment with detachments of Royal Artillery, Royal Engineers and Signals. They were to bluff their way through the perimeter defences and then set up a base in readiness for the assault on Mersa Umm Es Sciausc.

As Ronald Hill of the LRDG stated: 'The LRDG was in a ferrying/support role on this mission with supporting targets at Derna and Benghazi.'

In command of the SS group was Major Colin Campbell of the London Scottish Regiment, known as a 'hard' man with a fierce pride and a stickler for 'discipline'. Second-in-command was Lieutenant Graham Taylor, who had previously worked in the desert with the New Zealand squadron of the LRDG. Lieutenant H. Davidson Sillito of the Argyll and Sutherland Highlanders was third in command of the force. Another officer with LRDG experience was Lieutenant Michael Duffy, formerly of the Hampshire Regiment, and there were two Royal Northumberland Fusilier officers, Lieutenant M. Roberts and Lieutenant R. Murphy. Finally, there was Second-Lieutenant W. MacDonald, a New Zealander.

The other six officers were attached. To man the captured guns, the Royal Artillery detachment had four Coast Defence gunners under Lieutenant J. Poynton and, in charge of the AA gunner detachment and also chosen for his intimate knowledge of Tobruk itself where he had served during the siege, was Lieutenant H.

Barlow. From the Special Boat Squadron came Lieutenant T. B. Langton, ex-Irish Guards, who acted as adjutant. He had the responsibility of signalling to the MTB flotilla that the southern inlet had been secured so that they could come in and land their reinforcements on time.

The Royal Engineer officer in charge of the eight-man demolition party was Lieutenant G. Harrison, while the signallers were led by Lieutenant M. H. Trollope. The medical party was under a Canadian officer, Captain J. Gibson. There was also a detachment of the SIG under Captain H. A. Buck and Lieutenant T. C. D. Russell. These were anti-Nazi Germans who had settled in Palestine and had been recruited to play a special part in the proceedings. Included in their numbers were two British officers, Captain H. Bray and Lieutenant D. Lanark. Finally there was the RAF Liaison Officer, Pilot Officer Scott, RAF.

Captain Lloyd Owen with Y.1 patrol of the LRDG was to be the guide to Haselden's D Squadron, 1st Special Service Regiment, Force 'B', to the perimeter of the Tobruk defences by way of Kufra. Their task, as we have seen, was to seize and secure the southern inlet but first they had to get close enough by dusk to begin their operation. Here is where the Special Identification Group came in. They were commanded by Captain Herbert A. Buck, an officer in the Scots Guards who spoke fluent German. Dressed in German uniforms, speaking fluent German, even carrying love letters to fictitious wives and sweethearts in Germany and other cleverly forged documents, as well as completely authentic arms, they were to play the role of German soldiers guarding three captured British 3-tonner trucks crammed with POW's and on the way to internment at the Tobruk cage. This was high bluff indeed and required nerves of steel and much courage. Needless to say, the Germans would have shot such men out of hand as spies had their disguises been penetrated.

Finally, there was an added bonus or postscript to Agreement, the possible release of the many British and Commonwealth POW's locked up in cages at Tobruk. This was one of Haselden's special projects, very dear to his heart, although the official orders stressed this was to be done *only* if it would not hinder the evacuation of the main attacking force and only if there was enough and suitable captured enemy sea transportation for them to get clear.

Peniakoff described his views on the matter thus:

Haselden wanted me to join this party: discussing the plan with him I discovered that he relied for ammunition and supplies on what he would find in Tobruk.

'Don't be a fool,' he said, 'there will be no difficulty. Tobruk is full of everything.'

I decided to keep away from Haselden's party and told him I would rather go to Derna, as I knew the country so much better. The projected raid on Derna, which was to be an LRDG responsibility, was dropped and I got myself transferred to the Barce raid.

These were the land forces for Agreement. What of the sea and air side of the operation?

*

The commanding officer of the submarine *Taku*, part of the 1st Submarine Flotilla, and his two-man Special Boat Section folbot party (under Lieutenant Kirby, RN), had two heavy responsibilities. The first, and most important of all, was to act as beach guides to ensure that the state of the sea off the landing area at Mersa Mreira was such that all the landing barges from the two destroyers could safely make the passage to the beach and back. As we have seen, there was little confidence in these vessels, and they were derisively christened 'Shoeboxes' by the Marines and sailors alike. Nails had been used instead of screws to hold them together, only canvas kept the water out from between the two plank skins and they capsized easily. The verdict on the solitary rehearsal at Cyprus had been that it had taken far too long, even with no opposition at all. Furthermore, there were insufficient of these craft for all the Royal Marines to go in in one wave; they had to land in two stages, yet another hazard in the pitch-blackness. Only if the weather seemed good enough for this was the landing to go ahead at all.

The two folbots were to be disembarked at 0130/D 2 and *Taku* was to signal to Force 'A' at 0200, just prior to the landing. The second job was for the folbot party to get ashore and, in a similar manner to Langton's task at Mersa Umm es Sciausc, to affix the landing lights ashore to guide the destroyers into the right inlet. One folboteer was to mark the eastern side of the Mersa Mreira at the entrance while the other was to place his marker half-way down the inlet on the same side. They were to exhibit two signals by making two long flashes every two minutes between the north-east and

north-west only from 0245 until the landing boats arrived, these
being a Red Light, 'All Clear', or a White Light, 'Strong Opposition'. Finally, the folbotists were to co-operate with work in the
harbour area.

Once the folbots were away *Taku* was to get clear of the area
quickly by proceeding to the north-west at her best surface speed of
17 knots until she was some 40 miles offshore, there to await events.
The two folbots were to join up with Force 'A' and Lieutenant
Kirby was to assist Commander Nicholl in readying the captured
F-lighters. Meanwhile, the British landing craft were to wait at
Mersa Mreira until Captain (D)22 signalled for them to join him;
each power boat was then to tow one dumb craft round to the
harbour.

As for the two destroyers, having landed both waves of Marines
they were to await the signal that the harbour area was in British
hands and were then to go in with all guns manned to give whatever
support was required. They were already to have been painted grey
overall and *Sikh* was to paint out her flotilla leader's Black Top on
her foremost funnel, while *Zulu* painted out her pendant numbers on
the side of her hull. The broad red and white diagonal stripes, the
Italian aircraft identification markings, were to be painted on their
fo'c'sle's.

Once inside the harbour, both ships were to be listed over, oil
being pumped out over the side; black smoke was to be made by
their funnels and from smoke floats aft; all their guns (six 4.7-inch
low angle and two 4-inch high angle in four twin turrets) were to be
put at maximum depression and no men were allowed on the upper
decks. The aim was to generally make them look like they were in
sinking condition, 'and so avoid direct dive bombing attack'. As
such they would have been undefended sitting ducks to any Stuka
pilots who had the slightest doubts on this score!

The two destroyers were also to send ashore signalmen with Aldis
lamps and flags to help with the situation ashore. The challenge and
response for all those involved in the operation ashore was 'Who
goes there?' – 'George Robey'. Perhaps it was not inappropriate!

The RAF bombing attack was planned to commence at 2130/
D1, whatever the cloud conditions prevailing, and was to last until
0340/D2. The north shore was to be the main target area for these
attacks. They were to refrain from actually dropping flares after
0100/D2. Although the bombing would have terminated, several
aircraft were assigned to remain over the town until 0500 to

keep the Axis radar busy and split the AA gunners' targets between sea and sky. It was hoped their engine noise would also help drown that of the MTB's; a rather forlorn hope, one would have thought.

Air Officer Commanding 205 Group was requested to brief a certain number of picked aircrew from those engaged in the air attack to be on the lookout from the commencement of the bombing for a visual signal which was to be displayed at Mersa Umm Es Sciausc. This signal was to consist of a triangle, with 20 yard sides, marked by three special glim lamps and an Aldis lamp near the triangle directed at the aircraft and signalling 'OK'. On sighting this the aircraft was to flash back an acknowledgement 'TOC' and to transmit the codeword 'Nigger' to Captain Micklethwaite aboard *Sikh* on the 4205 kc's wavelength.

The AOC was also instructed to request a certain number of the aircraft to fly low offshore north of Tobruk and make diversionary attacks on Ju88 and Stuka bases in Africa and Crete, on D1, D2 and D3 (although later Crete was deleted from the list of targets), 'provided other commitments permit'.

To help plan the operation, up-to-date information on the state of the enemy defences was absolutely vital. In particular what was required was aerial photography covering the area bounded by the sea and harbour in the north, Wadi Sahal in the west and the old perimeter defences in the south and east. These would be annotated in ink. It was requested that this area of Tobruk be photographed on a scale of 1/16,800 (i.e. F/20″ at 28,000ft) to show the following subjects in particular:

1) Perimeter defences for new digging or new defence positions.
2) Extensions to the railway.
3) Possible new dumps and camps.
4) Topographical features with a view to revision of existing maps which do not agree with photographs, particularly in regard to wadis and escarpments.

The request from the DDMI concluded: 'In view of the valuable Military Information to be gained, may this Demand be given the highest priority.'

Therefore, on 30th August, Brigadier Davy of the DMO requested of the RAF that a master mosaic of aerial photographs of the Tobruk area be made readily available. He conceded, however, that he did not think there now remained sufficient time to obtain the necessary information and he did not want an increased scale of air reconnaissance over the port during the following three weeks in case the defenders be forewarned.

The reply from H. P. Wigglesworth, SASO, the next day, agreed that it would be a good idea to have such a mosaic, but:

> It is pointed out however that the existing operational commitments of PRU aircraft can barely be met with present resources and, as you know, they are likely to increase considerably now that the Western Desert battle has again broken out.
>
> I regret therefore that I cannot place the demand for special photography of the Tobruk area on the highest priority as from any given date.

All the raiding forces therefore had to go in relatively blind.

Finally there was the ticklish subject of fighter cover for all the various naval forces. It was stated that such air cover would be required for the two main naval forces from first light until dark on D1; for returning naval forces on D2 (Force 'D') and D3 (Force 'A').

*

In view of the huge numbers of allegations of breaches of security the following points on that subject were made at the time:

> All Marine personnel embarked in the destroyers are to be warned that they are not to appear on the upper deck in khaki while the destroyers are at Alexandria.

Colonel David Stirling made a strong statement when Len Deighton half hinted that the SAS or LRDG might possibly have let slip details of the operation. At a social meeting which he attended at the British Embassy in Cairo he had been warned by 'a particularly idiotic junior officer serving in MEHQ' that Churchill himself was a 'notorious security risk'. Stirling commented that 'the attitude of the higher echelons of the MEHQ . . . was always helpful – although I cannot say this of many of those junior regular officers unseasoned by front-line warfare.'

He also stated quite categorically that the operation failed, 'mainly because of loose gossip in Cairo. The training and

operational bases of the men of the so-called "private armies",
however, were miles away from Cairo and in no case were these men
even told about the operation until they were at Kufra – more than
800 miles away from base. The LRDG and the Special Air Service
Regiment insisted on the most stringent security discipline. Our
very existence depended upon this – we operated continually
behind the enemy lines, not sporadically.'

With this Lloyd Owen agreed and in one of his books gives details
of a talk he had with John Haselden in Captain Shan Hackett's
office at GHQ in which he says he warned Haselden that there was
much loose talk about the operation already, and that Haselden had
agreed although he did not think the enemy knew exact details.
Kennedy Shaw in his earlier book is more non-committal on this
issue, as one would expect.

However, Rear-Admiral L. E. H. Maund, who served at
Combined Operations, Middle East, makes a whole series of
allegations on the laxity of security, and did not confine his criticism
to the Royal Marines either:

The men to do the cross-desert journeys to Tobruk and Benghazi
collected at Kufra in the desert 400 miles south of Tobruk. An
airman who flew back from there said that at Kufra no one was
attempting to conceal what was afoot and men dressed up in
German uniforms were drilling in the streets to German orders.
These were the men to bounce the guard on the road leading
through the outer defences of Tobruk. A considerable convoy of
lorries was collecting, and it was said that only reason information
could not reach the enemy was because all the old camels capable
of the cross-desert journey had been dispatched. There was little
security – so many men of action just must talk.

At Haifa, too, the talk of the town was the training of the
marine battalion. People began to speculate – the one thing that
must be stopped at all costs if secrecy is to be maintained – and
it was difficult to speculate at all and not hit upon the proper
target, Tobruk. We had asked that the marines and their
destroyers should be moved to Kabret, thirty-five miles from the
nearest town and a place that could easily be roped off, but the
destroyers were badly needed on the Levant coast for moving
troops between Cyprus and Palestine and for escorting convoys
up and down the coast.

Then, just as the naval part of the expedition sailed, and well after the party had left Kufra, information reached GHQ that an officer of the New Zealand camp just outside Cairo had been heard discussing the operation. A cordon was at once thrown round the New Zealand camp and we still hoped the enemy had not picked up the story.

Rear-Admiral Maund was obviously speaking from inside knowledge and a unique position but he offers no sources or confirmations for these statements. Nor does Fitzroy Maclean who was even more outspoken:

> For obvious reasons, secrecy was vital, and only a very small number of those taking part in the operations were told what their destination was to be. But long before we were ready to start there were signs that too many people knew too much. . . . Worse still, there were indications that the enemy was expecting the raids and was taking counter-measures.

G. G. Connell, in a more recent account, writes:

> Operation Agreement was common knowledge in the bazaars and cafes of Alexandria; the men in the ships became aware of the total lack of secrecy when dhobymen came hurrying inboard with laundry and pressed for immediate payment with great urgency. When questioned, the fellaheen told the uneasy sailors, 'Officers baggage go to the Fleet club, you go to Tobruk', and in fact officers' trunks were going ashore, as they spoke.

Vague German confirmation of these allegations was put by Heinz W. Schmidt thus:

> Now agents reported that the British planned a sea-borne landing between El Daba and Mersa Matruh. Their reports resulted in a welcome change for my battalion. I was ordered to site defensive observation posts directly along the coast.

The Official Naval Historian, the late Captain S. W. Roskill, was to write that: 'There is some evidence that the highly efficient German cryptographic organization known as the B-Dienst had obtained warning of the Tobruk raid, but I have been unable to obtain definite confirmation.'

However the Official History of the war in the Middle East was quite positive: 'No evidence has been found to show that the enemy had become aware of any part of the plan.'

We shall return to the evidence and claims of both sides again. But meanwhile, for good or evil, and with Auchinleck's early fierce support, Operation Agreement was now a firm project. On the face of it a desperate gamble, only a few spoke out against it *at the time*. To their credit those who had their doubts were old desert hands, Stirling, Peniakoff, Lloyd Owen. Others were also less than wholehearted in their support of the plan. Air Chief Marshal Tedder was very uneasy, because of the obvious lack of fighter cover for the operation and having the whole force exposed for a full twelve hours' daylight to all the enemy cared to send. General Bernard Montgomery had no part in either the planning or the execution of any part of the operation, which was all done at MEHQ, but he *was* shown the full plan. He made no comment before, although afterwards was full of condemnation for it. It was typical of the man to distance himself from failure but in this case he was really *not* involved. His distaste for the small clandestine units was well known anyway and, whether they were successful or not, he had little time for such raids, a view shared by Tedder.

The Royal Navy C-in-C was the one whose forces, reduced to the bone as they already had become, stood to lose the most if things went wrong. However, he was the least opposed to the attempt. Harwood was in a difficult position; the failure of the June convoy, the loss of the three destroyers already mentioned and other setbacks had taken much of the lustre from his crown and he had immediate and first-hand witness of what happened to those who failed to please the premier with the abrupt departure of 'the Auk' himself. So he backed the plan, but that was not to ultimately save him from the same fate as the general.

Admiral Harwood described the operation *later*, as a 'desperate gamble'. It was noted how interdependent all these widespread forces were for overall success. It was estimated that the failure of Force 'A' or Force 'C' (but not both) would not necessarily mean the failure of the whole operation, but that failure of Land Force 'B' to take Mersa Umm es Sciausc would involve complete failure. 'The critical phase of the Operation is, therefore, the initial success of

Force 'B' and the immediate passing of this information to all other forces. Unless the success of Force 'B' is known to Forces 'A' and 'C' by 0200/D Two the operation will be abandoned.'

Not every objective survey of the scheme viewed it favourably, however, even at the time. For example, a cold hard look was taken by the Joint Planners on 29th August, as to the probable effects even a successful series of missions would have on the Axis army. They came up with the following disappointing estimates:

(1) They thought that there would be little effect on the enemy's maintenance position by reducing intake at Benghazi, unless the use of Tobruk was greatly restricted or totally denied.

(2) Owing to the fact that the enemy had by then moved eastward from the Jebel Akhdar, the majority of his supply dumps, guerilla operations by British raiding forces in that area would have little effect on his supply position.

(3) The enemy had established from one to two weeks' reserves in, and east of Tobruk, and intake through that port balanced daily consumption.

They continued:

> Tobruk cannot be blocked. Operations against the port would only result in it being partially out of use for the maximum of a week, by which time the enemy could probably replace the lighters which had been destroyed in the port. The effect of the operation therefore, would be to force the enemy to eat down a few days reserves and then only if active operations were proceeding on the El Alamein position.

But it was too late to stop Agreement now.

*

If, despite the differing opinions of the C-in-C's, the ironically re-named Agreement was to be the Mediterranean combined forces' *pièce de résistance* curtain-raiser for Alamein, it was to have a strong supporting cast. There were several other raids planned to coincide with the Tobruk attack. The Benghazi operation was reinstated, but in the simpler form urged by the specialists. Other attacks were also planned, the whole coming together in the hope of causing utter chaos the length and breadth of eastern Libya that would have great psychological, if not overwhelming material, results on the Axis forces.

The raid on Benghazi was code-named Operation Bigamy and, as we have seen, was to be made by Force 'X', also operating from Kufra. It also had the objective of blocking the inner harbour, sinking all the ships found there, and destroying the oil storage tanks and pumping plants. This accomplished, Force 'X' was to retire to the fastness of the Gialo Oasis, and from there continue with further raids. For this Stirling's group was to command 'L' Detachment with their forty Jeeps which would be led in by S1 and S2 Patrols of the LRDG, and were themselves then to 'beat up' Benina. Plans at first also considered two Stuart tanks and use of a battalion from Malta, but this was later dropped and the two tanks added to Tobruk's Force 'B'.

Stirling himself visited Eighth Army HQ on 25th August and outlined certain proposals for capturing aerodromes in the Gebel which were dependent on the success of the Benghazi operation, but it was pointed out that this was for GHQ to decide as this would have repercussions on Eighth Army operations. However, it was decided that once Bigamy had been successfully accomplished Stirling's party would retire on Gialo and half would then be sent back to Kufra. The remainder would be available from about 25th September to carry out harassing operations in which railway locomotives, motor transport, tank workshops, ammunition and food dumps and aircraft would be the targets. Stirling said that the best road blocks could be laid between Matruh and Sollum. On 29th August, Colonel C. D. Quilliam, DDMI, of the Joint Planners stated that although there were fuel storage tanks at Benghazi ('believed to be far from full'), the enemy depended almost exclusively on intake through Tobruk. At Barce there were railhead dumps, 'of *no* great extent' and that, in general, it had to be assumed that most of the contents of the enemy dumps as of last May had been moved forward already. 'It appears that sabotage of dumps and occupation of Derna would have NO appreciable effect on the enemy's effort.' This part of the scheme was duly dropped. As for the attack on Benghazi little immediate effect was likely on the enemy's effort. As for morale:

The projected operation should have a very considerable effect on enemy morale, but experience has shown that the Axis Higher Command in North Africa recovers its balance from unexpected shocks quickly. The effect however, is likely to be appreciable in the back areas.

To MERSA MATRUH and EL ALAMEIN —

ENEMY GUNS

High-speed Motor Torpedo Boats going in and coming out

Railway to TOBRUK

Attempt to tow off M.T.B.

MTB aground

PARTIES LANDED

BIG FIRE

DUMP BLOWING UP

Road to El Gazala

Road into Tobruk

TENTS AND MOTOR TRANSPORT WORKSHOPS ATTACHED.

ROYAL MARINES landing West of Town

Royal Marines hold out for 24 hours

STRIATED CLIFFS

Boat landing Parties towed by Power Boats

Landing on narrow 50 yard beach

DEFENCE AREA OF TOBRUK

BIG FIRE

LANDING PIERS

TOBRUK TOWN

BOOM

Headland at Harbour mouth

ENEMY BATTERIES & SEARCHLIGHTS

H.M.S. SIKH shelled from shore

SIKHS steering damaged

H.M.S. ZULU attempts to tow off disabled 'SIKH'

The Best-Laid Plans ... How it was done. This reconstruction of how the attack was to be carried out is accurate in its broad essentials, even if the achievements were vastly overrated by the British artist.

Stuka on the prowl. By dawn the Luftwaffe and Regia Aeronautica were early astir to take advantage of the long hours of daylight to make leisurely target practice among the many small ships struggling to safety along the North African coast. Here a pair of Ju87s of the German crack Stukagruppe 3 are seen over the coast.

An Italian Macchi Mc202 fighter of the type used by Major Viale's 13 Gruppo in the strafing and destruction of the British MTB's and ML's off Tobruk at first light on the morning of 14th September. These coastal craft proved very vulnerable to such attacks.

The German flak craft (Siebel-Ferry) SF110 of Flak-Abt. (Fahre) 144 carrying out a practice shoot of its main weapons out at sea.

Nor were any large or lasting diversions considered likely to result from the raids.

To establish Gialo itself as a British raider base it was to be taken on the night of 15th/16th September to coincide with Stirling's return from Bigamy and was to be held for three weeks. This attack was code-named Operation Nicety. It was estimated that there were two hundred Italian troops based there and that, as far as was known, no other Axis troops were on that part of Cyrenaica, apart from native Arab companies, one at Agheila and one at Marada, but who had little transport. There was no intention of holding Gialo, once captured, against any *superior* enemy attacking force. To accomplish this Force 'Z' was assigned to be made up from the garrison at Kufra. It originally was to consist of the following units:

One motorised battalion, less one company, Sudan Defence Force.
Detachment 3.7-inch Howitzer battery.
Detachment anti-tank battery.
Detachment light AA battery.
One LRDG patrol for navigation, reconnaissance and inter-communication purposes.

Force 'Z' was to leave Kufra on the evening of D1 and hit Gialo on D4 or by the morning of D5 at the latest. As at Tobruk the RAF was to lay on heavy bombing raids, with 205 Group attacking Benghazi harbour from dusk on D1 until one minute before midnight when all bombing was to cease, although the planes were to linger overhead for another hour to fool the defenders. No flares were to be dropped after 2200.

On 18th August, GMO Davy requested that:

I am particularly anxious that the enemy should not get any inkling that we are taking an interest in Gialo. So will you lay off any form of air recce or photography in that area.

The RAF was also to provide the Benghazi party with air reconnaissance over Benghazi harbour, Benina, Berka and Barce airfields and Coetia camp with aircraft from Malta. Also, as far as Gialo. If they asked for it (by radio signal 'Airsup'), the Stirling force was to be supplied by air and Kufra was to be used as a base to operate the six Bombay transport aircraft of No 15 South African

Air Force Squadron detachment, plus such transport aircraft as assigned by RAF HQ ME. Each Bombay could carry 18,000 lbs of cargo and therefore it was necessary to assign a RAF liaison officer to Force 'X' and another RAF officer was to be sent to Kufra by 28th August to supervise loading of the transport aircraft by AOC 203 Group.

Other operations consisted of a raid on the Italian airfield at Barce by two further patrols of the LRDG under the command of Major J. R. Easonsmith, with 47 men in five Jeeps and twelve 30-cwt trucks operating from Faiyum 700 miles away.

A demonstration against Siwa was to be laid on by a motor battalion of the Sudan Defence Force operating from the Bahariya Oasis, coupled with the dropping of dummy parachutists by the RAF. This was code-named Operation Coastguard. The land force, comprising all available vehicles then at Bahariya, were to advance along the Sitra track as far as Sitra itself. They had to be ready to move out at four hours' notice from midday on 10th September and be prepared to operate over a period of four days. 'The vehicles need not be filled to capacity but the force must have sufficient striking power to deal with any enemy patrols encountered en route.'

To comply with the hoodwinking requirement Group Captain C. Hallawell detailed six Hudson bombers of 216 Squadron, each carrying 40 dummy parachute troops, to be available for take-off from Khanka airfield on D1.

The Hudsons were to simulate a parachute landing at Siwa Oasis by dropping these dummies in waves in full view of the defenders, commencing at last light on D1. The attack was to be spread over one-and-a-half hours with each aircraft making several runs over the target area so that the enemy thought a much larger number were being used than was really the case. To help the Italians to get the full picture flares were to be dropped as well and each bomber was to drop a few incendiary bombs as well, for good measure.

*

And so the die was cast. From all over the Middle East hard-fighting units were being called on to supply an élite force to impress its mark on the enemy and weaken his resolve in readiness for what was confidently expected to be the decisive final round in the long and epic confrontation of Afrika Korps versus Eighth Army. Thanks to an extra 500 American tanks, an overwhelming artillery park and heavy superiority in infantry, only one result was expected by the

British: victory! But they had been wrong before. They could not be absolutely certain that somehow, yet again, that wily fox, Erwin Rommel, would again outsmart them, no matter what the odds.

'Rommel. Rommel. What matters but to beat him!' scolded the frustrated premier. Thus any diversion, no matter how small, *anything* that might cause their German and nervous Italian opponents to look over their shoulders and thus not see the knock-out blow aimed at their chin in time, was welcome.

The fighting men that were to bring about this feint came from all manner of units, some with long and honourable traditions second to none, like the Royal Marines. They were the very stuff of legend, a corps whose history of almost unbroken victory stretched back almost three-hundred years. Others, like the SAS and the LRDG, represented the new breed; small, compact, élite, wary, alert and honed perfectly to the peculiar logistics and style of desert warfare. With them were traditional units from famous regiments; sailors from the fleet adrift in a sea of sand; the odd RAF pilot grounded instead of aloft; two Greek interpreters; some German Palestinians; and representatives of almost every one of the Commonwealth country nations. There were professional soldiers and there were ex-lawyers, merchants and mechanics. But for all of them there was now no turning back.

CHAPTER THREE

Destiny's Chance

The last doting of I's and T's now was now all that remained to be done as the final days ticked away before the assault parties set off. Obviously the land columns would need many days' advance notice to get themselves into position before the attack date itself, which the moon period and the preparations for Alamein had made the night of 13th/14th September 1942. With so many forces criss-crossing the desert wastes and the Eastern Mediterranean, and most of them heavily dependent upon one another, it was essential that a tight timetable was drawn up and ME GHQ was in overall control to ensure that it was kept to, except for the vital period from 1200 on D2 to 1200 on D3 when total command and control was to be transferred from GHQ to HQ C-in-C Mediterranean. Force 'Z' was to come directly under GHQ from 1200 on D3.

This meant that several staff officers had to move around: DMO and GI Current Operations from Cairo to Alexandria between 0800 and 1100 on the first day along with a clerk and then back again. A special room was set up at the Naval Operations Room for use of the Army and RAF officers during this period.

The final operational movements of Agreement were finalised thus:

D – 7	Force 'B' was to leave Kufra Oasis and proceed to assembly area in vicinity.
D – 3/1200	Sudan Defence Force detachment ready to proceed to Bahariya Oasis for Sitra for Operation Coastguard.
D – 1	Force 'A' was to sail from Haifa.
D – 1	Force 'C' was to sail from Alexandria.
D – 1/1200	Force 'B' to arrive Sidi Rezegh.
D – 1/2130	Air bombardment of Tobruk was to commence.
D – 1/2145	Force 'B' was to attack and capture the AA and CD guns at Mersa Umm es Sciausc.
D – 2/0130	RAF to stop dropping flares.

D – 2/0140   *Taku* to disembark folbots north of Mersa Mreira.

D – 2/0200   Folbots to land and mark entrance.

D – 2/0200   Force 'C' to enter Mersa Umm es Sciausc, but *only* if 'All Clear' to do so had been signalled by Force 'B'.

D – 2/0230   Force 'C' to land from MTBs and MLs.

D – 2/0300   *Sikh* and *Zulu* to arrive off Mersa Mreira.

D – 2/0340   First flight from Force 'A' would have landed and be followed by second flight.

D – 2/0340   The bombing would cease but diversionary air attacks would continue.

D – 2/0415   All air attacks would end.

D – 2/0415   MTBs and MLs would enter Tobruk harbour and attack shipping there.

D – 2/0900   *Sikh* and *Zulu* would enter Tobruk and mop up.

D – 2   Force 'Z' to leave Kufra for Gialo.

D – 4   Gialo to be captured by Force 'Z'.

So much for the attack at Tobruk. The bulk of the forces were to be withdrawn by sea after a twelve hour occupation. (Some historians, even today, appear to think Tobruk was to be held until relieved by the Eighth Army. This is of course incorrect.)

However, after a conference held at GHQ on Friday, 28th August at which Stirling and Oldfield of 'L' Detachment, Haselden, Commander Couchman of the C-in-C Mediterranean's staff, Lieutenant-Colonel Calthorpe and Major Quill, SO(I), Mediterranean attended as well as the top brass, it was decided that the military forces under the command of Lieutenant-Colonels Unwin and Haselden should, after the completion of their task at Tobruk, retire to Jebel in captured motor transport. The priority of those selected to return by land was – first, LRDG; second, SS Troops; third, Argyll and Sutherland; fourth, Royal Marines. The decision as to the feasibility of this retirement overland would be reached by Lieutenant-Colonels Unwin and Haselden about noon on D2 and the result of this decision would be communicated to Major Stirling.

The force in Jebel would have as their object the destruction of enemy supplies. Their final retirement would be made across the desert. Lieutenant-Colonel Haselden would work in collaboration with Major Stirling while operating in this area.

Stirling was told to continue to plan and operate on the assumption that the object first given him, namely, to destroy shipping, lighters and gun positions and deny the use of the Benghazi aerodromes to the enemy, were still his prime objectives. If he was successful then this fact was to be communicated to the joint Headquarters in Alexandria. It was then for the Chiefs-of-Staff to decide, in the light of information at their disposal, whether a ship with one battalion should be sailed from Malta to reinforce Stirling's holding party at Benghazi. The object of this battalion, if it was in fact landed, was to co-operate with Stirling's troops, and any released POWs, and try to hold Benghazi as long as possible before retiring and continuing to harass them in Jebel. Their withdrawal would have to be made by captured enemy motor transport over the desert because their ship was to be sunk to block the approaches to the port. It can be seen how this old idea refused to lie down.

Also detailed at this period was the final allocation of RAF squadrons to provide air cover over Forces 'A' and 'C'. They were made by the RAF in this manner. On Day One, two Hawker Hurricanes of 274 Squadron were to maintain a standing patrol and one hour after first light they were to be relieved by another two from 335 (Hellenic) Squadron, all operating at 8,000 feet. From that time on, two naval squadrons combined four Hurricanes of 274 were to patrol, two at the same height and two up at 12,000 feet. From 1100 hours the single-engined fighters were to be relieved by twin-engined Bristol Beaufighters from 252 and 272 Squadrons in relays and from 1915 a specially equipped night-fighting Beaufighter of 46 Squadron was to take up the job until 2130 in order to deal with the first night shadower, if any.

For the sake of simplicity we shall follow the fortunes of the various diversionary parties, each in turn to their conclusion before we turn to the final description and examination of Operation Agreement itself.

Benghazi
Stirling's attack was a complete failure and, although they managed to extradite themselves with the customary skill, they failed to cause any damage to their targets and were subjected to prolonged bombing afterwards. The force was a large one and proceeded in groups to lessen the likelihood of detection, with Captain Mayne and Lieutenant Maclean in the leading one. Captain John Olivey commanded S1, Captain Ken Lazarus commanded S2, both under

the leadership of David Stirling and his SAS personnel. They were equipped with Jeeps armed with Vickers K-guns and Ford 3-ton trucks laden with ammunition, fuel, water and food. Included in the SAS group were Captains William Cumper, Maxwell, Paddy Mayne, Robert Melot, Lieutenants Stephen Hastings, Fitzroy Maclean, Carol Mather, Michael Sadler and Sandy Scratchley and the RAF liaison officer, Flying Officer Derek Rawnsley with 57 NCOs and other ranks. A group of French officers and men were included on this raid.

After the mishap with the two 10th Hussar tanks, in all of the prolonged crossing of the Sand Sea by way of the Bir Zighen gap and the delicate side-stepping of Gialo, there was only one untoward incident when one truck was destroyed by a Thermos bomb and two of its crew seriously wounded. It took several days to cross the 800 miles of desert but they were not detected at all. Finally, the party reached the Trig-el-Abd track that skirted to the south of Jebel mountains between Agedabia and Agheila in the Gulf of Sirte and the Tobruk itself to the north-east. Here the LRDG's S1 Patrol, with one officer and 18 men in six Chevrolets, rendezvoused with S1 Patrol and Force 'X' at Wadi el Devadeen on 12th September.

Once at the Jebel, Fitzroy Maclean in the leading party made a rendezvous with the help of friendly Arabs with Robert Melot, a British agent who had been in the hills for several weeks scouting the lie of the land around Benghazi itself. Both Melot and the Arabs confirmed that reinforcements had been reaching the Axis defences in the port area in recent weeks. Much to Maclean's reluctance an Arab deserter from an Italian native force was produced who was said to be willing to spy out the town itself for them and this risk was agreed to. The man duly returned to the rendezvous point and confirmed that the attack seemed to be expected; extra minefields were being laid and more wire put up while the garrison was on a high alert. A German machine-gun detachment had arrived and extra Italian infantry were ordered in. Even the date of the attack, the 14th, was alleged by Maclean to have been common knowledge.

This information was invaluable and was passed to Stirling when he arrived in the mountains with the last column to cross the desert. He in turn notified GHQ ME but was advised to continue as planned. Next day, the assault party set out for the target. One party, guided by Melot, set out to attack a fort which housed a radio transmitter; the rest headed for the main Benghazi road. Their objective was the harbour itself and then later Benina airfield east of Benghazi. The Liberator bombers made their attacks as planned on the night of D1 and their bomb burst could be clearly seen but owing to a guide taking the wrong track down the escarpment Stirling's force was late getting onto the main road into the port.

By the time they had reached the road it was 0300 with only a few hours of darkness remaining. The patrol set off at full speed to try and make up some of the lost time. But worse was to follow for they were still some three miles short of their objectives when they ran into a road block with the suspicion of a freshly laid minefield on either side beyond to prevent them by-passing it. All seemed quiet and so Captain William Cumper, a Londoner and former Royal Engineer officer and 'one of the best explosives officers in the Middle East', who was in the leading truck with Stirling himself, got out to investigate. He confirmed that they were minefields. He lifted the barrier to allow the convoy through but the fact that this was a carefully prepared ambush was immediately made obvious for a hail of small-arms fire broke out from concealed positions ahead of them. Somehow, Cumper regained the Jeep and a wild fire-fight at close range developed.

Fortunately, the excited Italian defenders were blazing away over the heads of the SAS column or else casualties would have been heavy at this point for they were well and truly surprised. However, they soon spread out and began shooting back with their Vickers K-guns which immediately brought about a slackening of fire from beyond the block. An attempt by one Jeep to crash the barrier and get to the other side of the defenders failed and Sergeant Almond's vehicle was set on fire. Soon, other British vehicles were hit and began burning. Surprise was obviously not to be had. Dawn was breaking. The full Benghazi garrison would now be on their way and the Axis bombers were probably already revving up on their runways. Stirling had little choice but to order his column to retreat forthwith.

By now it was also clearly far too late to try to make it back to the mountains. They would be caught long before they made the top of the escarpment so they camouflaged their trucks as best they could at the foot of it. However, it was not long before the German dive-bombers and Italian biplane fighter bombers located them and one of the first bombing attacks of the day blew up an ammunition truck which acted as a marker to lead further aircraft to home on them. All day the air attacks continued. Not used to sitting and taking it, the SAS this time had little choice although one French-manned vehicle started up and made a running fight of it with a CR42 which they shot down with their Vickers and Browning guns. This was an heroic but isolated incident, however. By nightfall some nine vehicles had been destroyed, but fortunately casualties were small: four men wounded.

Meanwhile, the group led by Melot had accomplished their task, for the cost of two more men seriously wounded. They rendezvoused that night with the surviving vehicles of Stirling's column and holed up in a deep wadi which they hoped would provide better protection the following day. However, one Jeep was late at the rendezvous, reaching at first light next day, and it was followed in by the bombers who allowed it to lead them to the main force. Further intense air attacks duly followed and by the end of it a massacre had resulted in the destruction of 18 Jeeps and 25 trucks from the combined force. This left enough vehicles to pack three men in each surviving Jeep and twenty into each truck, but little food or water remained to them. In two days of disastrous action, 75 per cent of his vehicles were wiped out and 25 per cent of his men were killed or missing, with nothing to show for it at all.

For four days they made their way south toward Gialo and what they thought would be safety. However, when they arrived they found that, far from establishing a base there, the Sudanese attacking force was still heavily engaged in fighting with the Italian garrison and that the bulk of the oasis still remained in enemy hands. They did, however, manage to get much-needed supplies and, when the main force was ordered soon afterwards to withdraw, the SAS retreated back across the Sand Sea to Kufra once more. In the meanwhile, Stirling himself remained in the Jebel looking for the many stragglers from his force. He rounded up a dozen in the end and brought them safely out by the same route a few days later.

The contemporary Italian view was given soon afterwards by Terravazzi who stated:

> The jeeps arrived from inland and attacked the three airfields, but they were checked by the barricades across the Via Balbia and beaten off by the airfield guards. They suffered a number of losses and achieved nothing.*

The C-in-C's viewpoint was this: 'Stirling seems to have been expected and consequently through no fault of his not to have achieved much.'

* Quoted in *Alamein 1933 – 1962* by Paolo Cacchia-Dominioni.

Barce

The attack on Barce was the only raid that was successful. Major 'Jake' R. Easonsmith with Major Peniakoff led an HQ section and two patrols, G1 and T1, along with S1 commanded by Olivey who were to break away later and make the attack on Benina airfield in conjunction with Stirling's force, as we have seen. The main column, which totalled 64 men in twelve Chevrolet trucks and five Jeeps, left El Faiyoum on 2nd September for the start of what was to be a 1,155 mile journey to Barce. In order to reduce the risk of detection, Easonsmith decided to use an old route to Ain Dalla, across the Sand Sea, to a location point known as 'Big Cairn' a six-foot high marker erected pre-war by Clayton and used by the LRDG as a rendezvous and store point, it being some 575 miles west of their base.

The first three hundred miles to Ain Dalla were on the comparatively good going but then after three days they entered the Sand Sea following Easonsmith's Jeep along a familiar, but hazardous route which he plotted at right angles to the big sweeping dunes. The column soon slowed down to an agonisingly slow pace and was subjected to frequent breakdowns, burnt-out clutches, broken steering-arms and vehicles becoming bogged down in the deep sand. There was also the occasional accident when a razor-backed dune was taken at speed resulting in a sheer drop the other side. In such a manner did the Guards patrols officer, Captain Alasdair Timpson, come to grief when he rolled his Jeep on just such a hazard. He had his head crushed, but his gunner Thomas Wann had his spine so badly bent that he was paralysed from the waist down. They were evacuated by air from Big Cairn.*

Time was by then getting short. After leaving Big Cairn the going became better and speed was increased. The Rhodesian patrol broke away and the remaining two patrols pressed on at their best pace. By the morning of 13th September they were two days behind schedule, and because of this they missed a rendezvous with two of Peniakoff's Seussi agents. A final halt was made at a position fifteen miles to the south-west of their target. They had already seen signs of increased enemy activity in the form of fresh tracks but were not challenged nor apparently sighted so the fifteen vehicles were laagered for the night in readiness for the attack the next day.

Having rested up they moved off again at dusk driving towards

* The unlucky gunner spent the rest of his life in a wheelchair, dying on 19 January 1987. His wife, Maisie, having nursed him for 45 years, died 13 days later.

the town, cutting telephone wires and destroying a police post on the way. They then split up to make their separate assaults but when T1 patrol was still five miles from the airfield they ran into two Italian tanks. They had no time to swop blows with such adversaries and took sharp avoiding action, their speed outmanœuvring the Italians, but it was feared that surprise had been lost. Far from it, however; they caught the enemy napping despite this.

G1 Patrol carried out a successful mission against the Italian barracks buildings in the town. They sped up to it and raked the building with machine-gun fire keeping the defenders' heads well down. A storming party of five men then closed under cover of this light weapons' screen and dropped several hand-grenades through the windows and door. This effectively silenced the garrison for good and allowed their companions to hit the airfield itself more or less unmolested.

'T' Patrol, having sped away from the two challenging Italian tanks, carried on with their part of the sortie as planned, driving fast straight through the main gates of the airfield. They then headed for the strip itself where they could make out thirty-plus aircraft parked on the apron and without any obvious defences barring the way. In typical LRDG manner they formed single line ahead like a squadron of destroyers and roared down between the rows of parked aircraft, shooting into them at close range with incendiaries and small arms fire. Any obvious targets that the first wave missed were tackled more methodically by the crew of the last truck with the placing of short-delay demolition charges.

The results looked spectacular and high claims were made but in fact the actual results of this daring assault were seven Cant Z10001 bombers, six Cacchia Ca311 and one SM79 bomber, one Ghibli and one German Fieseler Storch reconnaissance plane, totally burnt out and destroyed. They also destroyed a lorry laden with fifty-two tins of petrol. The remaining 16 aircraft were all damaged but were all subsequently repaired.

The surprised Italian defenders were totally demoralised and reported the attacks had been carried out 'by British armoured cars'. Although they did not offer much in the way of resistance, the LRDG had now well and truly stirred up the hornets' nest and all the Axis airfields in the area were put on full alert. This included a German Stuka base and they were to bring quick retribution for the Italians' losses. Not surprisingly then, the two patrols found their return journey was rather more tricky than the ride in and indeed it was to turn into a rout. They once again ran into the pair of Italian tanks they had met earlier. This time, rather than waste time avoiding them, the patrol tackled them head-on. They were rammed by the leading British truck and before they could regain their composure the British had scrambled clear and placed grenades beneath the tracks of both tanks, immobilising them. They then headed out to the desert to return to the rallying point. According to the general plan, this was to be at LG125, a former Allied desert airstrip. Here, they were to join up with the other parties in two days.

However, on reforming after the attack, it was found that only six of the vehicles were still operational, although three more were under tow. This was to slow them down fatally and before long the Junkers Ju87's arrived, attacking in pairs. For a long period, they harried and bombed and strafed the columns, dispersing them and picking them off one by one. There was little defence, caught out in the open this way, and the LRDG suffered heavily losing 21 casualties out of their total of 47 men and having 15 out of their 17 vehicles destroyed completely. By evening, only one Jeep and one Chevrolet truck remained. Easonsmith decided that the wounded should be sent on ahead to LG125 in the two vehicles. The rest took to shanks' pony to trudge back to the rendezvous point, hiding by day from the persistent air searches. They had naturally lost most of their food and water with the destruction of their vehicles, but luckily they were able to negotiate some supplies of milk and meat from some Arab tribesmen. Then they split into small groups and headed off to seek the relief column. Most of them were later rescued by S2 Patrol by 19th September except for two who became separated and lost, but who later surrendered at Benghazi.

Again an Italian viewpoint was given by Terravazzi:

'Here there were only jeeps. Very artfully they made straight for the town and then attacked the airfield from the town instead of from the desert. Naturally the defences of the airfield were concentrated on the far side, facing the open country, and the few guards on the town side were swiftly overcome. Some of the attackers went round setting fire to the aircraft, while others kept up heavy machine-gun fire on the airfield buildings, and effectively prevented any intervention on the part of the garrison. After this they withdrew, but it appears that some of them were caught in the desert.

During the daylight hours of the 14th, our air force attacked groups of trucks and jeeps withdrawing into the desert and towards Kufra. Some vehicles were destroyed, and a number of men were killed and wounded. On the 15th, two slightly wounded Englishmen arrived at Benghazi and asked for help for their more seriously hurt comrades immobilised in the desert.*

But in fact many of the wounded were evacuated from LG125 by air on the 18th September.

Another Italian was later to tell Popski, who himself had the little finger of his left hand shot off by Italian machine-gun fire during the fighting:

I know what happened because I took part in that action myself, with a machine-gun. I was a short distance from Barce with half a signals company. You succeeded partly as a result of your skill and courage, but above all because there was not an efficient garrison on the spot.

Gialo

While survivors of the other raids made their way to safety, the Sudanese Defence Force, led in by two LRDG Y1 and Y2 Patrols commanded by Captains Hunter and Talbot, had failed to establish the raiding base at Gialo. (Captain Tony Hunter commanded S1 Patrol with a detachment of the SDF.) Their attack on the night of 15/16th September was thought to have been the easiest of all to accomplish but they met with unexpectedly well-organised resistance. After establishing a holding base and dump at what Kennedy Shaw named the 'Middle-Lift Wadi' some 75 miles south-west of Gialo, three columns of the Sudanese force advanced under cover of darkness to within a few hundred yards of the fort itself.

After much confused fighting, the attackers managed to gain a lodgement in the fort itself and the western part of the oasis. But the Italians counter-attacked bravely and the fort was re-captured. During the 16th and 17th, they heavily shelled the Italian garrison holding out stubbornly in the eastern part causing fires and explosions but were unable to shift them at all. The Italians reacted from the air with attacks by bombers against both dump and lodgement. The Sudanese managed to shoot down one CR42 fighter-bomber and damaged another but could make no progress

* Quoted in *Alamein 1933 – 1962* op cit.

on the ground. On the 19th, while a second major assault was being readied, GHQ ordered them to pull back to join Force 'X' on its return journey to Kufra.

Siwa

The demonstration at Siwa was duly carried out by the motorised Sudanese Defence Force battalion on the 14th after the dummy paratroop drop. They returned the next day. Their outing had caused absolutely no enemy reaction on the spot, save that the enemy sent more troops to reinforce the garrison the next day.

One naval operation that *did* go according to plan was conducted in the early hours of 14th September when the light cruiser *Dido* and the destroyers *Javelin*, *Jervis*, *Kelvin*, *Paladin* and *Pakenham* carried out a night bombardment of the Daba area at 0001. They fired a total of 350 rounds, getting an estimated 50 per cent hits on the main target and 70 per cent of their salvoes in the area. All the warships returned safely to Port Said without further incident.

All that these raids achieved were a major overhaul of Axis defences along their lines of communication, whereby Gialo, Jarabub and Siwa all had their garrisons reinforced. The German replacement battalions were put into Sollum, and the Italian Pavia Division was retained at Mersa Matruh for a short period before moving up to the front line. The capture of Kufra was also on the cards but events at the front prevented this from taking place.

Tobruk

We must now retrace our steps several days to the eastern end of the Mediterranean Sea, in the much shrunken parameters of British control which now only extended some forty miles eastward of Alexandria itself and up northward through Palestine and French-controlled Syria. Hemming this area in to the north was Turkey, a wavering neutral, fearful of German expansion and proven power, harbouring a centuries-old detestation for the Russians and somewhat credulous of the ever-increasing list of defeats being suffered by the once-great British Empire in Europe, North Africa and the Middle East; even India to the rear seemed threatened at this date with the loss of Malaya and Burma to the Japanese and the humiliation of the Royal Navy in the Indian Ocean in April at the hands of the Japanese Task Force.

Here the much-reduced Royal Navy was utilising the bulk of its few remaining warships almost entirely to the needs of the Army and

Admiral Harwood was gambling that this devotion to the cause would not prove abortively costly.

As an example of how far his force was stretched, the two destroyers had to squeeze in the test landings between normal convoy escort duties. Also the ordinary ships' boats had to be used because the special craft were still being built (some would have said, thrown together) at Haifa. Many of these were still being rushed to completion to meet the deadline (some even had to have the engines fitted at the last moment).

Following this rather abortive test landing off Cyprus, some small improvements had been made to the two destroyers' accommodation. Thus in order to load the 'proper' landing craft both destroyers had their ships' whalers moved forward and slung from new auxiliary davits while the motor-powered lighters took their places on the davits at the break in the fo'c'sle. Further along, at the ship's waist were to be stacked, inside one another, six of the dumb lighters on each ship.

In the same rather casual and makeshift manner the MTB flotillas had made their own dummy landings on the seafront at Alexandria in front of scores of civilians of the Royal Egyptian Yacht Club. No warships were less suitable for the transportation and landing of parties of soldiers than these little craft. They were built exclusively for speed, with low profile and a small narrow 'hard chine' hull, and their tiny departments below decks crammed to bursting point to accommodate their powerful engines. The limited deck space on these little vessels was crammed with automatic cannon, machine-guns and depth charges. They could barely accommodate their crews, yet now they had to find room for nine sections of men armed to the teeth, plus a great deal of demolition gear and explosives, not to mention extra petrol tanks for the long sea voyage. These latter were strapped to the upper decks and turned the frail craft filled with men and machinery into floating time bombs.

Ashore, too, at Alexandria, the same story could be seen with small units training hard for their specialised role in the coming battle. Lieutenant Philip Myers, with thirty men of 261 HAA Battery, Royal Artillery, was completing training on how to operate various German and Italian guns at Mustafa Barracks, Alexandria. There was a sub-section of 296 Company, Royal Engineers with special demolition charges to get ready and pack. The Royal Northumberland Fusiliers platoon had been pulled out of the front line at Alamein and brought down to the coast under the command of Lieutenant E. Raymond. The Argyll and Sutherland Highlanders, commanded by Captain N. McFie, numbered five officers and 97 men in all. There were two Royal Army Medical Corps sergeants and an AA gunner detachment under Lieutenant Beddington.

It was hard *not* to realise something special was brewing with all this activity at Alexandria. To try and fool the German spies who tumbled this rather obvious fact during the training the Argylls had two Greek officers attached to them. It was hoped this might indicate that the target was Rhodes, the main island base in the Aegean, often listed as a target for attack over the previous two years, but still inviolate.

Admiral Harwood noted on 3rd September that: 'Security cover has been provided for by the inclusion of Greek offices and men in the military forces during the training period.' However it was to take more than that to convince the Alexandria grapevine that it was not Tobruk that was the object of all this frantic preparation.

Finally, however, and for some far too soon, the time came to embark the forces. Thus, on the 11th and 12th at both Haifa and Alexandria there was yet more movement down to the dock area. The commanding officer of 'A' Company, Royal Marines, noted:

> 11th Battalion Royal Marines embarked at 2100 hours on Friday 11th September on board HMS *Sikh* and *Zulu*. Battalion Headquarters and 'B' Company and Headquarters Machine Gun Platoon, together with attached Royal Artillery and Royal Engineers aboard *Sikh* and 'A' and 'C' Companies, with two Machine Gun Sections and attached Royal Artillery and Royal Engineer Detachments aboard *Zulu*.
>
> We sailed at 0600 hours on Saturday, 12th September, for Alexandria. On reaching Alexandria at 2000 hours Intelligence Officers came aboard and gave us last minute details, issuing us with small compasses, silk maps and special iron rations.

Aboard one of the destroyers was Captain Earle A. Graham who was a young film cameraman with the Army Film and Photo Unit. He had been sent out to the Middle East towards the end of 1941 and had been in Tobruk itself at the end of October when it was still under siege. He had filmed the break-out and had been closely involved in the desert campaigns throughout 1942, including a period with the Long Range Desert Group themselves when he

(*Above*) The low-lying but rocky cliffs skirting the bay of Marsa el Auda where the destroyers landed the first wave of the Royal Marines in error.

(*Right*) The narrow gully leading up the cliffs from the bay Marsa el Auda, up which the Royal Marines who managed to get ashore fought their way to the top.

Italian Marines of the San Marco battalion in action at Tobruk early on the morning of 14th September 1942.

The Italian destroyer *Castore* and various German and Italian landing craft acting as mobile artillery units in action against British MTB's off Tobruk harbour, morning of 14th September 1942.

joined a Road Watch. He was therefore an ideal choice to film Agreement and he was able to provide me with a trained observer's close-range view of events as they unfolded, including the preparations as the ships sailed for the target zone.

Just after the battle of Alam Halfa I was recalled to Cairo, and was told that I was to go on a commando raid. I went to Alexandria and boarded the *Sikh* in the early hours of Sunday, 13th September. It was then that I learned that our target was Tobruk.

The *Sikh* and her sister destroyer, the *Zulu*, had come from Haifa with the Marine Commando which was to carry out the attack. This was to be co-ordinated with a land attack ferried in by the LRDG. On board I met one of our sergeants – Crapper – who had boarded with the Marines at Haifa. We were briefed on the details of the raid; the attack was to be made in two waves as there were not enough landing craft for everyone to go together. Sergeant Crapper and I were to go with the second wave, and I decided that we should operate separately so as to get the widest coverage. The landing craft were big open boats and were to be towed ashore by some that had motors. I never knew the exact number. He was attached to one party and I to another.

Thus the seaborne part of the great raid got under way.

*

The land raiding force of the SAS had also assembled its vehicles at Abbassieh Barracks in broad daylight before beginning the first stage of its 1,200-mile journey from Cairo to Tobruk. This had been on 24th August and they had then started out to cover the easiest leg across to the Kufra Oasis. Here they joined up with the various other parties as related. Here, the LRDG patrols were subjected to the hard scrutiny of RSM Swinburn of the Leicester Regiment who did not approve of what he saw. There followed six days of rest and training.

Later, Hudson aircraft brought in Stirling and other SAS leaders fresh from the last-minute conferences and Bombay transports brought in the four Germans of the SIG with their two British officers, Bray, formerly of the 4th Indian Division, and Lanark an ex-Scots Guardsman. The four young SIG men, Corporal Weizmann, Privates Wilenski, Berg and Steiner, kept themselves

apart from the rest and constantly practised German drill. They
were looked upon with suspicion and downright distrust, especially
by the LRDG men, for one 'traitor' from a force of two such
Palestinians had betrayed one of their patrols earlier that year,
resulting in their deaths. Jock Fraser told me: 'We all distrusted
these guys though some were very brave men.'

Other ill-assorted guests looking out of place in the middle of the
Sahara were Pilot Officer Aubrey L. Scott, the RAF liaison officer,
who later fell asleep and fell off his truck during the night passage
of the Sand Sea, and two naval ratings who were to liaise with Force
'C'.

Finally, Colonel John Haselden arrived and the officers,
including Lloyd Owen and Stirling, had a meeting. It was here that
Haselden told them that Rommel had emptied Tobruk's defences
completely and that only low-grade Italian units would be met. He
was full of confidence. He revealed that there were an estimated
4,000 Allied POWs in a cage south of Tobruk which he aimed to set
loose and there were another estimated 16,000 in camps south of
Benghazi which he hoped Stirling would be able to use.

Following this, most of the combined force moved out of Kufra
on 6th September.

The next full officers' conference was not held until the force
reached Hatiet Etla, some ninety miles south of Tobruk, which was
reached on 10th September and here it was that the last rehearsal
of the drive-in was done.

*

David Lloyd Owen's Y1 patrol of the LRDG accompanied the
commandos from the Nile Valley to Kufra and thence to the vicinity
of Tobruk.

The two General Stuart (Honey) tanks did not last long, as
Gordon Fraser remembered:

We were on a huge sand sheet, 'A' grade going, flat sand for
hundreds of miles. Despite this, somehow the two Honey tanks
collided, coming together with a crash and both of them lost their
tracks. We hadn't the means to repair them so they were left
where they had stopped and we took their crews on to Kufra.
There was a sequel to this many, many years later. I was invited
to go with my family to the première of the film *Sea of Sand*. When

I arrived, the manager of the cinema met me at the door and took me to meet a chap who was posing for the camera and giving a vivid account of various episodes. The manager introduced me and said that of course I must know this fellow. I had never seen him in my life before – at least not that I could remember. It turned out he was one of the Honey tank drivers.

Gordon remembers other incidents along the way quite clearly as well: 'I can well remember the patrol and the commandos and that at one point we were running late and the skipper, David Lloyd Owen, switched some of us drivers from the patrol to take over the 3-tonners of the commandos in order to push things along.'

What better person could there be to recount accurately the movements of this force to Tobruk than their navigator himself, Jim Patch?

The Commandos were highly disciplined and quite unused to the casual behaviour of the LRDG men who were all well-trained individualists whose effectiveness depended much more on self-discipline rather than accepted army protocol. I experienced a vivid illustration of this before we left the Nile Valley. Our normal footwear was sandals – Indian chaplis – and no socks. This was fine in the desert but not so good in populated areas. We had just reached Asyut and were about to turn south-west into the desert towards Kufra when a hornet got itself trapped between my sandal and my big toe and stung me. At our next stop, my toe had begun to swell so I went to find the Commando Medical Officer. I found him talking to another Commando officer and, as they were just chatting, I interrupted and asked the doctor whether there was anything he could do about my ever expanding toe. Before the doctor could reply, the other officer gave me a glare and asked him whether he had any plans for holding sick parades and, if so, when the next one would be held. The doctor was a good deal more unbending and told me there was precious little he could do unless I thought that complications were setting in.

The journey to Kufra was, so far as I remember, uneventful. The journey north from Kufra towards Tobruk was routine enough until we began to get close to Gialo. Here we stopped, had our evening meal and, when the stars came out, I took a fix to be absolutely certain we knew where we were. We then took

Jim Patch continued:

a very careful bearing to take us between Gialo and the western end of the Great Sand Sea, keeping as far from enemy occupied Gialo as possible but staying on the good going just out of the sand.

Navigation has to be by magnetic compass. This meant that David Lloyd Owen, who was leading, had to get out of his vehicle every 15 minutes or so and find a star low on the horizon which happened to be on the right bearing. I had to do the same but more frequently because every deviation to get past large obstructions such as hills and wadis had to be recorded in case we were seriously diverted from our route. No headlights were allowed but each vehicle had its differential painted white and a small lamp under the body shone on this. Thus each driver was able to follow the truck in front. There was no moon. I had a tiny map-reading light. We travelled all night and when, in the morning, David Lloyd Owen judged it safe to stop, I placed my cross on the map a short distance from a hill called Qaret Something-or-other. Colonel John Haselden came to examine the map, looked about him and pointed to a hill about half a mile away, saying, 'Well, that's about the only thing anywhere near here which is anything like a qaret.' I have often wondered whether that hill was, in fact, the one marked on the map. I like to think it was. Not that we ever had any faith in those terrible Italian maps we had to use.

The journey continued through broken country with many hills and wadis. Every time we stopped and I marked our progress on the map one of the Commando officers would come over to me and want to look at the map and then take bearings on the different features shown on it in order to check our position. I had to keep pointing out that it was LRDG practice to rely far more on the navigator's dead reckoning than on bearings taken on anything marked on an Italian map. Taking a lot of fancy bearings might have been all very well at the OCTU but was a waste of time and, indeed, dangerous in the situation in which we found ourselves. When we stopped for a midday meal, I slept.

We arrived at Hatiet Etla in good time. Here was plenty of camouflage for the vehicles and we had a day or so to spare. The Commandos practised their drill in the event of their being challenged at the Tobruk perimeter. Ken Tinckler, who spoke German, acted the German guard who became suspicious and

Jim Patch continued:

called out to the Guard Commander. The dispirited British 'prisoners' at once leapt to life, produced weapons, wiped out the guard and drove off. I was impressed.

At the appointed time we arrived at a point on the escarpment above Tobruk and sent the Commandos off with much shouting of good luck. After dark we followed and in the broken country at the bottom of the escarpment we were fired on from a pill box. Ken Tinckler was driving the truck I was on – the wireless truck – and must have stalled the engine. He said, 'We've been hit' and we all piled out. There was Dave Searl, the wireless operator, Stacey, Ken and me. The rest of the patrol had stopped nearby and we joined them on foot. David Lloyd Owen said we must either recover the truck or destroy it, especially the cyphers which were on board. A party of us returned for the truck and located it with a Very light. It was just a few yards from the pill box. Under covering fire Sullivan and I ran to the truck. He got into the driving seat and I resumed my normal place in the passenger seat. He pressed the starter and the engine started and we drove to where the rest of the patrol were waiting. The only damage was a punctured tyre which was soon repaired.

As the patrol re-assembled, someone spotted a lone figure on the edge of the darkness and we all crouched down, weapons trained on this figure. David Lloyd Owen called, 'Who are you?' but there was no answer. We then tried to find out whether anyone was missing, each man announcing his name. It was – 'Harrison' – 'Here, sir!'; 'Fraser' – 'Here, sir!' and so on. Then, 'Hall' and from the figure we were all staring at came 'Here, sir!' He was called a few other names at the time.

We found the road which led to the main coast road into Tobruk. We were late and drove fast with headlights on. I switched to the large scale map of Tobruk and David Lloyd Owen stopped where he judged the perimeter barrier would be. There was a steam roller across the road which we simply drove round. If there were any enemy there, there was no sound from them. There was a lot of shooting going on from the direction of the town and harbour. A little further on we pulled off the road to the right into a hollow and Dave Searl tried to contact the Commandos on the radio. There was no response. He kept on trying but without success. The result was that we stayed in that spot all night because it would have been futile to go in without direction or being aware of what we would meet. A staff car came along the road from Tobruk. We stopped it but one of the occupants got away. Soon after, searchlights began to scan the area but we remained hidden because we were in the hollow.

At first light, David Lloyd Owen ordered us out. Titch Cave wanted to shoot up all the enemy camps we passed on the way back to the escarpment but was ordered to restrain himself.

Gordon Harrison recounted:

I remember waiting on the outskirts of Tobruk for instructions to go in and do our part. I think we had to go in and release the POWs and send them to the beach and then go and destroy the aircraft on the aerodrome. None of this happened because the commandos didn't manage to silence the Coastal Guns. I recall us driving out of Tobruk at dawn and driving through German camps with their cooks, etc., just getting the day's work started. We then turned into the desert driving like hell waiting for the Stukas to come looking for us.

Another LRDG man, Jock Fraser, has similar memories of this sickening end to their hopes and schemes.

My own small part was as a gunner in the back of a truck, always scanning the sky and the horizon as we escorted the commandos towards Tobruk. I spotted an enemy patrol; we ambushed them and killed them all. Nearing Tobruk we parted from the raiders and commandos and they took the road while we drove through a mine field in the dark and parked beside an enemy laager where we were to wait for the signal for us to enter the perimeter.

Heavy gunfire and bombing was going on, and the only way into Tobruk was by that same main road, as elsewhere there were tank-traps, slit trenches, barbed wire, machine-gun posts and mines. Had we gone in as planned our job would have been to attack the aircraft and the radar sites and then to release the British POWs. Sadly the signal never came and we were ordered to withdraw. By then the gunfire had almost ceased as daylight was creeping in. We then drove up the road past a huge enemy encampment; fortunately they showed little interest in us as they lit their cooking fires and such. Then it was through the mine field

again and we set about putting as much distance as possible
between us and Tobruk before the enemy began their air
searches, which were not long in coming. We got away all right,
but our thoughts were with the lads who didn't return.

One Italian version of these incidents was recorded by Paolo
Cacchia-Dominioni, in this manner:

> At El Adem on the afternoon of the 13th, a group made up of a
> lieutenant, a sergeant, four airmen and a civilian labourer were
> collecting spare parts from damaged aircraft to the south of the
> airfield when they were surprised and captured by the occupants
> of a truck which they had taken for German. . . . The seven men
> were shot down in cold blood. Two of them were only wounded
> and saved themselves by feigning death. When the truck left they
> managed to make their way to the airfield. That truck was
> certainly the advance guard for the main body following on and
> making for Tobruk.

*

When the raiders were last seen they were on the way in for the last
and most hazardous leg of their audacious journey.

The disguised party of prisoners and escorts drove boldly on
towards the town in their Canadian-built 3-ton trucks. Strangely
enough such vehicles in themselves evoked no particular interest in
the Italian sentries or any other onlookers. So vast had been the
booty taken during the Eighth Army's pell-mell retreat earlier that
summer that hundreds of such trucks had fallen in the grateful hands
of the Axis. They themselves were short of transport and such a
windfall had been a real bonus for their supply detachments.
Nothing much was done to the trucks other than to mark them with
the Afrika Korps motif and paint identification markings on the cab
roofs to keep the Stukas away.

The real German POW convoys usually contrived to cram forty
prisoners in each lorry. Apart from the driver, his mate, standing
on the seat, acted as the solitary armed guard with his weapon
trained on the prisoners. The need to conceal all the hidden arms
of the raiding party plus their changes of clothing meant that only
thirty men could be loaded in each of the six vehicles but it was

hoped that this discrepancy would not be noticed in the twilight; nor was it. With only four 'genuine' Germans they were hard-pressed to have enough men in the cabs who could speak the language if seriously challenged but overcame the problem by having three of the officers, Lieutenants Barlow, Harrison and Langton, volunteering to play this role, as well. Each of the SIG had his carefully prepared passes and ID documents to hand for close scrutiny.

There had been a slight delay in their descent of the escarpment before they reached the main road, and they had to take care in joining it at a suitably slack time but once safely on they merged into the normal base traffic flow and began to make better time down the metalled road to the perimeter fence, where they were merely waved through. It was all much easier than they dared to hope.

One version of what happened after that is given as follows:

Inside matters did not proceed quite so smoothly, as they quickly met a fast-moving convoy coming towards them and their middle lorry was struck a glancing blow by a German staff car carrying, according to another SIG man, a high-ranking officer. None of the lorries stopped – indeed they accelerated away – while behind them the Axis convoy slowed to a halt; various angry voices shouted after them but eventually the convoy started off again, doubtless with someone writing down the lorry numbers for disciplinary action to be taken at some future date. For another uncomfortable period the commandos were accompanied by three motor-cycle combinations bearing German military police who seemed unnecessarily inquisitive, and for a time it seemed that Very lights erupted on every occasion they passed an important Axis installation, giving the impression that their course was being charted; but no attempt was made to stop them, and the most memorable moment in their journey into Tobruk came when Haselden nodded casually towards an impressive rockface looming out of the near-darkness (for it was by now nearly 2100) and said, 'That's the bomb-proof oil-storage depot we must destroy later tonight.'

However, Langton's account is somewhat different to this:

Owing to a slight miscalculation, the party was late getting on to the El Adem road and it was dark soon after we had turned on to the main road towards Tobruk. However, the entrance went smoothly and no check posts were encountered. Further delay was caused by the fact that apparently considerable alterations (wire fences, etc.) had been made where the track along the southern bank of the harbour joined the main road. We were still some way off our debussing point when the bombing started.

In the event, all passed off smoothly as they drove steadily past the huge enemy airbase of El Adem and down the road past sprawling camps, dumps and activity. Two miles on they had reached the outskirts of Tobruk town itself and here the trucks pulled off the road, the 'guards' quickly removed their German uniforms and substituted the more normal British battledress. Likewise, the surly and apathetic 'POWs' threw off their lethargy and armed themselves for instant action. In Langton's terse words, 'After debussing, sorting stores, hiding German uniforms, etc., the two parties set out.'

Between 2225 and 0330 91 Wellingtons, Halifaxes, Liberators and Fortress bombers dropped 70 tons of bombs on Tobruk and started several fires. Under cover of this rising crescendo of noise and frenzy the small party of grim-faced men began moving out in earnest.

Haselden's bold, but exceedingly dangerous, gamble had seemingly paid off.

CHAPTER FOUR

Steadily Worse

The German reports are full of the massive RAF air bombardment of the town area and how both its length and intensity aroused their fears and brought their units to a high pitch of readiness. Although the bombing was spectacular and caused a few large fires, actual casualties were remarkably small and the damage inflicted was negligible despite claims to the contrary. 'At 0230 the Kommandant of the Reserve Army area reported the termination of about seven hours' continuous bombing of the Tobruk area,' ran one official account. The AOK at once put all land forces on full alert and brought reserve units further out in the desert in instant readiness to move. The Kommandant's own report states that between 2040 on the 13th and 0330 on the 14th air attacks on Tobruk were continuous and were carried out by 178 two- and four-engined aircraft. The Germans claimed that they dropped about 600 bombs while they claimed in return to have shot down seven of them. The attacks were carried out 'with great severity', and by 2300 a warning had been sent to Generalmajor Deindl, who, as was customary for one or two days of each month, was visiting the HQ of the 'Köruck' battalion, some twenty kilometres west of Tobruk town itself.

Under his immediate command in the Tobruk area, Deindl had the following German land units:

1. (a) The Staff company of the 'Köruck' battalion along with the Field Police and the 613th (Motorised) Military Police company.
   (b) Two companies of *Wachbatl.* (Guards Battalion) *Afrika* (the 3rd company of this unit was based at Mersa Matruh).
   (c) The reinforced Motorised 909 Pioneer Company.
   Altogether 35 officers and 680 NCOs and men.
   2. Under the command of Nachschubstab Tobruck, Major Hardt, the complete strength of the supply and back units based in Tobruk itself, in total about 40 officers and 1,400 men.
   3. Under the command of Luftwaffe Garrison Commander, Major Schewe, the Luftwaffe airfield guard and ancillary units, totalling in all some 20 officers and 292 men.

4. Under command of Major Hartmann was Flakgruppe Tobruck, the AA and light AA batteries defending the town and the harbour. (In the German line of battle the Anti-Aircraft (Flak) units came under command of the Luftwaffe, not the army as was the British custom.) Their weapons were very efficient and far superior to anything the Italians or British possessed in this line of equipment. The heavy flak, the famous and deadly '88', Flak 36, was already famed as the tank-destroyer *par excellence* in the desert and was as good a weapon firing horizontally as it was firing vertically. It had a rate of fire of between 15 and 20 rounds a minute. The German batteries around Tobruk could count no less than four dozen of these weapons in their armoury! The mobile multiple 20-mm weapon, of which some 85 were in place, was a superior version of the Swiss Oerlikon gun firing cannon shells at high speed and again could easily be directed against land targets.

5. A small naval guard detachment from the German Navy in the port area, consisting of two officers and 25 men under the command of Korvettenkapitän Meixner.

The Germans had already established a plan to repel any seaborne landing which had been well rehearsed and on the issuing of the codeword 'Landealarm' all these units were to be subordinated to Major Hardt in the fortress sectors along the coast north of Tobruk, stretching from the town along the heights with the main high road west, the Via Balbia, as their main supply and reinforcement route.

The Italians were supposed to co-ordinate their own plans with this but in the event, the Fortress Commander, General Giannantoni was in Bardia hospital sick and command had devolved on his second-in-command, Colonel Battaglia. The senior Italian commander was Captain Temistocle D'Aloja but, by coincidence, Rear-Admiral Giuseppe Lombardi of the Italian navy was visiting the fortress at the time, and because of his rank he was the overall senior Axis officer present.

The best troops the Italians had were the 160 Marines of the San Marco battalion commanded by Lieutenant Colotto. These had themselves just staged a much smaller-scale attack behind British lines when, on the night of 29th August, a force of fourteen demolition personnel from this unit had been put ashore from an Italian destroyer to cut a rail link and aqueduct between El Alamein and Alexandria, which they accomplished successfully. The coastal batteries, 6-inch and 4-inch, at Fort Peronne to the north and Mersa

Biad to the south, were not yet fully operational but were being modernised and extended and both had some guns in position behind strong concrete block-houses and entrenchments. There was also a strong detachment of armed police, the 18th CC.RR Carabinieri Battalion, and some twenty-five men of the Italian African Police, as well as the usual miscellany of behind the lines units, airfield, supply dump and harbour guards and the like. Like the Germans, the Italians had a mobile reserve force on hand ready to move out, in this case a Bersaglieri unit based at Bardia, which was indeed alerted but never reached the battle zone.

Both the Italians and the Germans had warships in the harbour, three Italian destroyers and some auxiliary patrol craft, plus a German motor minesweeper flotilla. These then were the Axis defences. The British reports on which the operation was based gave the Axis strength as follows:

It has been reported that there may be the equivalent of one Italian infantry brigade in the area and in addition up to 1,000 German troops at a staging camp some 15 miles to the east. It is believed to be unlikely that there will be sufficient transport available to enable them to take immediate counter measures but attacks upon the area by these troops may be possible later. Accurate dispositions of enemy forces in the area are unknown but a proportion will be employed in manning the AA and CD guns.

Another estimate stated: 'Enemy has a large number of AA guns protecting Tobruk, of which 12 heavy and 20 light can probably bear on the approaches to the harbour, in addition to 8 Coastal Defence guns.'

Alas, such opinions proved far too sanguine.

*

The intended survey of the landing beach north of Tobruk town was the first part of the complicated plan to fall down. The continuation of bad weather in the area for the two days prior to the landing was causing considerable anxiety even before the ships set sail and reconnaissance planes were duly despatched to look the area over. They reported on the 13th that surface conditions were good, with calm weather and only a slight swell. Thus it might appear from several thousand feet up but on the actual surface this was far from the case. The *Taku* was ordered in according to plan, but as a last-minute check she was also sent the following signal:

Report state of sea off landing by following codewords at 0130/14th to capt. (D) 22 and C. in C. Mediterranean. If assault craft likely to beach successfully and get off again codeword MALLARD. If likely to beach but not get off codeword PUFFIN. If unlikely to beach codeword SHAG.

Taku duly approached the designated beaches soon after midnight on the 14th and closing into the shore she sent out signal 'Mallard' which indicated that the assault craft should probably be able to reach the beaches safely and be able to get themselves off again for the second flight to embark from the destroyers.

However, when the submarine herself came to operating her two folbots she found things were rather more tricky than she had indicated to Alexandria. Both these small canoes in fact capsized during the actual launching at 0130. The actual beach marking had to be aborted and it was only with the greatest difficulty that the *Taku* was able to recover the two boats and their occupants. Italian post-war claims that their anti-submarine patrols drove the *Taku* away from the landing beaches by their aggressive action are, like much else from such sources, pure fiction. Another rumour that circulated among the British survivors after the war was that the two frogmen got ashore whereupon they were captured by German and Italian soldiers, and that they then shifted the lights to a new location and prepared an ambush. This remarkably persistent story is still doing the rounds but, like the Italian story, it bears absolutely no relationship to the truth.

*

The main force, with the anti-aircraft cruiser *Coventry*, sailed first from Port Said. The four Hunt class destroyers, *Belvoir*, *Croome*, *Dulverton* and *Hursley*, also passed the boom at Port Said at 1945 on 12th September and took station on the cruiser at 2150, and steamed at twenty knots. Later that night, at 2230, the whole force changed course to 340 degrees, then to 200 degrees at 0300 the next morning and finally to 256 degrees at 0630.

At 0545 on the 13th, the *Sikh* and *Zulu* sailed from Alexandria according to schedule with the 11th Battalion Royal Marines and other personnel embarked together with the four Hunt class destroyers, *Aldenham*, *Beaufort*, *Exmoor* and *Hurworth*, and, at 0900, the officers and men of the 11th Battalion aboard the two Tribals were informed that this was not an exercise but that they were now on their way to carry out Operation Agreement and all were put clearly in the picture. All the automatic weapons were tested and fired and then cleaned and oiled. In the words of the official Royal Marine report:

> Aerial photographs and annotated maps were combed through and through during the day. Every phase of the operation was explained to all Officers, NCOs and men, every man was shown and had explained to him by means of the aerial photographs the ground over which he was to travel. All means of withdrawal and escape were thoroughly explained. By 1800 hours, all were conversant with the whole operation. All were confident and happy at the thought and importance of the operation.

At 0925 the destroyer force sighted the *Coventry* and her four 'Hunts'. It was five minutes after this that both British warship groups were spotted by long-range German reconnaissance aircraft and reported. The enemy reports were picked up and gave both British groups' positions and stated that they were on opposite courses.

The track of this aircraft had been picked up at 0930 at a distance of 32 miles to the south and was being carefully monitored aboard the *Coventry*. The watchers considered she was flying at 6,000ft on a north-westerly course and she passed within 30 miles of the ships to the west, gaining height the whole time. The RAF Liaison Officer embarked for this operation, Squadron Leader Turner, was consulted and he gave the opinion that the plot was of one of the RAF's own PRU aircraft. No other hostile aircraft were detected at this time, however, either then or for the rest of the day and no enemy aircraft approached closer than eighty miles of the combined force throughout the rest of the daylight hours.

Junction of the two naval squadrons was made at 0950 whereupon the whole force changed course to 315 degrees at 0950 and increasing speed to 22 knots. They headed on throughout the day, course again being altered to 280 degrees at 1400. The RAF patrols, initially short-range Hurricanes and then from 1100 onward long-range Beaufighters, did appear on time and at regular intervals as planned and were good at identifying themselves via IFF or light signals but strict wireless silence was maintained throughout. They patrolled in pairs flying at 1,500ft to keep below German radar cover and so not to give the position of the force away by their being plotted circling above it. In all, nineteen Beaufighters were on standby and twelve sorties were conducted by two aircraft apiece. The whole of this stage of the proceedings was such to inspire considerable confidence in the efficiency of the planning so far.

One thing did mar this feeling of 'rightness'. During the afternoon, the radar aboard the flagship experienced several instances of interference over arcs of 180 degrees which blotted out the screens for periods. This was put down to either deliberate jamming of some kind by German RT transmissions, or else cloud ionization extending over the bearings 270 to 090 through 000 degrees the result of a small thunderstorm which moved over the squadron during this period. In any event, this interference both started and stopped very suddenly. A later disturbance from the south was put down to a sandstorm.

Most people aboard the escorts were still largely in the dark regarding their mission, as Geoffrey David, then *Coventry*'s young Paymaster Midshipman, recalled to me:

Having been appointed as captain's secretary, I was, of course, responsible for all the ship's correspondence, including secret operation orders, but the orders for Operation Agreement never passed through my hands. I presume they were given to Captain Dendy personally by some officer on C-in-C's staff, and that thereafter they were kept locked up in the captain's personal safe. Hence, when we sailed from Port Said on the evening of 12th September, I had as little idea of where we were heading as most of the rest of the ship's company. Much later, I heard that the captain had cleared Lower Deck before we left and told the ship's company that we were bound for a particularly dangerous operation; somehow I missed that announcement – probably, I was engrossed in secretarial business at the time.

Anyway, it was not until the day after we left Port Said that I learnt a little more, when our force was joined by *Sikh* and *Zulu*, and some more Hunts. Watching *Sikh* from our quarterdeck, and hoping (vainly, of course) to catch a glimpse of my brother, who was Flotilla Navigating Officer to Captain Micklethwaite, I noticed some odd-looking barge-like craft stowed on *Sikh*'s upper deck. I remarked on these to some other officer who was standing near me, and he told me they were landing barges to be used by a Royal Marine detachment in a raid on Tobruk that night.

At 2100 that evening, and the force having been detected only once during this crucial period, the two Tribals parted company and, working up to 24 knots, headed towards the port of Tobruk. Force 'D', on the other hand, reduced to 16 knots to mark time. Twenty minutes later they were able to plot the RAF bombers heading for Tobruk which 'were detected coming over in a steady stream at about 13,000 feet.' An hour after the two destroyers of Force 'A' had taken their departure, Force 'D' turned back to the east and increased speed to 22 knots, maintaining their anti-submarine zig-zagging pattern awaiting events.

Captain Dendy had still not received any reports of success from Force 'B' at 0155 and fifteen minutes later, believing the operation to have gone awry, he prepared to order Operation 'K' but a minute later he received Force 'B's signal of success.

> Your 1139 13th. Tobruk. 1st shore objective gained. Great hopes. Weather conditions for landing from destroyers good.

The cruiser and her escorts therefore continued to maintain their patient beat, all the time listening intently for more good news from over the western horizon. The *Sikh* and *Zulu*, still unaware of *Taku*'s complete failure to mark the correct beaches for them, had meantime steamed steadily on towards their target. While still some 70 miles offshore, they observed the first of the scheduled RAF bombing attacks commencing on the town which gave them a clear guide in.

The Reuters' correspondent, John Nixon, was later to give this view from *Sikh* of the target area at this time:

> Two huge fires were visible when we were still many miles away. We steered towards them. They resembled at that distance a couple of powerful car headlamps, but when we got nearer we could see the flames leaping high into the sky.
>
> One fire periodically burst out into a strange pink glow, shedding a lurid radiance far over the sea. Streams of coloured tracer bullets shooting up from the flames, punctuated by violent explosions, suggested a large munition dump had been hit.

But then the bombing, in fact, had quite an adverse effect when, at 0258, a direct hit appeared to have been scored on an enemy ammunition dump which blew up with a satisfactory explosion but which continued to blaze fiercely for some time. The smoke from this spectacular inferno drifted out over the cliffs and obscured the shore line at a vital time for the destroyers, making accurate landfall at the precise beach difficult. In fact, it led the ships astray and was one of the first contributory factors which were to lead to disaster.

*

None of this was known aboard the racing destroyers where the men were now keyed up and ready for their great ordeal. Aboard the *Zulu* last minute preparations were under way as 'Tug' Wilson recalled:

After we left Alex we made a feint towards the Dodecanese, Rhodes, I think, and then made a mad dash down to Tobruk. The main thing I can recall during this final dash was going down below, blackening my face with the other 'volunteers', checking my weapons and things like that. I had remembered being issued with an Italian Baretta pistol and wondered why we didn't have any of our own pistols and why we had to have this little Italian thing. We had special iron rations and we were also issued with Army-type uniforms with a tiny little compass which we had to sew in one lapel and a little silk map of the Tobruk area which we had to sew in the other. Of course, we were not really volunteers but were 'told off'. Each of the Assault boats had a crew of three with about 16 to 20 Royal Marines per boat. They were all blacked up as well, although after forty or more years I cannot recall what we used, boot polish, charcoal or grease, but I do remember blackening my face.

The Royal Marines were a splendid bunch and unlike us seemed to be looking forward to the scrap and a chance to contribute at long last as hitherto they had not had much chance to see action. They were to get more than enough as it turned out, those that made it as far as the beach anyway, which was not too many of them. I myself was young and in my prime and I too recall that I was looking forward to it.

Meanwhile, somewhere on the journey in we had painted the Italian flag on our fo'c'sle and the paint was still wet and sticky. We also had Italian ensigns to fly from our masts during the daylight hours while we lay at anchor in Tobruk harbour in the hope of fooling the German air force!

The Royal Marine report continues:

> At dark *Sikh* and *Zulu* broke away from the escort and raced on a westerly course. At 2359 hours we turned to the south and began to approach Tobruk. At 0100 hours on Monday, 14th September, we could see bomb flashes which lit up the coast and told us the RAF were bombing heavily. At 0157 hours we received the code word 'Nigger' which told us that the Operation was on. The Long Range Desert Group had secured a Coast Defence battery at the approaches to Tobruk harbour. Needless to say, a cheer went up from the *Zulu* when this was broadcast. At approximately 0215 hours we received a signal from Mr Winston Churchill to wish us luck.

John Nixon set the final scene before the men went over the side in typical Fleet Street language, thus:

> As they took up their positions on the deck in the star-studded darkness, the men were walking arsenals. Like their officers, they wore khaki shorts and shirts, steel helmets and heavy suede boots with thick crepe soles for silent walking. Armed to the teeth with tommy-guns, Bren guns, machine-guns and rifles, every man was also bristling with grenades, sticky bombs and guncotton. Each man responsible for demolition had 20 lb of guncotton. The ships themselves had been converted into floating arsenals. Besides huge boxes of ammunition of various kinds on our decks and tied to our forecastle, were several red and green boxes containing sufficient gelignite to blow the average city sky-high.

*

The MTB's of the 10th and 15th Flotillas, MTB's *260, 261, 262, 265, 266, 267, 268, 307, 308, 309, 310, 311, 312, 313, 314, 315, 316*, along with three Fairmiles motor launches, ML's *352, 353* and *349*, forming Force 'C' had meanwhile sailed as per schedule at dusk on the evening of 12th September, adopting the night cruising formation on passing the outer channel buoy, and headed west throughout that night at an economical speed of only six knots. Embarked in the MTB's were some 200 men of the Northumberland Fusiliers, while two of the MLs carried the demolition teams under Commander Nichol; the other acted as reserve. The only setback was that half an hour after midnight one of the MTB's, *268*, developed engine trouble. Rather than hold the rest of the force up from their strict timetable, her military passengers were transferred to *ML 353* and she was sent back to Alexandria.

The remainder of the night passed uneventfully and Force 'C' had an incident- and trouble-free passage throughout the daylight hours of the 13th, remaining undetected by both the enemy air patrols and coastal radar coverage. Each of the marked progress stages were passed on time, thanks mainly to the very precise navigation of Sub-Lieutenant M. Wallrock, RNR. This young officer received high praise for his work in ensuring all the MTB compasses were working correctly and that these vital positions were maintained.

Thus, the whole operation was initially favoured by good fortune and all the omens seemed excellent. Two separate forces, one consisting of one cruiser and 10 destroyers and the other of 16 MTBs, were unobserved by enemy air reconnaissance on D1 while proceeding westward, 100 miles and 50 miles respectively off the enemy coast. They were able to get within two miles of the shore without being detected by the radar stations which the enemy were known to have set up in the Tobruk region.

Thus, at 2030 on the evening of the 13th, the whole force increased speed to 25 knots for the final run-in to the target area. This caused the first problems, for many of the young officers in command of the MTB's were not fully certain of the individual performance of their vessels at these high speeds and thus lost touch. The whole of Force 'C' became split up and contact between the separate groups was never regained. By contrast, from 2300 onward, their position relative to the coast was made simple by the flash of the numerous bomb explosions in Tobruk as the RAF bombing continued unabated. However, these attacks seemed to cease some thirty minutes earlier than expected.

At 0030 on the morning of the 14th Commander Blackburn, embarked in *MTB 309*, ordered the boats still in company, MTBs *265*, *266*, *267*, *311*, *313* and *315*, to slow down to eight knots once more and they turned to a new course of 270 degrees on silent running. It was not until this manœuvre was undertaken that he first became aware that only a total of seven MTBs of the original sixteen were still in company. The CO never again had more than seven of his force in sight at any one time.

At 0145, he estimated Tobruk Point to be some two miles off on a bearing of 270 degrees and the anti-aircraft fire and searchlights probing the sky above the town were clearly visible.

At 0200 *MTB 261* (Lieutenant-Commander R. A. Allan, RNVR) closed and informed him that he had received the signal 'Nigger' from a holder of a call sign TOR. The signal itself from the troops ashore actually read: 'Only 2 MTBs arrived await remainder.'

On receipt of this information, Blackburn led the boats into the south shore and searched for the entrance to the Bay of Mersa Sciausc. Blackburn himself was later to state that he was convinced that his boat, *MTB 309*, actually made the entrance at this time due to the accurate navigation of Sub-Lieutenant Wallrock, but neither he nor his officers were able to see any of the red signal lights which should have been exhibited to mark that entrance.

All the other sixteen commanding officers reported that their boats arrived off Mersa es Sciausc off Tobruk in dribs and drabs that night having lost sight of each other due to bad station-keeping, but none of the others achieved anything at all. On the limited credit side, most of the MTB's had completed nearly 700 miles without refuelling or major breakdowns; and this reflected credit upon the officers and men concerned. It also showed up the reliability of the American-built Elco boats of which the force was composed. The British-built Vosper boats of 7th and 8th Flotillas were too unreliable to be included in the operations, which is why their numbers had been made up by the use of Fairmile motor launches.

The other MTB's in company were equally unable to spot any such lights, so Blackburn decided instead to scout the approaches to Tobruk harbour itself for enemy shipping. Quite what this had to do with the operation in hand is not clear; they were hardly in a position to carry out conventional MTB attacks, with so many troops crowded into their slender hulls, or to sustain the close-in fire fights such a policy would result in without suffering inordinate casualties from return fire. Nor would this in any way help the other arm of the pincer attack to be delivered by the Royal Marines to the north. Nonetheless, this was the action decided upon and the six MTBs nosed into the area and remained hunting up and down for half an hour, from 0245 until 0315, without finding any sign of enemy shipping. This is remarkable in view of the fact that there were three Italian destroyers, a flotilla of German motor minesweepers and a host of armed barges distributed throughout the area of the harbour at this time.

The MTB force then withdrew and returned to their original

mission – the landing of their troops on the southern shore. The German and Italian defences were by this time fully roused and were subjecting the whole area to searchlight probes from the north shore while a sustained artillery shoot was being conducted by them from the western end of the harbour area. But, although the MTBs diligently plodded up and down to the east of Mersa Biad almost up the boom, no lights or friendly signals were seen from the shore.

However, two of the MTB's *had* sighted the signals of the LRDG. They made out a single fixed white light to the eastward while the light inside the entrance was a group flashing six red at irregular intervals. Thus, the two of them (*MTB 260* and *MTB 314*) alone of the whole of Force 'C' actually entered Mersa Sciausc. The military personnel were duly disembarked but the latter boat ran ashore and later had to be destroyed by our own forces.

But what of Lieutenant-Colonel Haselden's party?

*

As we have already seen, they had reached the perimeter of the Tobruk defences and penetrated it quite simply, even if slightly behind schedule. They found the track eventually, after some scouring in the dark night, and the first of the RAF's bombs started exploding ahead of them as they made their way up it and surrounded a small building which was to become their base for the night's work.

Here, they stopped to regroup and form themselves into the Commando parties for the first series of objectives. Haselden, with the SIG and RA detachments, along with Lieutenants MacDonald, Silito and Taylor's sections, was to take the small house and gun position located on the west side of the bay at Map Reference 417431. The rest of the commando, under Major Campbell, was to similarly take positions on the eastern side of the bay. Once both flanks had been cleared and secured, success signals were to have been fired by each group whereupon Campbell's men were to continue on eastward for two miles more to the vicinity of 'Brighton' rest camp to see if any enemy guns were mounted there and if so to take them out. Haselden's group was to stay put at the HQ's (unless the enemy positions were found to be of the 'walk-in' variety) until the Argyll and Sutherland Highlanders company and the platoon of Northumberland Fusiliers got ashore.

Lieutenant Langton, meanwhile, had the vital task of signalling in the MTBs with the vital reinforcements and meeting them and guiding them inland. The signal, as we have seen, was to be three red 'T's flashed every two minutes from Map Reference 41784315 on the west coast of the bay, and also from a point to the east, just beyond the bay at Map Reference 41834313.

It was here that a vital error of judgement was made by Haselden, which, although understandable at the time, was to have severe repercussions on events. Campbell's dysentery was now severe but he insisted on carrying on. This the Lieutenant-Colonel permitted, but ordered Langton to accompany him and his group on the first part of their task as second-in-command. As the signalling was not due to commence until 0130 according to the strict timetable, it was thought there would be ample time for Langton to do this and resume his signalling position. It was a calculated gamble, like so much else in this operation, and, again like so much else, it did not come off.

Haselden's group's first job was to secure the building itself as quickly and silently as possible and for this Captain Buck, Lieutenant Russell and Haselden himself along with the four Palestinians carefully approached the building and all save the latter, who remained on guard outside, burst into it. Here, they found a solitary Italian whom they took prisoner and questioned, in German, with regard to the position of the defenders and the telephone system, reporting the results of their work to Haselden outside, who then resumed the interrogation, this time in Italian. As Russell laconically stated later, 'I believe this man was later shot when trying to escape.'

Leaving the small commando with Haselden to protect the newly established HQ, the rest then proceeded to the east to undertake their particular assignments. Before leaving, Langton had placed two Royal Engineers at the eastern signalling point, each with a torch, in case he did not get back in time. He gave each man a briefing on how to signal in that event. He also assigned Flying Officer Scott with the two powerful Aldis lamps to Haselden's party, the plan being for himself and Scott to take the RE's places in time for the actual signalling.

A small minefield was Campbell's first obstacle and this necessitated a careful and thorough search by the Royal Engineers team equipped with a mine detector. Already late, this hazard added yet valuable minutes to their congested timetable and the men had to carefully negotiate the cleared path single-file. For a heart-stopping moment, while in the middle of this delicate operation, it was thought that the whole force had been discovered by the enemy for there came a solitary rifle shot from across the wadi. The British troops were in a position of high vulnerability and immediately froze where they were. Strangely, this first shot was not repeated and, after many anxious moments one section was led forward by Lieutenant Roberts to see if the way ahead was clear.

Lieutenant Langton at the same time asked permission to investigate the sandy beach below them. He walked right across it without bumping into any sign of the enemy or arousing any hostile movement whatsoever, so he directed Roberts to lead his section up the high ground to get behind the lone sniper. Langton meanwhile returned to the minefield and reported the position to Campbell. Then, one section at a time, the whole force was led out to safety across the beach, again without incident.

While this was being done, Lieutenant Roberts' section had worked their way painstakingly round to the rear of the enemy and surprised a German machine-gun section manning a Spandau, which they duly engaged and wiped out. Why these Germans had not wiped out Campbell's party in the open remains a mystery; perhaps they confused them for one of their own patrols after that first warning shot, but whatever the reason the German gunners were given no second chance.

So the wadi had been crossed without loss, but a vital hour had now elapsed and the same cautious approach was necessary to gain access up the far side and beyond, with Langton going ahead and then awaiting the rest of the party, including Lieutenant Roberts' section who were re-joining them, burdened down with explosives and the like. Once they were up, he hurried to catch up with Campbell's team once more who he discovered had pressed on to the east, away from the bay area. Lieutenant Duffy reported to him that the enemy positions located so far had been empty and unused and from the distance the success signal from Haselden's group was seen in the black sky.

Joining Campbell at the head of the column, Langton pressed on and they stumbled on an enemy wireless station, which Lieutenant Roberts' section dealt with as quickly and effectively as they had the Spandau. So far, all was going swimmingly but Langton, glancing at his watch after this was done, found to his horror that the time was already 0130. He urged Campbell to fire his own 'first objective attained' signal, and hurried back on his own back to where he had left the two Royal Engineers at the bay.

Needless to say, this journey did not go smoothly either. In the

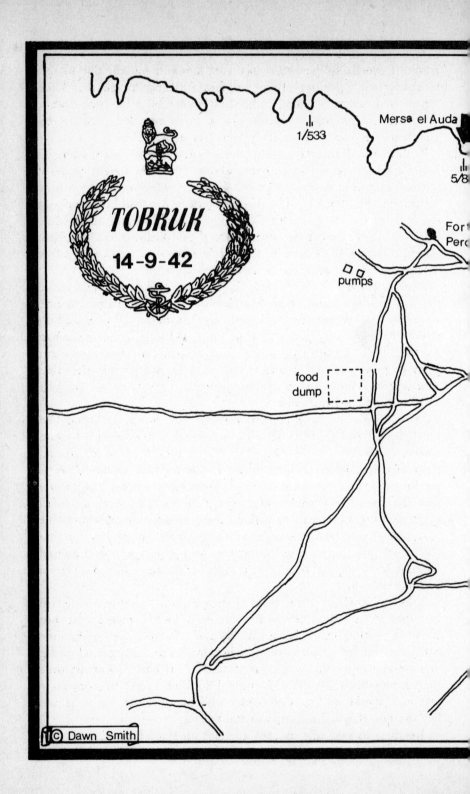

TOBRUK

14-9-42

Mersa el Auda

1/533

5/8

For
Per

pumps

food
dump

© Dawn Smith

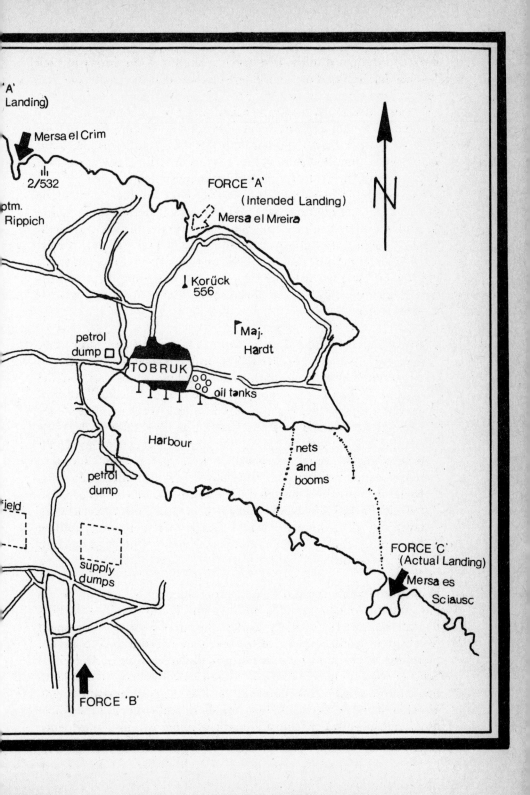

'A'
Landing)

Mersa el Crim

2/532

ptm.
Rippich

FORCE 'A'
(Intended Landing)

Mersa el Mreira

N

Korück
556

Maj.
Hardt

petrol
dump

TOBRUK

oil tanks

Harbour

nets
and
booms

petrol
dump

ield

supply
dumps

FORCE 'C'
(Actual Landing)

Mersa es
Sciausc

FORCE 'B'

darkness, Langton must have taken a slightly different route back because he stumbled on another enemy post that they had somehow missed (and strangely had not been sighted by, despite the firing) on the way out. He had to give this a wide berth and this further delayed him, but on arrival at the eastern signal point he was relieved to find that, although both the RE's had vanished, Scott had already preceded him to the western signalling point and was at work with the Aldis lamp. Unfortunately, Scott seems to have positioned himself too high up in the rocks for his signal to be effective. All Langton had was his torch and again, amazingly on a mission which depended so much on exact timing, he had no watch!

Nonetheless, the officer attempted to signal in the correct sequence basing his flashes on Scott's across the bay and was eventually rewarded with the happy sight of the first of the MTB's nosing into the bay. In his own words, Langton describes what happened next:

> After a short while, I saw two MTB's come in. After that, however, no more appeared. My problem now was whether to stay signalling or to go to meet the landing troops and conduct them to HQ as I was suppposed to be doing. I decided to try a compromise by wedging my torch in a rock and leaving it alight. I did this and started back but, before I had gone 200 yards, I saw a light flashing out to sea and it appeared to be on an MTB proceeding *away* again. I rushed back to the torch and started to signal again. But nothing materialised. After another half hour, I left signalling and started back towards the landing point. On the way back, I discovered that my haversack and T/G had been taken from the sangar where I had left them before climbing down to the rocks. I later ran into two enemy, one of whom I hit with my revolver.

With considerable aplomb Langton continued on his journey to the bay and on reaching the landing point found the two MTB's disembarking the Fusiliers under the direction of Lieutenant MacDonald. Collaring one of the commando and a T/G, Langton therefore returned to the eastern signalling position and rejoined Scott in continuing signalling out to sea for the rest of the flotilla to home in on. However, on arriving back at the eastern point enemy searchlights were active all along the shore and sweeping the whole area while a heavy fire from automatic weapons was also in evidence

from the opposite shore of the harbour out to sea, making any
approach by British light forces a hazardous affair indeed. Despite
this, Langton recommenced his hopeful signalling.

He resumed:

> Once the MTB's got caught in the searchlights and I could see
> their wake and tracer bouncing off one of them. They were still
> well to the east of us, however, and it was obvious that there
> wasn't much chance of them getting in. One of the MTB's
> slipped out past me during a slight lull, and appeared to get away
> safely. At 'first light' I decided to abandon signalling and I
> returned to the landing point.

Here Langton found just one solitary MTB hard aground and
abandoned while heavy rifle and light machine-gun fire could be
distinctly heard coming from over the western edge of the wadi
where the British trucks had been parked the night before. After
shouting to see if anyone was aboard the MTB and getting no reply,
Langton made his way up to Haselden's HQ to see what was
happening.

Back at HQ earlier, the colonel had ordered the wireless truck to
be brought up to the hut and the small group settled down to await
the return of the other commandos and the arrival of the MTB's and
their reinforcements. Time passed by but the MTB's failed to
appear as scheduled and, after a time, Lieutenant Taylor and three
commandos were brought back in a wounded condition, having
been shot in error by their own forces in the confusion. In the end,
Haselden sent Lieutenant Russell down to the shore to see what was
happening. As the latter later was to recall:

> I heard the engines of the MTB's and occasionally saw them in
> the searchlight beams. There was extremely heavy fire from the
> west point of Tobruk Bay, which effectively prevented all but two
> of the MTB's entering Mersa Umm el Sciausc. The greater part
> of the fire seemed to be small calibre automatic tracer cannon fire.
> Of the two MTB's which entered the bay, one ran aground and
> the other left about an hour before dawn. These two MTB's
> landed one section of Northumberland Fusiliers and their
> machine-guns.

These were No 14 Platoon, 'Z' Company, Royal Northumberland

Fusiliers, led by Sergeant Miller, and with Corporal Wilson, Lance-Corporals Ridley and Watt, along with Fusiliers Harbottle, A. Leslie and G. Leslie, MacDonald and Shields, with two Vickers machine-guns. These were the only reinforcements that the MTB force succeeded in putting ashore that night.

Thus it was that as the Germans and Italians closed in to within 200 yards of Haselden's HQ building completely undetected, despite the approach of dawn's first light, the strength of the little British party was little more than two platoons and these were taken completely by surprise when the enemy opened fire at this close range. A brisk fire-fight then developed but Haselden was determined to hang on for as long as possible to await the return of Major Campbell and the rest of the commando. For a considerable time then the brave little group fiercely defended the building and managed to keep the enemy at bay but, with only forty-five minutes to go before dawn, which would have made their position suicidal, it was decided to get the men away while there was still a slim chance.

Accordingly, the four wounded men were loaded on to one of the trucks together with the doctor, while he boarded the wireless truck himself. While Lieutenant Russell and the survivors kept up a hail of fire from their remaining automatic weapons and grenades, the two lorries then attempted to storm the enemy line and break clear by charging full-tilt down the hill. This was done.

The men left behind kept firing until the light broke clear and then they turned to thoughts of their own salvation. It was shortly after this dramatic bid for freedom that Langton arrived to find the HQ deserted and the heads of an enemy platoon about 300 yards distant. He beat a hasty withdrawal back to the bay and after again shouting in vain went on board her but found her completely deserted. He filled his water bottle and took what food he could find and prepared himself for a lonely walk back to friendly territory, but at that moment he heard shouts and was soon joined by four British soldiers. These proved to be Lieutenants Russell and Sillito with Privates Hillman and Watler, who, after the fire-fight had ended, had headed for the bay itself and the stranded MTB. Russell reported how he found Lieutenant Langton trying to get her started.

While he was doing this I operated the twin Lewis gun, which was mounted on the forward deck, at what I took to be the enemy. We were being shot at spasmodically and desultorily by SAA.

Langton and Watler, who was a mechanic, went below to look at the
MTB's huge engines but neither could get them going at all, so,
after gathering more food and water, they shifted over to one of the
equally abandoned assault craft lying alongside her being joined by
the others. Russell reported that:

> On failing to get the boat going we rowed off in an attempt to get
> round and down the coast. We were shot at, however, from the
> west side and as we should have come under heavier fire if we
> continued, we pulled into a small bay on the east side of Mersa
> Umm es Sciausc, where we landed.

Langton said that:

> We paddled out into the bay, but were forced to go ashore by
> being fired on from the rocks on the west side. We saw some of
> our own men dodging along the west side of the bay and there
> were large explosions coming from behind them. It was
> impossible to tell who they were but I think they may have been
> the REs dealing with the guns on the point.

Landing again, the little party climbed up through another
minefield and into a protecting wadi. They were joined soon
afterwards by Sergeant Evans and then they made for the hills, but
found they frequently had to duck for the nearest cover as enemy
aircraft were criss-crossing the sky above, obviously aiding the
enemy patrols who were closing in on the whole area. Their chances
seemed slim and reducing all the time. Once, on gaining a high
point, Langton glanced briefly out to sea. It was now daylight and
he could clearly see the *Zulu* trying to tow the *Sikh* clear far away to
the north. 'The latter appeared to be burning and shells were
bursting all round. We were fired on heavily going over the ridge
from the direction of 'Brighton' but got safely into a large wadi
where we found about 15 – 20 others waiting.'

Like the Commandos, the little section of Fusiliers, after firing off
all their ammunition, spiked their guns and joined up with remnants
from other parties. Altogether, some fifteen men had assembled at
the bay under Lieutenant McDonald and Lieutenant Barlow of the
Light AA and these were joined by the other three lieutenants and
the two privates. Such a group was considered too large a force to
escape detection and, in order that some at least might stand a

remote chance of making it back, they were split into two parties.

One group, with McDonald and Sillito, headed eastward along the cliffs in the hope of sighting the MTB's out at sea and attracting their attention. 'I do not think they had the slightest chance of succeeding', recalled Russell. 'No one knew quite what had become of Major Campbell's party. It seemed clear that Colonel Haselden had been killed.' His own group, with Langton, Barlow and eight other ranks, headed south-easterly at first and hid in a small wadi during the remainder of the day while the Germans and Italians quartered the area searching for them. That night they decided to split up still further into three groups of one officer and two or three men, the rations and water being equally divided. We will return to their fate later.

We must now retrace our steps to John Haselden's HQ. When the blockhouse had originally been taken with its solitary occupant, he revealed that his companions were at their posts on alert but the SIG team had little difficulty in taking these positions out one-by-one, the only bad casualty being Lieutenant Graham Taylor. What was not so good was that four of the Italians made good their escape back down towards Tobruk town. These raised the alarm in a very short time and this resulted, as we have seen, in Haselden's HQ being quickly enveloped by the enemy. When word was received at 0700 that the other landing had also failed, John Haselden had determined on breakout and sent word to Campbell to blow up the positions he had captured and fall back. When the do-or-die crash-through was being readied it was seen that the enemy were ready for them in ambush. The trucks indeed met with heavy fire but Haselden's truck, with Lieutenant Barlow at the wheel, had managed to break right through the Italian ambush and emerged, relatively unscathed, on the other side.

They might have got further but instead stopped their lorry and got out to take the enemy on the flank and thus facilitate the escape of the rest of their party, including it was hoped, the wounded who had the help of the landing party of men under Regimental Sergeant Major Swinburn. They had two heavy machine-guns which had been brought ashore and, once they all had re-assembled, Haselden personally led an heroic charge back at the enemy position. Haselden was joined in this attack by Lanark, Captain Bray and two SIG men, Berg and Steiner as well as Private Watler.

They were met with a hail of fire from the panicky and screaming Italian defenders and the colonel himself was hit at very close range. Lieutenant MacDonald ran over to his leader to see if he could help him but as he reached his side an Italian threw a grenade which burst practically on top of Haselden's body. MacDonald himself was stunned by the blast for a short period and his face blackened by the explosion, but he survived. In the interim, Lieutenant Barlow rallied the remaining men. They were covered in this by Lieutenant Russell manning the two Lewis machine-guns mounted on the stranded *MTB 314* but a burst of this came a bit too close for comfort so, still covered by the Fusiliers, the commandos decided to pull back. The Fusiliers themselves fired off every round of ammunition they had and then spiked their guns and joined in the general withdrawal and subsequent dispersal as described.

The RSM's party also fought on until but three rounds per gun remained. They were being assailed by German troops now as well as Italian and heavy mortars were playing on them in addition to light weapons. Bowing to the inevitable, this little party also surrendered. The Italians were vicious in victory and attempted to get at the British prisoners; many were clubbed or hit, but in the end the German troops formed a protective guard around them to keep their allies away and marched the small group off to the town, their heads held high. The Italians' version of the battle, which throws some light on their vindictiveness towards the surviving commandos, was recorded by Terravazzi in this manner:

During the night three heavy lorries crammed with British prisoners and guarded by German troops arrived in the town, having successfully passed through all the road-blocks. But the British were not prisoners, and the Germans were not Germans – and large quantities of arms were concealed in the trucks. In a small bay down near the port . . ., they massacred a group of Italian artillerymen in their sleep, having first silently knifed the sentries. They immediately established a strong-point.

He continues:

To the north of the promontory, enemy ships began to land men in the darkness. But we had completely broken up the raid before morning. Almost all the British who landed were killed; there

were very few prisoners. The massacre at El Adem had been
dearly paid for.*

Meanwhile, over at 'Brighton' camp Major Campbell's hitherto
successful and methodical advance also finally ran into trouble,
more than they could handle. They found the camp in a state of
defence with the old, formerly abandoned, concrete emplacements
repaired and enlarged and some Italian coastal defence guns
mounted there. Their gunners and the defending infantry were in
a state of high alert, no doubt forewarned by the earlier little actions,
and they had wisely shut themselves in tight. When the commandos
attempted to storm these guns' positions they were hit by heavy fire
from adjacent automatic guns stationed on the northern side of the
harbour and suffered some losses, including Campbell himself who
was severely wounded. They dropped grenades down air vents
causing many casualties but the recall signal was received before
they had completed their task. There was nothing else for it but to
pull back, and in the confused fighting which followed, they were
once more joined by the indefatigable Lieutenant Michael Roberts'
section rejoining after their latest mopping-up exploit in the rear.

The whole force now pulled back the way they had come with
Lieutenant Roberts and Lieutenant Murphy assisting Major
Campbell who was now in a very bad way with the wound and the
dysentery, at the same time coaxing on their sixteen Italian
prisoners. They sent Sergeant Evans on ahead with a small group
of men and it was this group that had been seen by the main party
escaping through the shellfire and which had joined forces later.
They all reached the HQ position safely, as did Flying Officer Scott
who stuck to his signalling post to the last before making a lone dash
through intense machine-gun fire. Miller and the Fusiliers, as well
as Sergeant Evans and Lanark, with Weizmann and Watler,
eventually all met, as we have seen.

For those commando troops, fit and wounded, that remained
aboard *MTB 314* some further attempts were made to get the
engines started or move her from her hard and fast position, both
to no avail but these efforts were terminated by the arrival of a
German motor minesweeper (mistaken by the British soldiers for an
E-boat) with a deckload of troops armed to the teeth with automatic
weapons. There was little choice but to surrender themselves and for
the wounded, this was the best thing that could have been done as

* Quoted in *Alamein, 1933 – 1962*, op. cit.

Two LRDG patrols with their converted Chevrolet trucks and guns meet in the middle of the desert.

All that remained of an LRDG patrol after the Stukas found them.

Wolf to the slaughter! Long used to being the hunter with an enviable war record against the Italian Navy in the Mediterranean the British destroyer *Sikh*, seen here entering Malta harbour, was to be one of the principal warships in an operation the lower deck christened a 'no-hope, death-or-glory' enterprise. And so it was to prove.

Too late! Crewmen from the destroyer *Sikh* picked out of the water by Italian vessels who later died of their exposure and wounds.

A wounded survivor from the *Sikh* aboard one of the Italian rescue vessels on the way back to harbour.

they were very well treated. The others were disarmed and made
POW's. Force 'B', initially so successful, was now reduced to
scattered bunches of hunted men, or lone survivors hiding out by
day and walking at night, all seeking to make their way either to the
rendezvous with the MTB or to reach Allied lines hundreds of miles
away across the desert. It was a sad end to an enterprise that had
initially seemed so promising.

In a way, but not in the scale, this had been foreseen. In the
preplanning, DAG had been informed that:

> It is impossible to forecast accurately either how many will return
> to Alexandria or when they will arrive as this is dependent on
> success or failure. The period over which their return is likely is
> from the morning of D + 2 to the evening of D + 3. It is requested
> that arrangements including medical, may be made for the
> reception and accommodation of these troops.

This clinical document also noted that: 'The troops on their return
will be somewhat disorganised and will require considerable sorting
out.'

Alas, it was all to be so correct, but for some, like Campbell and
Haselden, there was no coming back; for others it was a very long
walk indeed.

*

MTB 309, with the crew of *MTB 314* safely embarked, had run the
gauntlet to safety after landing her troops but back out at sea the rest
of Force 'C' was still very much in the dark. Commander Blackburn
complained later that had only one of these two who had actually
sighted the lights informed him of the fact, things might have been
different. With the benefit of hindsight one can perhaps contemplate
that, had *all* the MTB's landed their men, it would merely have
increased the casualties and POW's without greatly affecting the
final outcome but of course this luxury was denied Commander
Blackburn who agonised on the failure to follow-up. The Fusiliers
themselves were equally loath to accept the status quo. They wished
to join their comrades ashore and not leave them in the lurch, but
Blackburn was adamant that if they could not be landed in the
correct position then it was best they were not landed at all, and this
they had to accept.

The principal causes of the failure of the bulk of Force 'C' to get ashore were later put down to:

1. The dispersal of the two flotillas of MTBs during the night due to bad station-keeping.

2. Partial failure of communications between the Long Range Desert Group and the MTBs.

3. Inadequate leading lights.

In fact, it was only from the signal which he received at 0440 that Commander Blackburn was ever made aware that two of his missing boats had in fact carried out their task successfully. On receipt of this tardy information, Blackburn took the two nearest vessels of this remaining force, *MTB 262* and *MTB 266*, into the inlet. As they pushed into the bay, they were met by a hail of artillery and small-arms fire from the north shore of the harbour. This made it very obvious that either the British troops had not established themselves ashore after all, or that (as proved the case) they had done so earlier but had been chased away by the defenders since. Blackburn therefore had little choice but to beat another hasty retreat to the eastward in the face of this fierce fire.

The three MTB's were held in the searchlights throughout this little foray and were all subjected to merciless fire, both medium-sized shells and small-arms fire being received, but, miraculously, they survived all this, although they again became separated from each other in the process of extracting themselves.

Lieutenant Robert Allan, RNVR, had managed to keep most of the boats of his flotilla together, but had of course lost sight of the senior officer and Lieutenant Denis Jermain's force. Both men had considerable MTB experience, including combat fighting in the English Channel, but some of their junior subordinates were fairly green. Nonetheless, this second group also appears to have arrived off Tobruk only a little later than the first, but they never sighted them at all subsequently. What they did run into was the hornet's nest already well stirred up by the others, with searchlights and tracer flickering all over the approaches and the enemy defences obviously fully ready for them.

This group, *MTB's 260, 261, 262* and *316*, also nosed up to investigate the boom defences, but could find no break. Three of these MTBs even fired torpedoes in the hope of blasting a passage through, but to no avail, and heavy return fire was met each time they tried to penetrate. Like the SO's section, Allan's boats remained in the area until daybreak and then, equally frustrated and running short of fuel, straggled off together back to the east. They took fourteen hours to complete the voyage back to Alexandria, being restricted to slow speeds for the whole journey.

Dudley Pope commented that Blackburn was 'an RN captain who, as far as is known, had not previously handled a unit of MTB's.' What he failed to mention, however, is that Commander Blackburn *did* know, and know intimately, both Tobruk and the coastal sea approaches to it, having commanded the famous gunboat *Ladybird* which had made the hazardous trip many times during the long siege of the previous year. He was therefore an ideal person to lead this mission and by comparison few if any of the MTB captains had ever been to Tobruk before, either by day or night.

The soldiers embarked were largely philosophical about the outcome once they had resigned themselves to the fact that they were not going ashore to help their mates. After all, many were veterans who had seen many such foul-ups since 1939. In their regimental history, the comments about the remainder of the Northumberland Fusiliers is confined to a diplomatic, 'the rest of the platoon had no alternative to returning to Alexandria, which despite being heavily dive-bombed en route, they reached safely.'

A similar picture is painted by the historian recording the fate of 'D' Company, 1st Argyll and Sutherland Highlanders under Captain McFie and their two accompanying mortar detachments. 'Owing to inter-communication difficulties the Argyll company did not land, but received a very heavy baptism of bombs and machine-gunning from enemy aircraft when returning to Alexandria, during which Second-Lieutenant R. W. McLaren was killed and five other ranks wounded.'

In another summary of their work this night on the lack of positive results achieved, it was thought that the MTBs failed to land their troops because of: (a) straggling on passage; (b) recognition shortcomings; (c) communication shortcomings; (d) lack of 'dash'.

The MTB commanders themselves felt that this failure might have been avoided by more careful planning and much more practice beforehand. The more experienced of them felt that there was a lack of real understanding in the higher echelons about just what such craft could or could not do. The usual MTB battle group was of four boats only. Never had sixteen MTB's been expected to keep in close touch over such a long period. In the aftermath of the Great War the size of destroyer flotillas, much larger ships, had been reduced from sixteen to nine for much the same reasons, and this same principle was now abandoned for these vessels which had much lower profiles. They were used to operating at closer intervals also but in smaller packages than destroyers and the like. Utilising such craft as troop carriers and mini-destroyers also did not take into account their much smaller, *pro rata*, officer complement. Furthermore, most of the sixteen boats had never operated with each other before on operations at night. The necessity of using the much slower Fairmile motor launches did not do much to improve the overall compatability of the flotilla either.

Admiral Harwood commented that:

> The young officers in the motor torpedo boat flotillas were a little too untrained and inexperienced to take full advantage of unexpected opportunities. In the light of all that happened, they had a very difficult task, but there is no doubt that chances were missed.

The force was now more split up than ever before and in some disarray. Reporting that the bay was in fact still held by the enemy, Blackburn searched about and, by 0545, had managed to gather together four MTBs in all, and these he led back into the Mersa Sciausc only to be beaten back once more by the deluge of fire of all types from the defences. These repeated attempts to force the entrance are in stark contrast to Bragadin's assertion that: 'The enemy craft quickly withdrew, all of them hit to some degree and one of them burning. By a few minutes after 0300 the British operation had completely failed.'

The Light Brigade had only charged once but, contrary to the above description, even after this third attempt had failed in fact Force 'C' did not accept the inevitable. Blackburn again retired from the scene and tried to reconcentrate the flotillas with a view to yet a fourth attempt later, at first light, although many might feel that failure in the darkness would have made a full daylight attempt suicidal.

This was made obvious by the fate of the three motor launches at first light. These vessels, *ML 349* (Lieutenant-Commander Ball), *ML 352* (Lieutenant G. R. Worledge) and *ML 353* (Lieutenant E. J. Michelson), with their vulnerable Hall Scott petrol engines, were capable of a maximum speed of only 18 knots when unladen, let alone packed with troops, as against the MTB's 28 knots. Nor were these 75-tonners large enough to be so well armed as the 120-ton 'Dog Boats'.

They went to the aid of the stricken *Sikh* but were soon set upon by Italian Macchi fighters (of which more later). These aircraft conducted low-level strafing runs against the ML's which proved most difficult for the slow vessels to counter. They had not the agility of the MTB's to dodge and weave and the blind spot of their defence, forward, was quickly noted and exploited by their attackers. The cannon fire and machine-gunning of the Macchis proved more effective than bombing against their thin wooden hulls and soon incendiary bullets and cannon shells were ripping into them and setting their petrol tanks ablaze.

First to go was *ML 353* which her young New Zealand skipper handled with skill and fought to the last. After repeated hits, she was soon ablaze and her survivors had to be taken off by *ML 349*. She would burn down to sea level but to make sure that she was not towed in by the enemy, demolition charges were set before the last man left which scuttled her more effectively.

The same tactics were then used against *ML 352* which withstood a whole succession of such attacks from the Italian fighters while still within their limited range. Repeated hits ruptured her petrol tanks which quickly spread into the vessel. She was soon a floating petrol dump and explosive cannon fire from the next MC 200 ignited this inferno, causing a huge explosion which tore open her port side in a huge forty-foot rent. As she settled and the flames roared along her whole length her crew took to the water. They had to hurry to place a good distance between themselves and their erstwhile home and when the bulk of the men in the water had got about four hundred yards clear a final enormous explosion sent her to the bottom. None of her companions was in a position to come to their aid and, after treading water for a considerable period, the surviving members of her gallant crew were hauled aboard the Italian destroyer *Castore* and taken back to Tobruk as POW's. Later, the third ML was also hit and badly damaged, but she managed to struggle back to Alexandria.

The MTB's withstood the initial attacks much better, and with the troops aboard giving robust support with their Bren guns and rifles, were able to keep the enemy at bay by dint of high speed zig-zagging. However, their luck could not last for ever and soon the Macchis began to score telling hits on these evasive targets, as well. In all, three boats were sunk in these and subsequent attacks, eight officers and 48 men were killed and many more wounded from these light craft.

MTB 312 (Lieutenant Jan Quarrie) was the first to be lost. She took a direct hit from the Macchis early on and disintegrated in a ball of flame. Surviving crew and Argyll and Sutherlands scrambled into the collapsible boat or jumped for it. Most of them were picked up by *MTB 266* (Lieutenant Richard Smith) which was herself near-missed by Stuka bombs soon afterwards and had an engine put out of commission by a cut oil feed pipe from a bomb splinter, while another such splinter killed one of their Argyll passengers, Lieutenant R. MacDowall, who was below.

MTB 308 (Lieutenant Roy Yates) was taken under attack by the fighters around 0730 and had received several cannon hits which disabled one of her engines and slowed her down. In this crippled state, she was lacking the usual agility of her companions and thus attracted more than her share of attention from the patrolling aircraft, which now began to include German Stukas from StG3 and then, later on that day, the long-range twin-engined Junkers Ju88 from LG1, on their way back to their usual bases in Crete from whence they had been diverted. She was joined by her sister, *MTB 310*, and the two vessels were attacked by a pair of the latter aircraft at 0800 which failed to score any hits. No sooner had they gone than another pair appeared and repeated the process, then two more, and so it continued. Their assailants were not the First Team but finally one of the Ju88's approached in a very shallow dive angle. It was apparently hit and damaged by return fire from *MTB 308* and failed to pull up, crashing full-tilt into the craft whereupon both *MTB* and bomber exploded in the carnage of mutual destruction. There were no surviviors from either.

Although she safely got away from the immediate area of Tobruk unscathed, and had witnessed the loss of *MTB 308*, *MTB 310* (commanded by the Canadian, Lieutenant Stewart Lane) was not to survive her sister for very much longer. During the morning, she was attacked by a succession of enemy aircraft. Firstly she survived dive bombing from a force of eight Junkers, Ju87s. Next, the Macchis had another series of attacks on her, which she again came through (reporting her attackers as Me109s!). Then, around midday, the Stukas returned and this time they made no errors. A direct hit bomb detonated on the little vessel's bows smashing through the flimsy decks and out the ship's bottom, depositing a large section of planking on her bridge in the process. She slid to a halt and was quickly abandoned. Strangely, nobody, neither her crew nor her twelve soldier passengers, had been killed by the explosion but several were badly wounded. All got away as the aircraft came back to finish her off. Her skipper died soon after being lowered to the assault craft. The others were left bobbing on an empty sea under a merciless sun.

Several other MTB's were badly damaged and sustained killed and wounded, the chief hazard being the reserve fuel tanks on deck which they could not afford to jettison. They were not alone in their ordeal.

For the nonce, then, Force 'C' had failed, but how had the landings to the north-west of Tobruk fared?

CHAPTER FIVE

'Why were you late?'

Aboard the *Zulu*, 'First Flight on equipment', was piped and broadcast through the destroyer. It was the job of 7 Platoon, 'A' Company, to cover the whole landing and they were joined in the First Flight by 'C' Company under Major S. M. R. Wood, Royal Marines, with thirty volunteers from 261 Heavy Anti-Aircraft Battery, Royal Artillery, under Lieutenant Philip Myers to deal with captured 88's, a sub-section of 296 Company, Royal Engineers and detachments of the Royal Corps of Signals and the RAMC. There was also the small party of naval safe breakers, SBAs A. Brown, J. E. Gray and G. A. Kay. In all, about 150 officers and men with three power boats, each one towing two dumb barges. The leading power boat contained Acting Lieutenant-Colonel E. H. M. Unwin as well as the first lieutenant of the *Sikh*. This power boat had the portable W/T set in it.

Other Royal Marine officers included Lieutenant (Acting Major) J. N. Hedley, Temporary Lieutenant (Acting Temporary Major) S. M. R. Woods, Temporary Lieutenants (Temporary Acting Captains) C. J. Mahoney, G. M. Nixon-Eckersall, L. W. Norwood, B. H. Salmons and M. G. A. Wright, Temporary Lieutenants A. M. Burnford and J. M. Burnford, Lieutenant G. W. Clarke and Temporary Lieutenants H. H. Dyall, W. Gledhill, W. J. Harris, J. W. Palmby, C. M. P. Powell, D. B. Taylor and Temporary Surgeon Lieutenant J. O. De E. Sugars. Alas, many of these fine young men were destined never even to reach the beaches.

Engines were stopped aboard the ship at 0310 when she had edged, bows-in, to within two-and-a-half miles of the enemy coast. 'Boat Stations' were then piped and the men began filing out in the inky blackness as the first boats were lowered into the heavy swell. The slippery and sticky paint over the two ships' fo'c'sles caused further trouble and chaos to the naval party and Marines alike.

Almost immediately, things started to go wrong. As the starboard forward power-boat of *Sikh* was being swung down, one of the falls parted and had to be hastily repaired in the blackness. The swell

120

continued to make the loading of the boats a difficult business and some forty minutes elapsed instead of the allowed-for twenty before all was ready. The men were clear of *Zulu* by 0348 but it was not until 0355 that all the power boats and tows left with the first flight and headed in towards the dark shore. Even while the first wave of troops were being disembarked from the destroyers into the barges, they could see clearly the large fire which the RAF bombing had initiated, pulsing and flaring beyond the distant escarpment backing the landing beaches. The fact that this bombing had woken up the whole defence of the Tobruk littoral also passed through the minds of the more thoughtful men waiting in the boats bouncing up and down alongside the two destroyers.

Eventually, then, the first wave got underway and the two destroyers turned back out to sea and steamed out on a westerly course at 15 knots and were soon lost to sight from the bobbing barges. Fire was not opened on them at first but about five minutes later when the small craft were still half-way to the shore, the searchlight came on again and this time the guns opened up. The struggling barges soon came under heavy fire from many shore batteries as first light lightened the sky. Many of the boats were hit right away and there were many casualties at this time. The seas were heavy the water deep and the landing place was strewn with jagged rocks which created more havoc than the gunfire. Among other barges who were in trouble at this early stage was that containing Corporal Leslie Joseph Andrews. The tow rope parted and fouled the leading boat's propeller. He immediately jumped over the side in the darkness and the swell, with enemy shells pitching around him, and for an hour struggled to cut the rope free. He was finally rewarded and, although it was too late for his craft to join in the landing, it was instrumental in rescuing many survivors from the, by then, crippled *Sikh*.

Another prime example of cool courage and disregard for personal safety was made by Corporal George Thomas Hunt at this time, in his attempts to get his section ashore. He was to prove his bravery yet further in the desperate hours which followed the landing. Marine Edward John Foley's landing barge was one of those hit and sunk in deep water by the enemy guns. Foley struggled ashore losing his rifle in the process but, nothing daunted, he took the bayonet of a wounded comrade and joined the leading troops of the first flight.

'Tug' Wilson of the *Sikh* recounted to me how the first wave of the landing went in:

When we got there, all I can remember is being called up and loaded into the boats. It was pitch-black, about three o'clock in the morning because we were late. We were rolling about a bit but the sea was not too bad. At least, it didn't seem bad to us sailors; the Marines might have thought differently of course. But not too bad although there was quite a swell. Compared with the practice landings at Cyprus, the loading of the troops went fairly smoothly. We used the ship's davits (we, of course, had left our normal ships boats behind in Alexandria).

I don't know how far we lay offshore but it must have been quite a way for it seemed a hell of a long trip in these boats. It seemed like miles away and so it could have been rough to some people. But we seemed a long time going into Tobruk. Then, all of a sudden, the searchlights came on. We were still well offshore at that moment and we certainly hadn't hit the beach then. Then the guns started firing, presumably at us but then they later seemed to switch to the *Sikh* and *Zulu* as it all went over our heads. The searchlights had not locked onto us. In fact, I don't think the searchlights got onto our particular section all the way into the beach. Others were not so fortunate but to us it appeared that they were firing over our heads and had either not spotted us or were not interested in the small fry at this stage.

Anyway, when we got to the beach we hit these rocks. The boat was smashed up, but we managed to get ashore or at least two or three of us. The rocks were under water as well as on the beach, and we had driven straight into them and holed our bows. We began sinking almost at once and we went out over the side into waist-deep water. Deep, cold water and in the complete darkness, as well. Then there were rocks on the beach itself, when, according to the operation, it should have been a plain, sandy beach! But there it was, here were these rocks which should not have been there and, of course, this instantly made us realise we had been landed in the wrong place.

Meanwhile, at 0414, the *Sikh* and *Zulu* again reversed course and headed back in towards land again to meet the empty barges returning and load the second flight into them. Wireless contact was meantime established between Commander R. T. White aboard *Zulu* and Colonel Unwin in the lead power boat and it was learned for the first time that his boat had broken down and that another boat was standing by him. Of the rest of the wave, nothing could be seen or heard, at first. It was assumed they were well on their way in by this time.

Because of the delay in launching the first wave and the desire of Captain (D) to locate Colonel Unwin's boat and render assistance, the two destroyers pressed in much closer to the shore this second time, to under a mile in fact, and this was to prove their undoing. From ashore, all was still quiet but this did not last long. A very bright white light was observed flashing from the direction of Mersa Mreira which was initially taken to be the folbotist signal indicating strong opposition to the landing and it was considered that this was made by a torch from the first flight.

Contact with the broken-down power boat was established by *Sikh* and Colonel Unwin returned to the destroyer, going up to the bridge to confer with Captain Micklethwaite. The decision was to abandon the operation and the *Sikh* began to edge in yet further, in order to re-embark all those it could from the first flight.

It was now 0500 and things had really begun to hot up ashore. Mortar and machine-gun fire was seen and appeared to move eastward down the north shore. Five minutes later, while engaged in picking up the tow of one of the boats, the *Sikh* was swept by a probing searchlight beam. Commander White took *Zulu* out to sea again to avoid being similarly detected then turned back in, bows-on to the searchlights, to present the narrowest profile possible. Meanwhile, the fighting had continued on land.

Among those of the ill-fated first wave that managed to struggle to the shore was Marine Major J. N. Hedley. He realised that they had been put ashore in the wrong spot and that in view of the conditions and the enemy reaction, he was not likely to be reinforced as hoped for, if at all. There seemed nothing for it but to try and take the commanding heights as quickly as possible, silence those guns and thus help the second wave in. The beach itself was under fire by now and illuminated by Very lights and star-shells; very little cover was to be had from their pitiless gaze other than the rocks themselves. Nothing daunted, Hedley began organising his survivors for the attack. Among his team were Lieutenant C. N. P. Powell, commanding 7 Platoon, 'A' Company, who on his own initiative collected what men he could and led them inland to establish a bridgehead.

A similar feat was accomplished by Sergeant John Povall who led his platoon in a bayonet charge which swept through several machine-gun nests and entrenched positions with great gallantry.

He also used his rifle to pick off troublesome strong-points as they made their way up the wadi from the beach. Accompanying this charge was the dauntless Marine Foley, armed still just with a bayonet with which he attacked an enemy machine-gun post at close quarters. This tight-knit little group got the men who were still in fighting trim together and they moved off up the beach firing as they went.

They found a wadi leading up the cliffs and used this as a convenient scaling point, advancing up it in extended line, under fire the whole time from enemy machine-gun posts. These were taken at bayonet point and beyond them they stumbled upon a tented camp which they took as well. The terrorised Italians were soon swarming up with their hands held high eager to surrender but Hedley's little party had neither the time nor the numbers to deal with these and ignored them. While the Royal Marines concentrated on the remaining defensive positions that were still firing, they left the Italians to wander off down to the beach and surrender to the boat party there.

'Tug' Wilson was among the small group left behind on the beach.

The Marines charged straight up the beach and got on with the job, leaving the beach landing party behind the rocks wondering what to do with ourselves. We couldn't go backwards because the boats had sunk, two or three of them. Then the enemy mortars started opening fire. Obviously, they knew we were there on the beach. I felt a bit lonely after the Marines vanished and the shooting started. I can recall one more of the landing boats crews nearby being smashed up, because we were spread out so much. There was some comfort in the fact that I had the stripped Lewis machine-gun out of the boat which kept me busy. Trouble was, the blasted thing kept jamming. Even so, we captured three or four Italians. Previous to that we had seen some Italians coming down the beach, about three or four of them, about 50 or 60 yards away and I opened fire with this Lewis and they all hit the deck. Then all of a sudden there were these three or four Italians near us. I can't remember how we did it; I really cannot recall what happened, but after a few bursts they had surrendered, much to our surprise and there they were, our prisoners!

When they all laid down I emptied their pockets and took their pay books, photographs and letters and kept these in my pockets.

(Anyway, going ahead a bit, after the Germans captured us these Italians started screaming their heads off because I had got all these photographs and personal papers. And so I had to give them back again quickly.) But for now, these Italians were just laying there. But where they came from I don't really know except we had these prisoners, although they were not prisoners for long.

Meanwhile the survivors of the 11th Battalion's first wave were being inspired by Major Hedley to continued advances. Hedley himself personally used a hand-grenade to destroy an enemy machine-gun mounted on a truck which was holding up his little group and a little later closed an Italian prepared position and with his service revolver quickly shot dead all five defenders. He then ran out of ammunition and would surely have been killed but for the intervention of Corporal Hunt, once more. His own platoon commander had been killed during the advance and when the rest of the section dived for cover Hunt continued to charge alone, almost immediately being shot above the heart. How he carried on defies belief but carry on he did with this wound, rallying his section and clearing the enemy posts. He reached Major Hedley just as an enemy NCO was advancing on the defenceless officer to despatch him but instead it was Hunt who shot dead the Italian. The wound was now finally taking effect and his arm became paralysed. One of the officers gently relieved Hunt of his rifle, at last. Lieutenant Powell's platoon took the right flank of the advance and, leading from the front in proper Royal Marine style, Powell urged his men on, wiping out several pockets of Italian resistance and cutting enemy telephone wires in the process to hamper their movements.

In such a manner, the Marines had fought their way to the top of the wadi by first light. Here they came to a halt.

Ahead of them lay a steep slope, swept by machine-gun fire and completely open. Hedley again determined on continuing to the top; to go back to the open beach and wrecked boats would have been pointless. A heavy fire was opened on the enemy defences and after a fierce fire-fight these machine-gun posts were also silenced. The Royal Marines were then able to clamber up the final slopes to the top of the wadi and gain a brief respite from Axis automatic fire. For the first time they had time to take stock. The position was grim; Hedley had but seventeen men left to him!

Ahead was a building, deserted, and they sought its cover to regroup, re-ammunition and take stock of their situation. Weapons were cleaned but no water was taken for Hedley determined that the only hope for his little party was to lay up during the daylight hours and try and make an escape to the east that night. After a short rest, it was obvious that a better concealment place was needed until then and so they pushed carefully on, but, with enemy aircraft criss-crossing the sky above them hunting for such groups, they were forced to make frequent dives for cover and progress was slow.

They eventually reached another wadi, pushed on up it and came upon some caves at its head. Hedley determined to lie low here and, once inside, the radio was found to be working still and attempts were made to get in touch with either the ships offshore or other British force still at liberty. But the results were disappointingly and totally negative. Nor was their presence a secret from the enemy for very long. As the day wore on, large numbers of enemy troops could be seen slowly converging on their hiding place. It was painfully clear that they had been pin-pointed and were totally surrounded. There were still many hours of daylight left and thus only a hopeless suicidal battle faced them. Bowing to the inevitable, Major Hedley surrendered his force after destroying the radio. It was the end of a most gallant foray, and among the very deserved decorations subsequently awarded when news of it reached home, was the DSO for both Hedley and Powell, the Conspicuous Gallantry Medal to Povall and Hunt and the DSM to Corporal L. J. Andrews and Marine E. J. Foley.

*

Back out at sea things had not gone well for the British force, either. The *Sikh* was illuminated and quickly held in the probing beam of the searchlights. She was so close into the shore that the German gunners could hardly have missed her. She was a destroyer, not a battleship, her slender hull was built for speed not to withstand salvoes. Very little steel lay between her highly vulnerable sophisticated machinery and the enemy shells. As the salvoes crashed out against her, she was soon in dire trouble.

A direct hit from one of the powerful 88-mm guns, used by the Germans to knock out heavily armoured British tanks, was taken in the crucial gearing room which put out of action the forced lubricating pumps, after switchboard, fire and bilge pumps. The starboard main engine immediately seized up but for a brief ten-minute period steam was possible on the port engine only. Unfortunately, very quickly a second hit was taken, this time in the steering compartment, and the steering gear was rendered completely inoperational. The rudder was jammed fast. This blow effectively finished the destroyer off, and, although she continued to fight back valiantly for a considerable time, she was clearly doomed.

The *Sikh*'s Gunner (T), Mr S. G. MacDonald, gave me this account of the landing and his ship's final moments:

> We were aware that the Royal Marines had landed in the wrong place when the first flight section, under the command of Colonel Unwin returned to the ship. The other section, under Major Jack Hedley, got ashore and made a magnificent attack which took them well inland but were forced to surrender eventually through lack of reinforcements – we met many of them later 'in the bag' and were able to learn how bitterly they felt at the way their expedition, apparently so successful at the beginning, was frustrated through no fault of their own.
>
> The *Sikh*'s pom-pom was not used in action against the German 88's. The range of this gun wouldn't make it effective and it was the chief AA armament for close-range use and would not be of much use because it would not depress sufficiently to engage a close low target.
>
> The 88's were clearly visible when firing in the dark but it would be hopeless to try to engage them other than by sight and guess. They would be reasonable targets for guesswork, for the original shore fire was from batteries to the north-east of the ship's position, and it seems to me that the Germans brought the 88's to come close to the ship's beam where we would be a very easy target, I assume. After all it was pretty portable, besides being a potent, weapon.

Able Seaman A. K. Collins was serving *Sikh*'s 'A' gun and gave this description of events as he saw them:

> The enemy's first salvo scored a lucky hit on the tiller flat and put all methods of steering out of action. *Sikh* commenced to circle helplessly and was unable to collect the remaining two flights of her boats. 'X' and 'Y' guns' crews were out of the ship manning the landing craft, so the gunner officer and four AB's went aft and manned 'X' gun. Shortly afterwards, the ship was hit in the gearing room and thereafter was purely a hulk. *Zulu* came alongside at 0545 and attempted to take her in tow.

While closing her damaged flotilla leader, *Zulu* sighted a single power boat and two dumb barges stopped in the distance and apparently immobile. They hailed Commander White but he had to leave them behind in order to get a tow to *Sikh* as quickly as possible, as with dawn lightening the sky the two destroyers' position, already critical, would clearly become untenable within a very short time. The first attempt failed as *Sikh* still had considerable way on at ten knots and dawn had broken by the time the second attempt was under way at 0625. It took ten minutes to get the tow across and Commander White ordered all the guns' crews down to the deck to expedite this vital work, but *Sikh* herself continued to blaze away. Aboard *Sikh*, 'A' gun's crew worked on the fo'c'sle whilst 'B' continued firing.

Within a minute of the tow being established both destroyers were hit several times in quick succession, the tow rope was cut, two men killed and several wounded. Commander White went ahead and laid smoke, at the same time asking Captain Micklethwaite if he should come alongside and take her crew off. Captain (D) replied, 'Wait ten minutes', which White assumed was to give *Sikh* more time to lay more smoke to cover this risky operation.

But it was not to be; *Zulu* took two more hits and *Sikh* many more and a short time after the tow had parted Captain (D) ordered *Zulu* to get out of it and join *Coventry* to the east. Commander White described his feelings thus:

> At the time, I, myself, had decided that this most dreadful decision was the right one as I was sure that *Zulu* would not have avoided severe damage if I had again closed into a mile of the coast. Courageous signals were received from the *Sikh* as we left her to her fate and she was last seen firing with her forward guns and being repeatedly hit.

Before she left *Zulu* went very close to the shore and laid a thick smoke screen. As she made her way out to sea, *Zulu* remained under continual fire from the shore batteries until some six miles out, by which time she in turn had fired off all her SAP ammunition (and also some of her timed HE with maximum fuses set), in reply.

Back at Alexandria, only fragmentary evidence was being received on how the operation was faring. At 0200 the signal, '1st Shore objective gained', was sent but the initial euphoria rapidly changed as the morning wore on. The next signal, timed at 0345,

Death throes of the famous ship. The anti-aircraft cruiser *Coventry* had fought many hard fights against dive bombers, from the fiords of Norway to the coast of Greece. But off Tobruk she was to fight her last fight. Hit by Stuka bombs she is seen heavily on fire forward.

Death throes of a veteran. Seen from one of the Luftwaffe's circling Junkers Ju88 bombers on her way back to Crete from north Africa, the *Coventry* receives her death blows as two torpedoes slam into her starboard side.

(*Top left*) Hands reach out to aid the unfortunate. A Carley float laden with *Coventry* survivors comes alongside one of the escorting destroyers. (*Top right*) Firm hands on a scrambling net pluck more wounded men from the oil-laden sea.

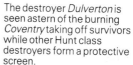

The destroyer *Dulverton* is seen astern of the burning *Coventry* taking off survivors while other Hunt class destroyers form a protective screen.

Seen from an escorting destroyer, the crippled cruiser is closed by escorting destroyers.

read, 'Awaiting remainder MTB's', which gave rise to the first niggling doubts that all was not well; then came a succession of disasters that steadily mounted in scope as the day wore on. At 0526, Captain Micklethwaite had signalled, 'Force "A" failed to land. *Sikh* hit and disabled.' This was followed at 0604 by another from the same source, '*Zulu* closing in to take in tow', and at 0623 by, 'Force "A" withdrawing – landing failed.' Then came Commander White's poignant farewell to *Sikh*, timed at 0655, 'Must leave you.'

Back aboard the *Sikh*, the fires had by now got a complete hold on the ship below decks and 'B', 'X' and 'Y' magazines had to be flooded in case they blew up. It did not prove possible however for 'A' magazine to be so dealt with because of the fierce cordite fire in the forward messdecks which cut off access to the flooding position located there. Very soon the whole fo'c'sle was red hot and the ship took on a heavy list to starboard.

Nor did *Zulu* escape at this period, being hit three or four times as well, including once on her quarterdeck which parted the tow and later more hits cut away one leg of the tripod mainmast and the W/T sets were all damaged. Less seriously, holes were punched in her hull in the wardroom aft and the torpedomen's and chief petty officers' messes but the flooding was of a minor nature.

Major R. W. Sankey, Royal Marines, aboard the *Zulu* also provided an account of the action:

At about 2000 yards and approximately 0445 hours, a coast defence gun to the west opened up. At the same time, the harbour entrance searchlight kept up a sweep to seaward. About the third salvo from the coast defence battery, *Sikh* signalled that she was hit and disabled . . . We moved slowly along the coast just off the landing beach, the coast defence battery still firing. *Sikh* opened and *Zulu* followed suit. Range was then 2000 yards. Star-shells were put over *Sikh* and also at times *Zulu*. Other coast defence guns had joined in, mortar fire was heard and we could see tracer being fired by the Royal Marines ashore, also heavy firing at the harbour entrance. During darkness a constant barrage of star shells lit up *Sikh* and *Zulu*; we made smoke but more guns opened, both *Sikh* and *Zulu* replying.

At 0530 hours, as first light approached, it was decided to leave the boat rendezvous and try to take *Sikh* in tow. She had been hit and was in a bad way. Three searchlights were now making a seaward sweep and several heavy anti-aircraft guns were firing at *Sikh* and *Zulu*. There were also signs of heavy fighting on shore. I ordered all Marines under Captain Ellis, RM, onto the quarter deck to work the wire. At approximately 0600 we attempted to take *Sikh* in tow, we were being heavily fired on from the shore and during this attempt *Zulu* was also hit.

The first attempt failed as *Sikh* was under way; she had one boiler working and was making about 3 – 4 knots. By this time it was broad daylight and we were between 1500 – 2000 yards from shore, a number of Coast Defence light and heavy batteries were firing at *Sikh* and *Zulu*, also light and heavy anti-aircraft guns, pom-poms and in one case a machine-gun post. *Sikh* and *Zulu* were still answering.

Zulu approached a second time; *Sikh* had now stopped and was drifting inshore. Again we attempted to take *Sikh* in tow, and this time the wire was being secured aboard *Zulu* when we were hit just below the quarter-deck, parting the wire. This shell killed Captain Ellis and severely wounded several seamen and Marines. by this time we were being straddled by all guns firing at us. We were hit again just abaft the foremast, this shell killing Marine Richards and wounding several more seamen and Marines. This shell set alight reserve grenades and small arms ammunition stored on the upper deck of *Zulu*. Without thought of personal safety, Corporal Murphy, Lance/Corporal Campbell and Marine McFarlane seized the blazing boxes and threw them overboard. *Sikh* was being hit frequently and what appeared to be 'B' turret magazine blew up.

Zulu went around once more to make another attempt but Captain (D)22 ordered *Zulu* to return to Alexandria. Under heavy smoke, we turned and steamed away. We left *Sikh* drifting shorewards still answering with 'X' and 'Y' turrets. As we left, a large column of smoke arose from the shore about the area where 'B' Company would be operating, heavy fighting was still going on ashore.

After *Zulu* had steamed away the *Sikh* continued her hopeless fight alone. Three or four more direct hits were taken. Eventually, when there was no hope at all remaining, scuttling charges were fired to ensure she sank as deep a water as possible. Able Seaman Collins again:

At this time *Sikh* was being heavily hit fore and aft. A shell on the mess deck set fire to cordite, and a number of the supply parties and Marines there were killed or badly burnt.

Captain (D) now gave the order to abandon ship, although 'B' gun still went on firing. Before leaving the ship, Collins assisted badly wounded men to get away and had to push a number of the Marines – who were so badly burnt that they could not face jumping – into the water.

After Collins himself had jumped in, he witnessed Captain Micklethwaite, Colonel Unwin and the first lieutenant, still going round the ship helping to get the men away and at one time manning 'X' gun to fire at an enemy aircraft. He initially grabbed a bundle of paddles to keep himself afloat then managed to get to a net raft. *Sikh* herself took three hours to sink and during all that time the enemy continued to pepper her, but many of their shells fell among the men in the water. A large number of casualties were caused at this time.

Sikh eventually rolled over and sank without having been approached by any of the enemy small craft in the vicinity, but German boats later put to sea to search for survivors.

S. G. MacDonald gave this account of *Sikh*'s last moments:

At the close of the action I was still engaged (in fact trying to get down to wreck the Asdic gear – which proved unnecessary anyway – it being ruined by fire) and did not hear the order 'Abandon Ship'. Captain Micklethwaite at the stern of the ship ordering the remaining survivors overboard. 'Come on, Guns', he said, 'over the side for you – no boats or rafts left – you'll have to do the best you can.' Seeing the beach not all that far away I took off my shoes, tied them together thinking that they would be helpful for the long walk to Malta or Alex (what an optimist) and jumped overboard after deciding it was no good going down to my cabin nearby for some tinned fags and photos.

Swimming well clear of the ship I found the sea crowded with boats, rafts, landing craft, Carley floats and floatnets. Many others were also swimming, the boats, Carley rafts and floats having been loaded with wounded and sick people – already some were screaming or plumped heavily in or on the craft, so that the only thing left was to seek a spot on a float or a net (a hempen cargo net fitted with cork floats along the edges and

down the net lines). By the time I'd found a spot it was fully
loaded but soon we obviously made to get just on the edge and
cling to the next man and this is just what all the rest of the
'crews' were doing – our heads and necks protruded above water
and heaven help those who lost their footing! I didn't see any
place free on the net where I was so spent a very miserable few
hours just keeping afloat and supporting each other.

It was impossible to register time but some time after
disembarking the *Sikh* slowly but surely rolled over on to her port
side and lay there for what seemed ages before she slowly sank by
the bows and eventually the screws appeared, after which to my
(and I suspect other people's) relief, she slid under. During the
time she was afloat constant machine-gun attacks were made by
Italian planes who raked backwards and forwards among the
wreckage and despondent survivors – the only protection we
were able to seek was to bob our heads beneath the waves as we
saw the bullets splash into the water towards us. The language
used was less than gentlemanly and to this day I wouldn't believe
it could happen had it not been for my own experience.

Shortly after the *Sikh* disappeared German harbour vessels
appeared – some towed those boats and floats capable into
Tobruk and others scurried around rescuing those of us who had
minimum support. Gratefully I saw the German ensign above
one of these small personnel carriers, a hand came down and I
was hauled up by a pleasant German boy in his natty Naval
uniform. When the carrier was full and that didn't take long –
the boat set off for Tobruk pier where we were landed under
scrutiny of the local Italian garrison – the newsreel cameras
having a field day. From there we were separated, officers and
men and trucked up to the Naval port headquarters to undergo
prisoner routine.

Earle A. Graham described how he saw events from aboard the *Sikh*
in the early hours of Monday 14th September.

We arrived off Tobruk in the early hours. There was an air-raid
going on at the time, but I saw nothing of it as the personnel of
the second wave had to stay below decks while the first moved off.
Word came down that they had got away safely, then we waited
for the order to go on deck in order to disembark. When this came
I went on deck aft with the other members of my party, which was

mainly made up of various specialists who, like myself, had come to do a specific job. One of these was an American war correspondent; he was called Larry, but I have forgotten his surname. Sergeant Crapper was forward and was going with a group of Marines. We waited in the dark, then there was some sort of commotion – I found out later that one of the motor launches had broken down and the craft it was towing had drifted back to the *Sikh*.

While this was being sorted out, one of the shore searchlights swung out to sea and picked us out. We were about two miles from the shore when the first wave went, but had gradually come in closer, probably to shorten the run for the second wave when the landing craft returned. There had been a lot of trouble with the first wave; the boats were very unsatisfactory, but of course, those of us waiting did not know this at the time. The Marines from the drifting craft were brought aboard, and suddenly the shore batteries opened up on us. We were hit and a fire was started forward.

For what seemed like an age we sat there with everything being thrown at us, and when at last the ship started to move she kept going round in circles. At the time, I was very puzzled by this and wondered why we were not trying to get out of range. As the ship circled round everyone was dodging round also, in order to have the deck housing between us and the shore. I remember quite clearly seeing one of the Maltese stewards moving round near me with the ship's cat in his arms. Our guns were firing back, and at one point I was in a bad position and as a result I suffered from gun deafness in one ear for some time. The reason, as I found out later, for the circling was that one of the hits had damaged the steering and the vessel could not go straight. The gearing-room had been hit and before long the engines seized up and we stopped. The *Zulu* came up and attempts were made to attach a tow, but after two or three tries this idea had to be abandoned, and she moved off to save herself. I think that she had been hit, but not as badly as the *Sikh*. I had no knowledge of what happened to Sergeant Crapper; in my movements about the deck to dodge the shellfire, I had not come across him, and could only hope that he was safe, though I knew by then that there had been numerous casualties forward when the ship had been hit at first and the fire started.

It was now getting quite light, the vessel was still on fire and was listing slightly. Then came the order to abandon ship; this meant that it was up to everyone to save himself if he could. Unfortunately, there were no ship's boats: all the room had been taken up by the landing craft. This meant that we had to rely on lifejackets and anything which would float. I had not been able to film anything during the night as it was too dark, and now it was pointless to try to do so. I put down my camera, which I had been carefully carrying, and took off my haversack with the film, and prepared to save my life if I could. There was one landing craft still on deck and I joined a group trying to get it over the side, but it was jammed in some way and we could not move it. It was now broad daylight.

I was wearing a 'Mae West' life jacket, which I had put on in order to go with the second wave. This I now inflated and went down one of the scrambling nets into the sea. Luckily, as I am not a good swimmer, there was a Carley float near by and I made my way to this and got in to it. There were several men in it already, and others joined us. Soon it was very full, then some decided to swim off to other floating debris. It was fortunate that the raid took place in September because the water was warm and that morning the sea was reasonably calm, though at one point the float did tip over. We paddled with our hands and bits of wood, which some of the men had, in order to get as far away as possible from the sinking ship for fear of being sucked down as she went under. She went down with her colours still flying, which was a nice defiant gesture, though I learned later that the captain had ordered them to be struck but the lanyard had stuck. Maybe it was because of this that when some planes came over they machine-gunned us. Finally, they turned away and shortly after the *Sikh* disappeared.

It was soon after this that some of the Axis surface craft at Tobruk, including an Italian destroyer and the motor minesweepers of the German 6th Flotilla under the command of Commander Reischauer, came out and picked up the survivors as Earle Graham recalled:

Shortly afterwards an Italian lighter came out of Tobruk and took us all aboard. There was nothing anyone could do for the wounded except to make sure they were safe. I felt exhausted and was only too glad to squat on the deck in the sun to get dry and warm again. We came into Tobruk harbour and were put ashore. Here I had a stroke of luck: I was wearing desert shoes, suede shoes with thick rubber soles which most members of the Eighth Army wore against regulations (the Eighth was noted for its peculiar style of dress) – these I had taken off in the water, as not being much of a swimmer I had feared that they would hamper me, though this did not seem to be the case with others. So I went ashore in stockinged feet. The captain of the *Sikh* – Captain Micklethwaite – saw me and gave me a pair of plimsolls which for some unknown reason he had stuffed into his pocket. I had every reason to be grateful for his generosity because it was some time before I was able to acquire a pair of boots. The wounded, including Sergeant Crapper, were taken to hospital but sadly, as I found out later, he died there.

Two of the landing barges with engines made a forlorn attempt to get away at a speed of one knot to reach Alexandria but these were quickly rounded up also. Collins recorded that he was taken to a rock dressing station where the Germans gave first aid treatment and, like 'Tug' Wilson, recalled how he was very well treated by the Germans. The Italians were another matter, being vindictive, spiteful and bullying on the rare occasions they got the upper hand. Two officers and twenty ratings from *Sikh* did not join them in the POW camps; they found their last resting place with their ship off the coast of Tobruk.

*

We must now turn again to examine the Axis viewpoint of the night's events. Hans-Otto Behrendt, then serving with Intelligence Section G2 at Panzer-Armee Afrika's HQ, which at that time was located at Sidi Abd-El-Rahman, was emphatic that the Germans had no prior knowledge at all of any landings. He told me that they had 'heard, only casually, that an attack on Tobruk had taken place and had failed. We had enough other tasks – and sorrows – of our own at that time that Tobruk seemed to be far away, and since this affair presented no immediate danger it did not call for special attention.' Even General Rommel's personal interpreter, when asked in 1986 about the raid, stated that he 'could not remember this affair at all.' So much for the impact Operation Agreement had on the German force in North Africa, both at the time and since! It seems pretty conclusive then that the landings did actually come as a complete surprise to the Axis with regard to prior knowledge, but that the RAF bombing had served to arouse their suspicions that something special was going on at Tobruk. Certainly, the German War Diary recorded at 0230 merely that the commanding officer of the Rear Army Area had reported that the enemy had landed near Tobruk after heavy air attacks which had lasted seven hours. As Behrendt says, 'Seven hours of bombing was enough alarm, at least for German troops!' As for the prior knowledge by the Germans or Italians, Behrendt adds: 'I know for certain that we had no spies in Egypt or any other Near Eastern country. But I do not exclude the fact that the Italians suffered from British attacks and raids so often that they expected them all the time, even against Tobruk.'

Let us now examine the detailed fighting that brought about this spectacular result. That it was undoubtedly the British air raid rather than any subtle source that alerted the defenders is made crystal clear by the German signal sent to Generalmajor Deindl at the Command HQ of Stab Köruck which was located 20 kilometres to the west of Tobruk, as early as 2300 on 13th September. This was originated by Major Liehr, the Kommandeur of the Guard Battalion Afrika who expressed his alarm and suspicion following the 'Strong and prolonged air attacks', which had been directed against Tobruk that day. He and his fellow officers regarded this as being consistent with a softening-up barrage for some special event and he recommended the immediate issuing of the alarm to initiate Operation Landealarm.

Half an hour later, Hauptmann Schultz-Ingenohl was made acting Commander in the event of an attack on the harbour and fortress area. Although Tobruk was nominally under the overall command of the Italian Admiral Lombardi, in reality, as in most cases in the German-Italian Axis, he was largely a figurehead whose control was only absolute over the Italian Marines of the San Marco battalion and other units. Schultz-Ingenohl organised most of the German units in the subsequent fighting, reporting directly back to Generalmajor Diendl as events moved on.

The alarm had also been raised as early as 2245 on the 14th by Oberleutnant Grelli of Kommando DICAT whose Luftwaffe troops were with the Flakgruppe unit based at Tobruk itself. They reported enemy landing craft had been sighted and all 200 men were put on instant alert and told to hold themselves ready to repel attack. Only later did they get any Italian help in their sector covering the harbour. They moved their mobile four-barrelled 2-cm light flak guns down to the harbour area and awaited events.

At 0020, Schultz-Ingenohl telephoned the Kommandanten that: Lieutenant Petzel (5./Nachschub.Kol.Abt.686) had informed him that the enemy were landing 3 kilometres east of Tobruk. He also reported the dropping of bombs as well as artillery fire in the town and fortress area, but that with Landealarm given, reinforcements were on the move.

Deindl told him in reply to resist 'the hostile landings with all his immediately available strength.' He added that he would soon be driving along the Via Balbia to reach Tobruk with advance forces while in Tobruk the Guardbattalions were to be fully alerted. Simultaneously, Generalmajor Deindl, through Schultz-Ingenohl, ordered Nachschub-Kol.Abt.909:

> Enemy landing at Tobruk. Move out to cover the line Gazala to Via Balbia road. HQ of 909 to the Via Balbia at Kilometre Post 19 to be at my disposal.

And at 0030 on the morning of 14th, the Kommandant issued over the radio, 'Landealarm'. Major Hardt reported that on the issuing of the code, German troops moved into their combat positions in Sectors II, III and IV. Their patrols from then up to 0400 established that there was no sign of any enemy troops having established themselves ashore at all even though the Italians were blazing away willy-nilly in the darkness, so much so, reported the German commander, that the lives of his own men were in mortal danger at times! The Italians were firing off Very lights in some directions but directing their fire in completely different directions to the positions illuminated, all for naught. Thus, 'from about 0100 onward along the whole eastern littoral of Tobruk the nervous Italians staged much wild shooting.'

When, between 0200 and 0300, two enemy destroyers were eventually sighted and taken under fire, it was found that many of the forward positions, supposed to have been held by Italian troops, were in fact still unmanned. For example, Oberleutnant von Rosenstiel, commanding the IV Sector garrison, reported that the Italians in his part of the sector had failed to set up any posts, that they were nowhere to be found and that the whole of that section of line was held solely by German troops. Similarly, in Sector III the commander, Hauptmann Rippich, stated that the Italians had one artillery gun and one machine-gun post manned in the line, at Fort Peronne; everything else was held by German troops. And these were the sections where the English were reported to be coming ashore.

At 0210, the commander telephoned the CO of Guardbattalion Afrika, Major Liehr:

> Enemy landing at Tobruk. Wachbatl. to assemble on the Via Balbia at Kilometre Post 19 leaving behind small forces on the way to protect the coastal section north of the encampments. One company with suitable vehicles to immediately proceed to Kilometre Post 19. After assembling there they were to move along the Via Balbia to Tobruk.

Beyond these immediate moves, other forces were set in train to seal off the area inland from Tobruk. Just what these reinforcements entailed is made clear in HQ reports which shows that the Royal Marines struggling ashore faced hopeless odds.

The initial reports coming into Generalmajor Deindl at Rear Army HQ gave no exact details about what kind of British landing was taking place or the strength of the forces coming ashore. It was assumed however that 'the enemy will try to take possession of the fortress.'

That was enough for the Army High Command (AOK) to assemble a German motorised force for possible combat use in throwing the British out should they establish a toehold. Accordingly, orders were rushed out to three units. These were:

1. AA 580 (Reconnaissance Battalion 580) who were ordered to move to Mersa Matruh at once.

2. AA 3 (Reconnaissance Battalion 3) who were told to get ready for an instant notice move.

3. Battle Group 'Everth' of the DAK which was to immediately assemble for combat one Panzer Grenadier battalion and one light artillery battalion and be ready to move out at once.

Major Hardt in command of the main reserve force in Tobruk town itself telephoned in a report through *Sonderführer* Dr Geiger:

> Flak Command Post reports: English landing 3 kilometres east of Tobruk presumably in the Bay at Mersa Umm es Sciausc. Italian coastal battery surprised and overrun. In Tobruk itself nothing happening. Complete telephone links disturbed. The men closest to the lodgement, the Guards and Koruck detachment, are assembling and are on their way. Major Hardt is already there.

The flak batteries have the enemy landing craft under fire now.

Hardt himself recorded:

I found myself at about 0330 at Height 42, in the middle of Sector IV. The Italian troops had established posts on Heights 40 and 42 manned by Naval personnel and AA gunners. They were covering the coast which lay some 800 metres in advance of these positions.

I was twice called up on the land line here and informed that the enemy landing craft had been sighted off the coast (at a distance of about 1,000 metres) and had been picked up and held by our searchlight batteries. In their glare our flak guns had opened fire and in return the English destroyers were shelling our searchlight positions in the Bay of Mersa Mreira area.

I at once sped off there with one car and one small truck with about twenty men, some from the Luftwaffe armed with hand weapons and stick grenades. On the way, I requested a meeting with the Italians' officer who I only knew as the man in charge of their coastal artillery. I must place on record that I found them over-nervous and without any discipline. At the Bay I saw in the glare of the searchlights the two destroyers who were firing at our searchlights. Over to the west there appeared to be much small-arms, infantry and machine-gun, fire taking place. I, with the Luftwaffe troops proceeded to reinforce these due to their apparent lack of operational readiness.

At 0430, Oberleutnant Soldt of 1./Wachbatl.Afrika, reported from Kilometre Post 19:

Company is moving quickly up to the road junction just to the west of Tobruk. From here we are continuing as commanded and a despatch rider is returning to bring up the rest of the battalion.

Ten minutes later on the Via Balbia report came from Hauptmann Schultz-Ingenohl from Tobruk command: 'Reports of further landings to the east of Tobruk false. Further attacks in the northern have not been made.'

Major Hardt continued his narrative:

Dawn was beginning to break and I could clearly observe the

small boats out at sea and the excellent gunnery against the two destroyers who were by now heavily engaged by both our flak batteries and the Italian coastal artillery. I despatched my twenty men under command of an officer to about 800 metres from the landing area to hold that sector. One of the two destroyers had by this time been disabled and was only firing with machine-guns while the other destroyer was trying to disengage. About 0900 the first destroyer was seen to sink. Others counted twelve small craft, many of which were wrecked, and estimated four to five destroyers and also a cruiser and a torpedo-boat off the coast, about 10 kilometres from the shore.

It is clear both from their contemporary reports, maps and subsequent claims, that the defenders did not realise that the *Sikh* and *Zulu* were in fact the same ships appearing at two different places after a slight interval. They were convinced at the time that all the comings and goings off the coast were by one force of four destroyers, hence their miscalculations. They were accurate enough when it came to the light craft closer in, however.

Down to the south of Sector IV at about 0500, the multiple machine-guns of Flakgruppen Tobruk's 3./914 unit opened heavy fire on light craft attempting to approach the entrance to the Bay of Mersa es Sciausc and they were joined in their defence by the multiple-2cm cannon of 4./914 under Hauptmann Frintrop which proved deadly in their effects on the thin-hulled MTB's. They were joined in this by fire from seventeen Italian motor barges which had been hastily armed and distributed around the harbour area, by the only two 4-inch guns of the Italian *Dandalo*, and by the light guns aboard three Italian destroyers which were in port at the time. This wall of shells from the fully alerted Axis defences was more than enough to quickly repel this attempt at a landing and they mopped up some 35 prisoners in the aftermath of their work here.

As the fighting progressed, it quickly became clear to the Axis commanders that these units would be sufficient to contain the small segment of the 'Invasion Force' that had managed to get ashore and that it was no more than a raid in strength.

While on his hurried journey through the darkness along the coast road to Tobruk, Majorgeneral Deindl felt confident that strong resistance would be put up by, 'my light and heavy flak batteries eastwards of the harbour, in addition to the coastal guns located to the north of Tobruk.' His one worry was that, isolated as they were from each other on the heights north of the harbour, they would be targets for individual attacks. In his mind they presented, 'concentrated targets for the ground forces from my reports and impressions of the pcninsulas north of Tobruk.' Those located south-west of the harbour were less split up and presented fewer dangers but if the earlier reports *were* true then the Army radio station itself was endangered. 'I verbally ordered the Kommandant and the Kompaniefuhrer. 1. Company Wachbatl. "One company move immediately to the Army radio post and protect the perimeter."'

At 0550, he received a reply from the Adjutant that 3./Wachbatl. and 1/60 Transportunit 'Speer' were on the way to protect the radio station from any new landings to the north.

Back at the cliffs overlooking the actual Royal Marine landing beach, Major Hardt on the spot was able to send a further encouraging report at 0545:

Altogether about twelve enemy units in sight, from two to ten kilometres out to sea. Two destroyers, respectively three and six kilometres out, are burning. Good, well-aimed flak fire directed against the landing craft.

The vital hits which had reduced *Sikh* to a helpless hulk to be finished off as mere target practice come the dawn were all scored by the 88-mm Flak battery, 1/60, commanded by Hauptmann Nitzki.(One post-war German source credits Major Wegener's 1/43, but this unit and this officer are not mentioned in any of the official German papers on the battle!)

Between 0530 and 0600, Deindl also received updates on the moving into action of the combined Army and Luftwaffe units under Adjutant Koruck from Staff HQ at Tobruk, as well as those units already in action on the beaches north of the harbour. This included word through the adjutant of the flak command post, that 1/36 AVL at Tobruk was on the move to reinforce the danger zone. There were also two more highly encouraging reports concerning the British seaborne forces. The first, at 0600, from the Kommandant of the command post atop the cliff stated that the surviving landing craft were withdrawing out to sea and the second, which the Generalmajor received at 0630, stated that a mass of enemy ships were sighted steering away on an easterly course, which indicated a British withdrawal rather than further assaults. All seemed well in hand, as indeed it was. By the time he arrived at the HQ, there was nothing much left for Deindl to do as his troops had already won the day.

Around 0700, Hauptmann von Rippich, commanding the three sections north of the harbour reported that the attempted English landings in the Bays of Mersa and el Krim had been defeated and some seventy prisoners had been taken so far. He also reported his own losses to date as: a) Pioneer Land Company – 3 seriously wounded, 2 slightly wounded; b) 5./Supply Battalion 85 – 2 seriously wounded, 2 slightly wounded; c) Company Workshop troop – 1 man killed, 1 slightly wounded. According to statements from Field Hospital there were about 30 German dead all told.

There were also reports of English parachute troops dropping out towards Kilometre Post 19 on the Via Balbia but these proved false readings of the German reinforcements' assembly signals. Another coup was the discovery by men of the 2./532 unit of a landing boat in which was found the complete British attack plan in full detail as well as an address to the Arab population. The capture of these secret plans was claimed by Admiral Cocchia as being achieved by an Italian naval signal rating, named Zinni, but perhaps there were two sets of the top-secret British plans recovered that day.

In either event, it certainly facilitated the Luftwaffe's operations during the rest of the daylight hours, as the precise details of the covering force were also made open to them. It also supplies the answer to one source of rumour that the Axis knew in advance of the operation. According to some post-war British sources, when Captain Micklethwaite was subsequently interrogated by an Italian officer he was asked the question, 'You were two hours late. Why?' As we shall see, other British prisoners were given the same demoralising treatment and are convinced to this day they had been betrayed. However, as the Germans and Italians had already recovered the full plans intact that morning, they could ask such questions easily and thus give the appearance that they knew all along! They also recovered intact two heavy machine guns, two bren guns and a rifle.

Also at 0700, Deindl requested the Italian air force to conduct missions over the fortress to help track down remaining British units and also to scout to sea and locate the full extent of the Royal Navy presence and its location, but this initiative too had already been seized and Italian fighter aircraft were already doing just that. There really only remained the mopping up. At 0717, the construction battalion was reporting to HQ, 'The attack by the English north-west of Tobruk has been shattered.' They added, 'Over 75 enemy troops and 5 landing craft destroyed, and with them the threat of invasion is lifted.'

Deindl was not lowering his guard yet, however, and signalled at 0743, 'Landealarm is still to be maintained by Wachbatl Afrika.' At the same time, he reassured Major Hardt: 'Harbour area is all secure.'

*

At 0830, there was a council of war between the officers of the Italian fortress commander and Stabsgebaude Köruck. It was decided to place all troops of whatever nationality in two groups for the rest of the operation. The Germans would control all forces north of the Via Balbia to Mersa Matruh and el Krim to the west; the rest of the fortress would remain under the Italians. This was confirmed at 0840 by Rear Army HQ who issued their direct order on this with regard to the defence of Tobruk. It was later further confirmed in the morning report to the Commando Supremo of the Italian Army when again it was proposed to put all Italian troops in the Tobruk area itself and to the east, under the operational orders of Panzer Armee.

Later in the morning, more detailed reports began to come which showed clearly that the troops on the spot had more than sufficed to repel the landings, and to inflict severe losses on the attackers as well. During the morning, under the new organisation the mopping-up of those British troops who had managed to get ashore and still held out began. 5/Construction Battalion 85, with Landingkompanie 778, plus 1 and 2 Groups of Italians, under the command of Hauptmann Rippich, was assigned the Mengar el Auda promontory and they diligently searched all that area and, as we have already seen, either destroyed or took prisoner all the surviving British Marines that they found there. The Army radio unit with 1./Wachbatl., deployed from 1800 metres north of the north-western area of the harbour itself, had prevented any landing attempts. The Flak Group under Major Hartmann and Hauptmann Nitzki, with the victorious gunners of 1/60, were deployed to the west down to the area around the bay, five kilometres south-west of Tobruk; there, they successfully took part in overcoming the British force. Guards Battalion Afrika covered from Wadi el Caf westward to Marsa el Auda against scattered groups of soldiers of the enemy force.

5./*Bau-Btl.* 85 took 55 prisoners (not counting 20 – 30 Italians who had surrendered to the British), while the men of the *Flak-Gruppe* bagged 35. Another two dozen were captured by Wachbatl. Afrika while the various Italian forces netted 50 more in these sweeps. The German commander noted that the prisoners consisted mainly of men of the Royal Navy, Royal Marines, one Canadian artilleryman, all mainly from Palestine, who had sailed from Alexandria on the night of the 12th/13th. As well as the complete plans of the operation which they captured intact, they itemised their other booty thus: 1 barge with six landing craft; 1 enemy boat with two barges; 4 machine-guns; 1 grenade-thrower; 2 automatic cannon; rifles; 1 radio set with large aerial; 1 radio telephone; 2 signal lamps.

German casualties in inflicting this humiliating defeat on the British force were minimal: eight men killed in action, eight seriously wounded and eleven slightly wounded. Of the dead, six died while patients in Field Hospital 36.

There was little harmony of effort or love lost between the Axis partners, even in victory. Bragadin claims in his version, which was published post-war in America, that the Italians bore the brunt of the fighting:

A company of Italian and German sailors, together with some Carabinieri, blocked off and then repulsed the 400 demolition men who had been landed from the British destroyers. A group of Marines from the San Marco Battalion halted the advance of the other 500 coming from the shore battery area.

Quite apart from the fact that less than 200 Royal Marines finally got ashore and not the combined total of 900 claimed by Marc Bragadin in the above version, the German C-in-C also vigorously refutes the latter and cites much evidence to the contrary, which is, of course, now supported by British survivors' accounts of Italians rushing to surrender to the nearest British Marine or seamen as fast as they could. It was the Italian report that stated that 'in the end the German troops had intervened', and which gave the impression that this spoilt the smooth-running Italian defence measures. Such an allegation, said Deindl, was completely false. 'Two reports, those of Reserve Major Hardt and Flakgruppe Major Hartmann, demonstrate the exact opposite!' He details, for example, the fact that at 0600, while the battle on the heights was raging, the German

Flak commander stopped to hold discussions with one of the Italian officers (Battaglia) and that the Italian was said to have pleaded during the conversation that he had only been made 'Acting Fortress Commander' for a period because his section commander, General Giannantoni, had gone sick and was in hospital in Bardia.

'The defense was led,' wrote Bragadin, 'by the Italian naval commander, Admiral Lombardi.' General Deindl himself, however, cited in his official report on the battle that he could not assume that the Italian C-in-C, Admiral Lombardi, or the Italian Senior Naval Officer, Captain D'Aloja, responsible for defence of the dock area, both being sailors, were men who could organise a land battle; that was not their forte. So he had to organise this himself just in case. As we have seen from the reports, it was just as well that he did.

On the role of the Italian senior officers, Admiral Cocchia, states:

When it became clear that a major attack was in progress, the two local commanders joined the admiral and a combined headquarters was formed. It was thus the naval command-post which became the nerve-centre of the defence.

It continues in much the same vein:

The order of battle of the defence was not imposing – very much the reverse. Yet it was those 160 cooks, orderlies, etc., who held the position in the north against the 400 marines from *Sikh* and *Zulu*, and Colotto's 120 seamen who pinned down the Commandos and the LRDG to the south of the naval 6-inch battery, and so enabled that battery to open a well-directed fire on *Sikh* and *Zulu* as they were withdrawing at dawn. Both ships were sunk.

Bragadin also claims that the *Zulu* was sunk by Italian fighter aircraft, which spoilt the claim made by Cocchia, but as both are incorrect perhaps that is not important. But Cocchia goes one better and thus he also claims for the fighters a share in the sinking of *Coventry* as well! Bragadin concludes by claiming that: 'The principal credit for this outcome indisputably belongs to the Italian Navy.'

The German Signal Log shows that as a result of the decisive repulsing of the British force, the considerable German forces being assembled were no longer necessary. Therefore, at 1030 on the 14th, Battle Group 'Everth' of the Afrikakorps was disbanded and ordered back to Corps. Half an hour later, Panzer AOK received a more in-depth report from the Commanding Officer RAA which stated boldly that by 0900 the British landing can be considered to have failed. At that time, they were reporting some 75 prisoners in their hands and that two units ('apparently destroyers') had certainly been sunk by AA guns while their own losses were small.

Final reports on the 14th stated that the British Force which landed at Tobruk at dawn, 'was annihilated or taken prisoner with only small losses of our own troops. Several enemy landing boats, plus arms and equipment, captured.' It went on: 'The enemy landing attempt was repulsed by German troops of the CO RAA and Italian units together with Navy and German AA artillery, the latter fighting with special distinction.' They estimated that off Tobruk itself three destroyers and two landing craft were sunk by Coastal and AA artillery. 'Captured documents show that the enemy had the order to destroy the harbour installations and to sink the ships in the harbour.' Out at sea to the east they estimated the Luftwaffe and Regia Aeronautica air attacks had destroyed a further 5 – 6,000 ton cruiser, one destroyer and two small craft, and had damaged another 4,000 ton cruiser, one destroyer had been heavily hit and three to four more damaged by bomb hits.

By 15th September, the final German tally of captured British prisoners had reached 590.

*

'Tug' Wilson, with the remnants of some of the *Sikh*'s boats' parties, was still pinned down on the beach with his Italian prisoners when the fighting petered out by early light. He told me what happened to them next:

When it became dawn, the Germans knew we were behind the rocks and were firing mortars at us from an escarpment on the right. And the German officer, when it became dawn, demanded our surrender. He told us to stand up. The Marines had gone on and had by then all been captured; we were the only ones left on the beach at this time who had not been captured. This German officer stood up and told us to stand up and hold our arms, rifles, etc., in the air, right up in the air, then throw the weapons down. He spoke very good English. This is what we did and then the Germans came charging down.

I think that there were about six of us, a couple of boats' crews; one man was badly wounded in his leg. The next thing, I remember quite clearly. I had a pack on my back, with spare boots and a clean pair of socks which we all had to carry. The Germans made us all sit down; as we were sitting there I asked this German soldier, we were talking to them, if I could change my boots and socks. He nodded and so that is what I did, believe it or not. There and then, the first thing I did in captivity was to get the old, wet boots off and change into the new ones. Then they marched us up to Tobruk itself, into this big compound. Inside they split us up into groups of five.

Tobruk in the daylight was disappointing to me. There seemed to be no damage at all and it was all dead quiet for it was all over and done with by then. Nothing at all; the Marines had all been captured. We were marched into this compound about 100 yards long and put in groups of five. Then the German officers came round and they were picking out one man at a time and taking him into this doorway. We were all wondering what have we got to go in there for, of course. Eventually my turn came.

There was a German officer sitting behind a desk, two Afrika Korps soldiers standing either side of him and two more standing behind me. And he started, 'What's your name?' – Answer. 'What's your Number?' – Answer. 'Oh yes! You are off the *Sikh*, are you not? You left Alexandria at so-and-so, made a diversion towards Rhodes at so-and-so', and he carried on telling me all our movements. Seeing my face no doubt, he said, 'Yes, we *know*!' They evidently knew all about the attack by then. Then he pretended to lose his temper with me, shouting and screaming at me. It frightened me to death. I thought they were going to shoot me.

After the interrogation, we were put into a smaller compound, not the original one, and left sitting there hour after hour waiting for the interrogations to finish. Next thing was that German officers came round and went round everybody, picking people out, you see. They picked me out. 'Walk over there', and there were about 11 or 12 of us, all been picked out. We thought, this is it, they are going to shoot us. But what it was really was that we were all about the same size, you know, about six foot, and the official German photographers came to take pictures of us as the prisoners of the failed attack. They picked out the tallest of us. But at first, we really thought they were going to shoot us.

Next then, we had a little tin of bully beef given us. We had emergency rations in our packs which the Germans allowed us to keep, chocolate and things like that. Biscuits and tablets, etc. We had all had a hot meal aboard *Sikh*, it was standard procedure, before the landing. But we were hungry again by then. Anyway, the Germans gave us Bully Beef, or the German equivalent. Then the next thing I remember, these lorries arrived and they put us all in these and drove us to Derna.

*

It was as the *Zulu* was heading back out to sea that she came across the remaining British light forces. Commander Blackburn had withdrawn to the eastward with the intention of forcing an entrance either to Mersa Umm es Sciausc or into Tobruk harbour at dawn, although how he was to effect this with his lightly armed small vessels against such powerful defences, now obviously fully alert, is not clear. It clearly would have been suicidal had he attempted it. In the event he did not, for at dawn they could clearly see the two destroyers under heavy fire to the north-west of Tobruk. When *Sikh* was seen to be stopped and making heavy smoke, the little flotilla steered to close her to see if they could render any assistance but, in Blackburn's words, the *Sikh* 'got way upon her before I closed. HMS *Zulu* steamed away to the northward at high speed.'

A similar account of these events was given by Commander White:

At 0730, four MTBs were closed and the Senior Officer asked if he could assist *Sikh*. I replied: 'No, I regret she must be left' and they turned to the eastward. By this time, *Zulu* was working up to full speed.

Commander Blackburn mentioned that, in view of the serious depletion of the striking force, he had only had seven of his sixteen vessels in sight since 2030 the previous night and had no idea of the whereabouts or fate of the others. He added that it was now obvious that the landing of Force 'A' was by no stretch of the imagination going according to plan and because of the unexpected strength and vitality of the enemy opposition, 'which would prevent the capture of the north shore batteries by the Royal Marines until late in the day, if at all, I reluctantly gave the order to MTB's and ML's in company to retire to Alexandria.'

This general retirement of the survivors commenced at 0810,

although the two ML's were still trying to effect a rescue of *Sikh*'s survivors. Soon after this, the whole force was attacked most seriously by six Macchi fighters and this resulted in the loss of two MTB's and one ML hit and set on fire initially, which reduced the force left to Blackburn to four MTB's and two ML's. Further attacks were made by the fighters on MTB's and Fairmiles off Tobruk, the official report stating that these were 'especially successful and resulted in the loss of three MTB's and two Fairmiles', which is in direct contrast to one post-war account which stated blandly that 'only a few of them were actually sunk.'

The attacks by the fighters were made by the 13 Gruppo CT led by Major Lorenzo Viale. This Gruppo comprised three Squadriglia, 82 equipped with 17 operational Macchi MC200 fighters, and 78 Squadriglia equipped with two operational MC202 fighters and five operational CR42 biplane fighter-bombers. They had a very busy morning, commencing at 0530 when they flew off an offensive reconnaissance with two MC200's followed by a second pair at 0550. They reported several groups of British warships off the coast, one consisting of nine units, including what they took to be a cruiser, sighted about 60 km north of Tobruk, while another group, a cruiser and three destroyers, was reported two kilometres north of Mersa el Auda, heading north. Finally, they reported a group of two motor launches and nine MTB's north of Mersa es Zeitun heading north-east. Apart from confusing *Sikh* and *Zulu* for cruisers (all airmen, Allied or Axis, tended to up-grade their warship sightings by one step; warship recognition was universally abysmal on both sides throughout the war), their reports were fairly accurate.

On his own initiative, Major Viale took off with all available machines to attack these warships. From 0550 to 0810, he scrambled away his fighters on a shuttle to the ships from his base, mounting in all some twenty-one MC200 sorties in this period without any loss to his Gruppo. They attacked with what they had, light bombs and their machine-guns, and the latter were particularly effective against the wooden, petrol-packed hulls of the MTB's and ML's. Frequent strafing attacks caused numerous casualties. One aircraft, as we have seen, made a bombing attack on the sinking *Sikh* but failed to hit her. Nonetheless, the Italian airmen laid claim to have done so in good faith. Bragadin credits them with giving the *Zulu* the *coup de grâce* when she in fact was sunk many hours later by the Germans. Equally erroneous are Cocchia's claims that both destroyers were sunk by Italian coastal batteries. Such baseless claims should not detract from the true achievements of the Italian forces, both airborne and on the ground, that night, however.

The remaining fighters strafed the light craft, and, as we have seen, to some good effect. One motor launch was claimed sunk by a bomb hit and five of the remaining nine sunk by machine-gunning which set them ablaze.

In addition to their offensive action, the Gruppo also managed to mount a standing fighter patrol over Tobruk with one and two MC200's respectively between 0555 and 1850 that evening, but there was no RAF activity at all during those daylight hours. Three more MC200s were sent out on another offensive reconnaissance to the zones around Tobruk itself between 0810 and 0910, and with one MC200 between 1005 and 1040, to help track down any surviving British troops still loose in the perimeter. Yet another MC200 mounted a protective patrol over the Italian destroyer *Castore* while she made a patrol off the coast searching for any stragglers or survivors from the dawn battles. She returned to harbour at Tobruk at 1230.

Not surprisingly, their hot little action quite rightly brought effusive praise to the Gruppo from their superiors. General Fougier sent a telegram from Superaero, the Air Ministry HQ in Rome, praising their 'Magnificent daring in defeating the invasion force', while General Marchesi, the commander of 5th Squadron Area of the Regia Aeronautica to which 13 Gruppo belonged, was equally fulsome in his praise, praising the 'Magnificent results' of their action that morning. The unit suffered no casualties of any kind from any of the AA fire from the ships.

Even when drawing out of range of the Italian fighters, the light craft were pursued by Junkers Ju88's from Libyan bases who made a series of attacks while on their way back to their normal Crete bases later that day. During the whole forenoon, the MTB's and Fairmiles were subjected to numerous other air attacks spread over a wide area by about 25 German bombers, but these were generally ineffective.

Zulu was also suffering heavy air attacks on her high-speed run to the east. The first sign that the enemy was onto her was at 0850, when she was dive bombed by a single Ju88 which was well clear of the mark, missing her by at least 50 yards. This was amateur stuff but there was still a long way to go. *Sikh* had been crippled 270 miles behind enemy lines and, even at thirty knots, there would be no safety for her sister until many more hours had elapsed.

Another alert was caused at 1000 by the sighting of a large surface vessel to the northward and the interception of radio signals from the same ship. *Zulu* duly closed to investigate but on getting within five miles of the target identified her as a large enemy hospital ship and so turned away and resumed her withdrawal.

Further air attacks now continued at regular intervals, growing in both intensity, weight and accuracy as the day wore on. These can be summarised as follows:

1116 Attacked by seven Ju88's.
1234 Attacked by six Ju88's.
1430 Attacked by four Ju88's and five Ju87 Stukas.

From all these she emerged unscathed. Meanwhile, distressing news was being received from the supporting squadron as they closed the gap between them. For a while, they had been undergoing their own trials and tribulations to support *Coventry* and the 5th Flotilla had been steaming to her aid.

It is to this squadron we must now turn our attention.

CHAPTER SIX

Grave Concern

Some 20 Beaufighters of No 201 Naval Co-Operation group were available to give fighter escort for the main force on the morning of the 14th. They took off at first light and were ordered to patrol at 8,000 feet unless ordered otherwise. The decision was taken to provide protection at the rate of one pair of Beaufighters at a time, to start with. Subsequently, fighter cover was as follows: two aircraft from 0700 to 1010; six aircraft from 1010 to 1330; four aircraft from 1330 to dusk; one aircraft from dusk to 2130.

The first Beaufighter patrols actually arrived over the main squadron at about 0500 on the 14th. This gave a superficial feeling of security but not until two hours later did the *Coventry* receive from them notification of their HF frequency (4350 kilocycles) so that the ship could actually communicate with them. This was the only such notification the squadron ever got. Lieutenant E. L. Gardner and Sub-Lieutenant E. F. Shales, respectively the fighter direction officer and radar officer for the operation, worked with Squadron Leader Turner of the RAF throughout and submitted their own report on the matter. No further information was received of times of arrival of relief aircraft which meant that there were long periods of tense expectation as to whether incoming aircraft picked up were friendly, or not. This was compounded by the fact that many of the RAF aircraft failed to show their IFF (Identification Friend or Foe) beacon until close in to the ships. Nor were any details of the strength or call signs of the fighter patrols received.

From the RAF side, they reported that their IFF was switched on during the whole flight and was tracked by the shore radar station as the aircraft left for the patrol and no failures were reported. 'R/T with *Coventry* was good and all aircraft received well, but it appeared that *Coventry* was unaware of how many aircraft were escorting her and only gave instructions to a few of them.'

Group Captain Streatfeild commented that:

Once again, the disadvantages of having IFF which cannot be

152

detected by destroyers was apparent and naturally resulted in the
Beaufighters being fired on by our own ships. We will never
achieve results until we have a certain means of identification
when the pilots may feel reasonably certain that they will not
constantly be taken for the enemy during their patrol.

Aboard the flagship of the covering force, the early morning
euphoria received a sharp setback with the arrival at about 0630 of
(D) 22's signal regarding the withdrawal of Force 'A' and also the
arrival of Admiral Harwood's signal ordering him to steer for
position 'P.P.' The whole force was turned to the westward and, as
Captain Dendy was uncertain of the fuel situation in the Hunts,
notoriously 'short-legged' ships, he decreased the squadron's speed
to a mere 20 knots while they submitted such details to him. From
their returns, Captain Dendy came to the unpalatable conclusion
that even at this low speed most of the destroyers would only just be
able to get to the new position, or just beyond it and still be able to
get back to Alexandria. However, that would leave them no margin
at all for emergencies, and emergencies would appear to be what
they were in for in the coming hours of daylight and with the stirred-
up hornet's nest of Axis bombers eager to inflict vengeance for the
night's work.

Just how determined they were was demonstrated early on when,
at 0700, an unidentified plane approached within ten miles of the
force. From then onwards, two or three unidentified aircraft were
continuously detected in the vicinity of the squadron shadowing
from between ten to thirty miles out. Clearly the enemy had located
them and was monitoring their every move.

Half an hour later, 0730, came *Zulu*'s signal that she 'had been
hit', which obviously meant that, although still afloat, she would not
be able to steam very fast, if at all. This also meant that, due to their
aforementioned fuel situation, the Hunts would be unable to go to
her assistance and still return with her as escorts. Nor was it
considered wise to risk taking *Coventry* further west to provide such
cover on her own, especially in the U-boat infested seas.
Reluctantly, therefore, Captain Dendy decided to turn the whole
force back to the east to refuel his destroyers.

Even before the signal telling Harwood of these intentions had
been sent (it was drafted), a different complication on the matter was
raised by the next signal to come in from *Zulu*, which made it clear
she was still capable of a respectable thirty knots. The Hunts' best

speed was 27 knots while the old *Coventry* could not manage more than 22 herself and this was therefore the maximum speed of the whole squadron. The news from *Zulu* indicated less severe damage than at first thought and a rescue bid by the bulk of the squadron was therefore again a practical proposition. Both *Aldenham* and *Belvoir* were too low for this to include them unfortunately, and these two destroyers were accordingly detached to Alexandria to refuel, while *Coventry* and the remaining six destroyers once more turned back to the west. The signal to Harwood was cancelled before transmission.

The shadowing from the air was unrelenting. Around 0800, 252 Wing reported radar plots of 45 plus moving out north-east from the Daba area. This heavy raid fortunately missed the ships and was soon returning in small formations shortly afterwards. An estimated 1½ hours was thought to be the time needed for the Germans to refuel and send out a second strike. In order to have a good number of fighters overhead in readiness for: this, at 0915 a further six Beaufighters were despatched by AOC of the group.

Back with the naval squadron, at 0830, Captain Dendy had decided to try and drive away some of the shadowers and perhaps thereby hide from their prying gaze his rendezvous with *Zulu*. There was no longer any need to preserve R/T silence now the enemy had them plotted exactly so *Coventry* endeavoured to put the escorting fighters on the enemy aircraft, but all efforts to make contact proved abortive for almost two hours! All attempts to contact the British fighters by HF and VHF were unsuccessful. A single Beaufighter flew across *Coventry*'s bows and acknowledged a visual signal sent by Aldis lamp asking her to check her R/T and climb to 8,000 feet but failed to do so and it was assumed the pilot had not understood. All the RAF patrols thus continued circling strictly at 1,500 feet. Thinking it might be their fault, the *Coventry* team tested their own R/T to *Hursley* but this confirmed that it was in fact working perfectly.

Meanwhile, at 0930, the C-in-C signalled *Coventry* to keep further from the coast, and the whole force turned 360 degrees and stood out to sea. Captain Dendy therefore sent back a signal giving his position, course and speed and told Harwood that he intended to turn west again at 1115 in order to rendezvous with *Zulu*'s estimated position at 1330 and escort her back to Alexandria. The turn to 270 degrees was made five minutes earlier than planned when *Zulu*'s further signal, giving her course, speed and position was received and Harwood's directions to her were also intercepted. A Visual signal contact was finally established with the two of the RAF fighter aircraft, 'Charlie 1' and 'Charlie 2', at 1020. These immediately climbed to 8,000 feet and established R/T contact and both reception and transmission were good.

Twenty minutes later, when some two or three single unidentified aircraft were picked up separately to the south, Captain Dendy had them vectored out to intercept. They 'Tallyhoed' at twenty miles but reported the aircraft as friendly. With the approval of the captain, the fighters were brought back down to 1,500 feet and they resumed standing patrol. Again, at 1110 more unidentified aircraft were picked up to the south at an estimated height of 11,000 feet, and 'Charlie 1' was instructed to climb to 10,000 feet. The cloud base at this time, 1115, was 4,000 feet; radar kept up steady sweeps on all other bearings at three minute intervals all this time, but no other shadowers were picked up on the screens. There seemed therefore no undue cause to sound off Air Raid Warning Yellow.

The unidentified aircraft kept boring and had now penetrated to within 25 miles of the ships. 'Charlie' was vectored on to a converging course of 170 degrees. At 15 miles, he was signalled 'Port About' and both friendly and unidentified plots merged on the *Coventry*'s radar screen following the same course and keeping the same range. Signals were constantly sent informing the British fighters of this situation but they replied that they could see nothing. Cloud base was now down to 2,000 feet which gave excellent cover to low-flying bombers. 'Charlie' was kept on the same course as the unidentified aircraft and the radar plot kept reporting them both still together all the time since they first merged some 15 miles out, but 'Charlie' insisted he could see no other aircraft. However, as both the RAF fighter and the unidentified aircraft closed still further 'Charlie' came through with, 'There's a lot of planes ahead of me.'

The bridge was duly informed of this alarming fact by the FDO up the voice pipe. This shouted alarm was the first and last received on the bridge and as soon as the fighter direction officer had yelled the warning of a large number of enemy aircraft, simultaneously the attack commenced. The 15 Junkers Ju87 'Stukas' peeled off over the *Coventry* in their all too familiar classic attack sequence from astern on a bearing of 090 degrees. The scream of the first Stukas on their way down was drowned by the concussion of the cruiser's after guns getting into action along with the crack of the 5th Destroyer Flotilla's 4-inch weapons as well. In vain! A moment later and the

RCO next door to the fighter direction position was blown up by a direct hit and the radar damaged beyond repair.

Lieutenant W. J. P. Church, commanding the *Hursley*, recorded how the attack was made by an estimated 13 aircraft, 'out of the sun', and that after she had been hit and set on fire *Coventry* steamed round in a circle for ten minutes or so and then stopped. He also commented that with the departure of *Aldenham* and *Belvoir* earlier, their positions on the rearward of the screen were unoccupied and that this was pertinent because the Luftwaffe 'invariably attacks from abaft the beam, especially if the sun is that way.'

The captain of *Croome* admitted that the force 'was completely surprised by three formations of Junkers 87s who approached from the starboard quarter. Two of these formations made a dead set on *Coventry* and the third on *Croome*.' He added that the first indication that the destroyers on the screen had was of the aircraft diving and he didn't think any ship opened fire before the first bombs fell. *Croome* herself went to full speed and her wheel was put hard to starboard. Thus, by this action and 'the greatest good fortune', no hits were taken although the shock of near misses put her radar out of commission.

Back at Alexandria, the first news they had was a wireless signal which read: 'Enemy aircraft attacking. Position 32.50, 28.15'.

How did the Stukas achieve such devastating surprise? Captain Dendy considered it was due to the possibility that the enemy were using IFF which thereby confused the radar operators when vectoring the fighters and the fact that the Type 279 radar had a 'Astern Danger Angle' when sweeping, a kind of 'black spot' astern. As this was the dive-bomber's favourite approach when attacking warships he considered this might have contributed to their undetected approach. In contrast to the reports of the officers aboard the *Coventry*, all the RAF pilots reported that her R/T was excellent and that her orders were clear, 'but she appeared to have no warning of this raid and was engaged in vectoring our fighters on to shadowers when it developed.'

The RAF estimated the number of Stukas as 20 to 30, the weather being 6 to 7/10th cloud, with base below 2,000 feet and the tops 6,000 feet. Here again, standard RAF doctrine was that dive bombing was impossible unless clouds were much higher than this. Again, they were proven in error. Some seven Beaufighters were over the ships, two were up at 11,000 feet, three at 8,000 feet and two more at 1,500 feet. As we have seen, just before the attack broke the top pair were vectored onto a shadower to the south but failed to sight him and were returning to the ships when they saw a larger formation of Stukas just starting their dive at the top of the cloud from the northward at about 6,000 feet. 'The ships apparently had not seen them and our aircraft were too far away to get in an attack. The leader gave a warning over the R/T and both aircraft dived below the clouds in an attempt to intercept the aircraft on their way out. No combat developed.'

The three aircraft at 8,000 feet were not vectored or warned of the approach of the enemy and their first warning was seeing bomb splashes amongst the ships. 'They dived down and made attacks on the Stukas who were retiring in loose formation. Some of these may have been circling for another attack as five or six jettisoned bombs when attacked. The Stukas were aided in their get-away by use of cloud.'

Finally, the low pair also had their first indication of the attack by seeing bombs falling among the ships and also tried to attack retiring Junkers Ju87's chasing them for fifteen miles before returning to circle the ships. One Beaufighter continued the chase for forty miles before returning home, damaged by the Stukas' return fire. They claimed in all that day to have 'probably' destroyed one Ju87 and 'possibly' destroyed one Ju87 and one Ju88 and to have damaged four others.

Air Vice-Marshal Slater, AOC 201 Naval Co-Operation Group, later stated that, in his estimation,

> The task of providing adequate protection on the 14th September, during the withdrawal of the seaborne forces was almost impossible. Had treble the number of Beaufighter squadrons been available for this task, attacks on the ships could not have been prevented. The cloud conditions prevailing on this day were ideal for attacking bombers and with the enemy employing all available aircraft (including fighter bombers) it is indeed remarkable that losses to our forces were as low as they were.

This is in marked contrast of course to the claims, repeated ad infinitum during the war (and since), that Stukas were mere 'Fighter Bait', easy, helpless prey and that short-based fighter cover would always guarantee protection against such attacks. Thus, a Middle East Air Force appreciation issued at this time made the following profound statement:

The failure of the Ju87's was most noticeable. The Stukas almost invariably jettisoned their bombs on sighting Spitfires or Hurricanes and made for home. By the end of the battle, moreover, the Stukas had abandoned dive bombing and were hurriedly dropping their bombs on the level. The bogey of the dive bomber had been finally exposed; when opposed by a determined fighter force it proved to be a crow masquerading in an eagle's feathers.

Similar statements had been made during the Battle of Britain two years earlier, then had come Russia and Crete. Not for the first time, nor for the last, the Stuka crews immediately made the RAF's deskbound pundits (who never ever missed any opportunity to deride all dive bombing), eat humble pie! For yet again the German dive-bombers had achieved the classic prerequisite of surprise and taken due advantage of it to deliver their untenable trump card, accuracy. And this, despite the radar watch, the overhead fighters and the general alertness of the force. They had perfected their technique over the years, of course. Off Norway, Holland, Dunkirk and Calais they had inflicted heavy casualties on Allied shipping. They had struck at coastal convoys and anti-invasion destroyer flotillas in the Channel during the same year, stopping the former and driving away the latter. When the Luftwaffe moved the gaunt crank-wing dive bombers down to the Mediterranean in 1941, they had immediately crippled the aircraft carrier *Illustrious* with a precision attack of enormous skill and had followed that up by sinking one cruiser and damaging another. So it had continued, year-in, year-out.

Despite ceaseless propaganda by the RAF (who had no dive-bombers of their own) that the Junkers Ju87 was 'fighter-bait', these self-same aircraft had contributed enormously to each German victory and British retreat. And they had also continued relentlessly to inflict loss after loss on the Royal Navy. Off Crete, the list of sunken and damaged warships was a melancholy one and included the *Coventry*'s half-sister, *Calcutta*. Off Tobruk, during numerous Malta convoy battles and at Malta, the toll had steadily mounted. Now, again, the deadly dive bombers had struck, and, as usual, they made no mistakes. The Stukas concerned were from III/StG3, based at Daba and Fuka airstrips and the III Gruppe had joined the rest of StG3 in May in readiness for Rommel's push east and they were equipped with the new Junkers Ju87D – 1 *Trop* machines. On this raid, they were led by Lieutenant Göbel who unhesitatingly took his aircraft down through the cloud layer, which extended from 6,000 feet down to 2,000 feet and carried out precise and exact bombing with great skill and panache.

Coventry was hit by no less than four bombs in addition to being strafed by the Stukas with both their forward-firing cannon and their rear-mounted flexible machine-guns. One bomb hit her bow, just forward of No 1 gun, gouging out the whole of the upper deck down to the waterline and starting a severe fire forward. Captain Dendy managed to turn the ship under helm after she had taken this hit but this did not prevent more bombs piling into her ancient little hull. Her exact position at the time of the attack was 32 degrees, 50 minutes north, 28 degrees, 15 minutes east.

A second, and most likely a third, exploded almost together on the fo'c'sle deck under the bridge, demolishing the SDO, Charthouse, RCO, and bridge structure itself before penetrating the deck itself causing further structural damage and starting a fire below. Both the flag deck and the radar receiving office were wrecked. The receivers were blown on the deck and the position was filled with smoke and caught fire. The bridge structure was rendered useless by these explosions, only the compass platform remaining usable. All communications were severed as a result.

Yet a fourth direct hit was taken abaft the after funnel, the bomb plunging down into 'A' boiler room before detonating and wrecking the deck between 4 and 5 guns and demolishing the radar transmitting room in the process. The *Coventry*, staggering like a punch-drunk boxer, eventually came to a stop and preliminary damage control operations were put into effect. The captain signalled *Dulverton* to report this attack as his own command was clearly unable to do so.

Geoffrey David, then an eighteen and a half year-old paymaster midshipman, gave me this account of the attack. It was about 1100 and the commander had just made a broadcast over the ship's communications speakers that the raid had failed and that *Sikh* (aboard whom was serving his much-loved brother, Lieutenant J. R. David), had been sunk and that *Zulu* had also been hit and damaged and that they were steaming to her assistance.

At the time of the broadcast, I was sitting in the Wardroom, as we were not at Action Stations, only Defence Stations. [As his own Action Station was the 'Action recorder' by the forward

Oerlikon gun just forward of the bridge, close to where the first bomb hit, this was his good fortune.]

I was just digesting the sad details of the Commander's broadcast, and hoping against hope that my brother was safe, when there was a sudden loud bang on the deck just above me. Everyone in the wardroom looked up, startled, but before we had time to do anything more there came the unforgettable throaty scream of a diving Stuka. My messmates leapt out of their chairs, and lay flat on the deck, and I followed their example. The first diving Stuka was followed by a number of others – I cannot remember how many – and there were several loud explosions, each of them causing the after end of the ship to whip violently up and down. After one of these I caught a glimpse through the Wardroom skylight of debris flying through the air, so I realised that one of the bombs at least had scored a direct hit. Then there was silence, and in the silence I heard the comforting rumble of the ship's turbines suddenly die away to nothing.

My first thought after that was to get to my Action Station, so I dashed out of the wardroom to the foot of the companion way – but as I started to climb I found to my anger and shame that my legs were trembling so much that they would not obey me. To add to my embarrassment, some one on the deck below shouted 'Gun's Crews *first!*' and I was very conscious that I was blocking the gangway. However, I somehow got myself to the top of the ladder, then went out through the port screen door onto the upper deck and tried to make my way forward to the bridge. After picking my way over a scatter of debris, and seeing to my horror a headless corpse draped over the side of the seaboat, I got almost as far as the break in the forecastle, but then found my way barred by a fire just abaft the bridge. So I turned round and came back aft, clambered up over the after superstructure and then down to the upper deck on the starboard side. I tried to make my way forward along that side, but found my way barred there too, so I turned round, uncertain what to do. As I did so, I noticed a wounded rating lying propped up against a stanchion, and completely black all over – presumably from flash burns. He was alive, and moaning faintly.

I could not think of anything that I could do for him, so I carried on aft, and stopped by a large jagged hole in the deck just abreast one of the funnels. Somebody – I cannot remember who

Three of the makeshift British landing craft used by the Royal Marines from the two destroyers, being examined by their German captors on the morning of 14th September 1942.

A captured British ACP speeds by the wreck of a landing craft after the British raid on Tobruk. In the background can be seen German F-lighters (*left*) and the Italian destroyer *Castore* (*right*).

A soldier of the German 5./B.B.85 unit at one of the inlets the British force mistakenly landed at.

Men of the Pioneer Company resting after their mopping up of British survivors on the cliffs overlooking the scene of the night landings.

– suggested that we climb down into the hole to see if we could rescue any wounded, but after inspecting the hole more closely we realised that this would be impossible – it was a sheer drop for about 20 feet, with nothing to cling onto. Just at that moment, as I was feeling particularly useless, I met the fighter direction officer – a lieutenant RNVR, whose name I have forgotten – and asked him if there was anything useful I could do. 'Nothing!' he replied, 'But just keep smiling!' A few moments later, Captain Dendy appeared, standing on the superstructure above me, and I heard him give the order 'Abandon Ship!'

Claude Nice was a gunlayer at No 1 4-inch gun and during that fateful forenoon was closed up here at Defence Stations, i.e. with one watch on and half the armament manned. He gave me this personal memoir of the subsequent events:

I recall it was a fine, sunny day, but chilly for the Med. Around 1100 the Skipper had advised us that the operation had run into trouble and that *Sikh* had been disabled at Tobruk, *Zulu* being on her way back to join us and return to Alexandria.

Very shortly after this we had an alarm bearing aft and action stations sounded. My gun could not bear at that stage and I almost immediately saw a number of Ju87's diving on us from astern. We had had something of a charmed life in *Coventry* until then, but this time my instincts told me we must be hit. Several explosions shook the ship abaft and then one Ju87 appeared almost over the top of No 1 gun and his bombs fell away. I froze and there was an almighty crash just forward of the gun. Everything went black for seconds as smoke, water and debris enveloped us round the gun. When this cleared, the ship was still going ahead and as we looked around we found that the whole gun crew were unharmed!

Most of the forecastle however had disappeared, and a fierce fire was raging beyond the breakwater. Amazingly, the ship remained on an even keel as she slowed down. The paint shop had been in the blown out section and when we on the gun surveyed each other we realised we were all covered in colours of all shades, which gave rise to some amusement despite our circumstances.

We ran hoses in an attempt to fight the fire under our feet, but the mains had been ruptured aft and we had no water pressure.

We quickly realised the ship was mortally hurt and that there were many casualties. Everyone later was completely astounded that it had happened to us at long last. We did what we could for the wounded and tried to get those badly hurt over the side to rafts, etc, as gently as possible. Certainly our poor old ship was in a hell of a mess but I recall no panic in evacuating her. It might have been different if a further attack had come at this stage.

Geoffrey David remarked that: 'It has always seemed to me surprising, that this specialised anti-aircraft ship, with well-tried air-warning radar and highly-experienced crew, should have been caught so completely unawares by 15 Stukas in broad daylight.' Admittedly, there was low cloud at the time, which would have prevented visual sighting until the last moment, but why were they not detected by radar? He mentions that one former radar operator who was on watch had affirmed 'that the screen was clear'. Another of *Coventry*'s radar operators has suggested an alternative explanation – that the radar at the time of the Stuka's attack was not carrying out the usual 'all-round sweep': instead it had been – for several minutes – concentrated on a single echo some miles away which was thought to be a shadower (and which later turned out to be a Beaufighter). 'Fighter Direction from a ship was, I think, a relatively new art at that stage of the war. . . .'

One of the radar watch that day was 'Tiny' Gough. He was wounded in the attack (and today, he still has pieces of German shrapnel in him). He states, 'the RDF were as close as anyone to know what was going on – and how we did not pick them up. We never had a chance to.' He adds that, at the time they were 'concentrating on the Beaufighters (under orders).'

In a subsequent examination by Their Lordships, the Director of Signals noted that:

A study of the RDF Officers' Report shows that RDF warning was in fact received, but was identified as 'few' – and therefore presumably not distinguished from shadowers. The interception carried out by Beaufighter 'Charlie' failed until too late to be of use. This may well have been due to a poor height estimate. At the time, the fleet's experience of height-finding (always a difficult matter with the types of RDF set at present fitted) was very limited.

In the uncanny lull after the din of the Stuka assault, Captain Dendy took stock of his command. The little cruiser was clearly badly hurt, being on fire forward and although the 4-inch magazine had been flooded to prevent further explosions there the pom-pom magazine could not be reached because of the existing fires and the upper flooding positions being wrecked. The bow was practically demolished so there was clearly no chance of towing from there. In addition, what remained of the bridge was also on fire. Both the radar and the W/T were gone. Down below, only one boiler room was totally out of action and the cruiser could steam slowly on one engine, but the fires were gradually spreading and steering had to be by hand. Efforts to curb the flames were hampered by lack of adequate water pressure and the Foamite machine fought a losing battle on its own.

There was also the problem of the many casualties. Captain Dendy had a hunch, which only captains of ships can understand, just a feeling, that the poor little *Coventry* was even harder hit than even her general appearance showed and that, if she went under, it might be quickly. Although she might be towed stern first at a very slow speed by two of the destroyers, steering her in this way would be hard. They were still only one hundred miles from the Stuka airfields and the German airmen would obviously be flying shuttle missions to finish her off. Conversely, they were still 160 miles from Alexandria with most of the day before them. The *Zulu* was flat out toward them and also needed their protection. All in all, it seemed that to try and save *Coventry* might mean the loss not only of her but other ships in the squadron. Thus, with heavy heart, the captain gave the order, 'Abandon Ship'.

To facilitate this, *Beaufort* and *Dulverton* closed in and by skilful ship-handling managed to take off most of the cruiser's crew, including the wounded men. The first lieutenant of the *Dulverton*, Lieutenant R. T. Wilson, went into the water several times to help survivors. All the secret documents and confidential books were thrown overboard in their steel safes and a good search was made in all parts of the ship that the fire had not made impassable, for any further survivors, but, in the event, none were found. By the time all the men were off and the two destroyers had pulled clear, the flagship was burning furiously and ready-use ammunition lockers were exploding.

Scuttling charges were carried for such eventualities but, following explosions of some of these charges aboard the old

Centurion which had been caused by near-miss bombs during a earlier convoy to Malta, on *Coventry* these had been placed below and left unprimed. They had in fact been wiped out by the fourth bomb hit.

On reaching the safety of the *Beaufort*'s bridge, Captain Dendy ordered the Senior Officer of the flotilla, Lieutenant-Commander Petch, aboard *Dulverton*, to finish off *Coventry* with torpedoes, not realising that most of the Hunts were built without these destroyer weapons. It was an ironical fact that the only two ships of the flotilla that carried torpedo tubes were the two he had already sent back to Alexandria to refuel! In view of the fires and explosions taking place aboard the cruiser, there was no question of sending a boarding party back to open the sea-cocks and so attempts were made by the two destroyers to sink her with gun fire and depth charges dropped close. None seemed to have any effect whatsoever, only redoubling the blaze on board but not putting her under.

Meanwhile, *Dulverton* had got away two further signals to Admiral Harwood. The first, at 1140, read:

Attacked by 14 dive bombers. *Coventry* hit badly forward. On fire.

This was followed, at 1213 by:

Coventry on fire. Abandoned.

Despite Captain Dendy's feelings about his erstwhile command's chances of staying afloat, the little twenty-five year old cruiser proved remarkably reluctant to succumb to her fate. Even with the huge fires and the awesome bomb damage, her innards were intact enough. She was built by Swan Hunters between 1916 and 1918 – In Captain Dendy's own words, 'They all tried firing 4-inch shell at her, but her old armour belt stood up to that. In any case, they were getting low in ammunition, and couldn't afford heavy expenditure.'

There has been a lot of rubbish talked about these little light cruisers being armoured on the scale of the old German armoured cruiser *Blücher*. They actually had 3-inch armour over their machinery spaces and 2-¼-inch plating abreast their magazines and oil tanks (against *Blücher*'s 7-inch belt), but this proved sufficient to keep out 4-inch SAP. The bulk of the Hunts' magazines would contain 4-inch HA, for they very rarely required surface action shells in the Med but always fired off hundreds of AA rounds. The fact that the Hunts were 'no longer fitted with torpedoes', has also been presented by some to have come as 'astonishing information'. It was nothing of the kind, far from no longer carrying torpedoes, the first two groups of these destroyers, to which the remaining six belonged, had *never* been designed to carry them anyway. This was common knowledge in the service and no secret. Not until the third group, to which *Aldenham* and *Belvoir* belonged, were Hunts fitted with torpedo tubes, mainly as a result of East Coast and Channel actions.

The distasteful job of trying to destroy their erstwhile companion commenced at 1226 when *Croome* signalled *Dulverton*, 'Keep clear I am firing SAP (semi-armour piercing)'. *Beaufort* signalled six minutes later, 'I will fire after you.'

Beaufort pumped several salvoes into the cruiser with no obvious effect and then withdrew and her place was taken by *Croome*. The cripple was proving to be far too tough for the Hunts to deal with without torpedoes. As *Croome*'s Sub-Lieutenant A. H. L. Harvey recorded at the time:

> We fire 4-inch guns at point-blank range at *Coventry*'s waterline, and drop depth charges, but fail to sink her.

In all, *Croome* fired some 124 rounds of 4-inch SAP into the hull of the cruiser at ranges between 1500 to 2000 yards. By 1245, *Croome* had to admit ruefully to *Dulverton*: 'My 4-inch is having very little effect', to which the latter replied, 'Try depth charges.'

Croome then tried 18 depth charges with depth settings of 50 feet to explode below her and blow her bottom in. Many did indeed detonate directly under the cruiser but apart from the fires blazing as fiercely as ever and a list to port there seemed no sign of her settling. By 1306, the other destroyers had left and *Coventry* still remained stubbornly afloat. *Croome* was now Senior Officer and signalled to *Hursley*: 'Have a bat'. Lieutenant W. J. P. Church described his efforts thus:

> This proved a much harder job than I had expected. Between 1315 and 1420, 22 depth charges were fired from the throwers and a similar number must have been fired by *Croome*, and of these quite a number hit her side but with no apparent effect apart from causing her to shake badly.

The precious minutes kept ticking on. As *Zulu* was only some fifteen miles off and closing fast, the Captain (D) was told to signal to her to do the job with her torpedoes, just one of which was considered to be sufficient. At 1327, *Dulverton* therefore signalled to *Zulu*, repeated to Harwood: '*Coventry* abandoned on fire. *Croome* and *Hursley* attempting to sink her without much success. Can you sink her with torpedoes. Her position 32.50; 28.15.'

Croome sent another message to Harwood, at 1401, which stated plainly that: '*Coventry* still afloat in position 32.48; 28.17. Burning well but very stubborn after gunfire and depth charges, *Hursley* is in company.'

Back at Alexandria, Harwood was not happy to see the force become further split up. Their only chance he felt was to remain together. Although he did not know it, he was already too late to prevent this happening, but, at 1420, he signalled to all the ships concerned:

> Your 1310 Force D remain concentrated and join *Zulu* as soon as possible. *Zulu* is subsequently to sink *Coventry*, and all Force return as in my 0905.

But this signal was never received aboard *Dulverton*. Her W/T department was at the time keeping a continuous watch on 480 kcs and 4205 kcs and did not shift from these frequencies at any time. At about 1555, the W/T Operator on watch on 480 kcs, in the D/F Cabinet, which was the usual practice, received an order from the bridge to get a D/F bearing of Alexandria. It was exactly at this time that Harwood's message was being made. *Dulverton*'s operator in fact picked up the call signs and number of the message but as he thought the D/F bearing was required at once, he ceased reading the message in order to switch over to get it, and he thereby missed the text of the message. The message itself was repeated back by Beirut, but was unreadable owing to atmospheric conditions. Although the operator passed the W/T bearing up to the bridge, he failed to inform them that a signal that might affect the ship had been missed. this uncharacteristic error by a man described by his captain as 'a most reliable and conscientious operator', meant that the destroyer force remained split up, with *Dulverton* leading *Beaufort*, *Exmoor* and *Hurworth* back to Alexandria, while *Croome* and *Hursley* stayed behind to put *Coventry* under.

Lieutenant-Commander R. T. Wilson of *Dulverton* described the reasoning behind this splitting of the force. The *Exmoor* was very low on fuel; his ship and *Beaufort* were laden with survivors several of whom were severely wounded and finally he hoped the Luftwaffe might concentrate their attentions on the larger group and leave *Zulu* in peace. He did not intend that *Croome* and *Hursley* should have joined *Zulu*, 'but *Coventry* proved a tough proposition to sink.'

In the interim, both *Aldenham* and *Belvoir* had safely arrived at Alexandria at 1330 and completed refuelling by 1615. The other group followed. On their sad way back to base, the bodies of five of *Coventry*'s crew, Lieutenant W. H. C. Rees, DSC; Warrant Engineer A. M. Woods, Chief Ordnance Artificer Simpson, Chief Cook Randall and the radar AB, Grason, were committed to the deep. The *Beaufort*, *Dulverton* and *Exmoor* finally returned to Alexandria at 1935 on Monday 14th to disembark survivors.

The loss of the cruiser and the splitting of the destroyer force into separate groups had a bad effect on the air cover for the rest of the day, also. The destroyers found great difficulty in communicating at all and, in attempting to split the protecting Beaufighters over each group, merely confused the pilots even more. One group used the call sign 'Agent' and the other 'Agent One'. The space call sign allocated for just this contingency should have been used but was ignored. No directions were passed to the fighters as to which party they should cover. 'After the *Coventry* had been hit, another ship took on direction. This ship employed a 'cockney' on the R/T and although the signals were of good strength, pilots complained they could not understand half of what was said. The information passed was vague and was of little use to the fighters', said the official RAF report. The net result was to once more prove fatal.

Lieutenant Church wrote how, 'At 1415, when it was apparent depth charges would not sink her, *Croome* ordered me to join. A few minutes later a destroyer was sighted bearing 260 degrees steaming very fast towards us. This was assumed to be the *Zulu* which she soon proved to be, but guns were loaded with SAP just in case.'

Zulu had indeed finally turned up at the scene of *Coventry*'s defiant stand and, at 1443, *Croome* signalled to her, 'Can you put a torpedo into *Coventry* as I am unable to sink her.'

To which *Zulu* replied, 'Yes, Close *Coventry*'. *Croome* thought that those aboard *Zulu* might have thought there were crewmen still aboard; she hastened to reassure *Zulu* that this was not so. 'She is abandoned'.

At this point, the Luftwaffe reappeared in the forms of six Junkers

Ju88's and *Croome*'s next signal was to the C-in-C again. 'Enemy aircraft are dropping bombs.'

From this time onward, the three destroyers were subjected to continuous dive bombing attacks by the big Junkers Ju88's from Crete. The first of these took place at 1430 just as *Zulu* joined them but their bombs were avoided. More aircraft kept joining from the north and circling to await their opportunity. *Zulu* signalled at 1449, 'Dive bombed. No hits. Am about to torpedo *Coventry*', adding '*Hursley* and *Croome* in company.'

In between attacks, *Zulu* took the fleeting opportunity to turn and put two torpedoes deliberately into *Coventry*. For this, Commander White reduced speed to 12 knots and the torpedoes ran straight and true, striking the cruiser amidships. She sank immediately, reported Commander White, and speed was increased to 30 knots as a further attack by six Ju87's developed.

These were again avoided and single line ahead was ordered, with *Hursley* in the van, followed by *Zulu* and *Croome* with a 1½ mile gap between the ships; speed was set at 25 knots, the maximum the Hunts could attain. This done, the next signal was sent to Harwood by *Zulu* at 1515: 'Attacked by 10 more dive bombers. No hits, *Hursley* and *Croome* in company. *Coventry* torpedoed.' She also signalled *Croome* at 1542, 'Is your W/T all right? Have you reported us joining up and destruction of *Coventry*?', to which *Croome* replied, 'Yes to everything'.

Overhead, one German pilot witnessed the last moments of the *Coventry* and took photographs. This was historian Gerd Stamp who was serving with I/LG 1, the renowned 'Helbig Flyers', the crack anti-shipping unit flying twin-engined Junkers Ju88's based at Heraklion in Crete and which earlier had sunk three out of four British destroyers in these same waters. He recalls the day's events thus:

I and II/LG 1 were called in from Heraklion and we landed at an airfield south of Mersa Matruh where we were kept waiting for further orders. *Coventry* was hit by Ju87's. Some of our 'Young Lions' were sent to attack destroyers and MTB's on their way back to Alexandria, but as they were not experienced enough they hit nothing. Meanwhile, we 'Old Hares' were kept waiting and then told that we would no longer be needed and that we should fly home to Heraklion. On the way home, in the early afternoon, I saw the burning cruiser and flew around the ship. I saw that the cruiser was alone. There was no other ship around. While doing so, I saw two torpedo traces coming from below the sea. There was no surface ship around. *Coventry* was hit by both torpedoes, which must have come from a submarine or U-boat.

He adds: 'I am surprised to read that the sinking was done by a destroyer. There was no destroyer.' He also is at variance with the official British accounts as to the exact location of the sinking. These are given by the British as 32 degrees 48 minutes north, 28 degrees 17 minutes east, but Gerd Stamp says that by his estimates, the latter figures should read 27 degrees 2 minutes east. 'We were on our course straight back from Quasaba to Heraklion. Quasaba base was south of El Daba, so 27 degrees east would fit as I saw the burning and abandoned cruiser straight ahead, slightly to starboard.'

Quite a little mystery, but there is no doubt about the photograph which was taken by the Junkers Ju88 ahead of Gerd's. Yet all three destroyers' captain's reports state clearly that *Zulu* fired the two torpedoes which did the job and no other unit, Axis or British, surface ship or submarine, ever claimed to have finished her off later. Besides, we have it clearly stated by Commander White that she sank, instantly. It may be that the range the torpedoes were fired from meant that *Zulu* was not immediately visible from the air, although Gerd Stamp is adamant that there were no other ships.

Another dispute is about the type of aircraft which delivered the fatal blows. Again, the Junkers Ju88 pilots maintain that no Ju87's were present, but all British reports clearly identify attacks by *both* types. There could be no doubt of the difference between the two, the Ju87 Stuka being a single-engined aircraft with inverted gull wings and a fixed undercarriage, quite unmistakable for any other aircraft, whereas the Junkers Ju88 was a much larger twin-engined dive-bomber with normal wing configuration. There seems little doubt that StG3 was flying shuttle missions and LG1 was attacking the same targets in small numbers, but that the two German squadrons were not co-ordinating their attacks; nonetheless they frequently arrived over the ships at close intervals. Both Stukas and Junkers 88's were clearly identified by the protecting RAF Beaufighters, also. For example, a single Beaufighter had found the three destroyers in the vicinity of the burning cruiser at 1438. This force was being attacked by about twelve Stukas who were being engaged by AA fire. He gave chase but was too far away to get an interception so he returned to patrol.

The RAF continued to despatch fighters at the rate of two every hour for a two hour patrol thus keeping four Beaufighters in the air, but these were initially sent to the estimated position of the combined force, long after it had become two widely separated ones. The naval viewpoint was later given by the Admiralty, thus:

> Though we are inclined to consider fighters can operate at considerable distances from their bases, they seldom prove completely effective outside 40 miles from land. Beaufighters are poor day fighters against modern bombers.

Down below, the three British destroyers now set course to the east at their best speed to undertake the final dash in this eventual operation. By 1525, *Hursley* had taken station one mile on starboard bow, course 140 degrees and speed a good 25½ knots. But the Luftwaffe had not finished yet.

Croome's captain commented on the fighter protection problems.

> Little is known in destroyers regarding the policy of fighters protecting aircraft. Towards sunset on Monday, 14th September, Beaufighters were plentiful and good communication was established, but the difficulty of stationing them in the most advantageous position to counter attacks was always present. It is considered that fighter pilots and commanding officers of HM ships should confer on these matters.

He made special comment on the bravery of the RAF pilots, however.

> During the initial attack on *Coventry*, I was dumbfounded to see our two Beaufighters diving down on top of the Junkers, in an attempt to engage them, which won the admiration of us all.

At 1510, a solitary Beaufighter overhead was fired on by the flotilla despite her twice firing off the identification colours of the day. Unable to stop them shooting at him, the pilot dived down to sea level and retired out of range, being followed by heavy flak bursts all the way. The ships made no signals to him but the pilot could hear them talking on the R/T to other ships. Nothing daunted, he continued to protect them from a distance, making an attack on a group of Ju87's and damaging one of them, but being badly hit himself by their return fire which he described as 'very heavy'.

At 1600, he closed the ships again and found them again under a cloud of flak bursts and being attacked by Ju88s. He attacked one and claimed to have severely damaged it, leaving it with both engines on fire and flying very slowly. Two more Ju88's closed in and tried to protect the damaged aircraft, the Beau closing to within 100 yards but the cannon ceased firing as they had run out of ammunition. He described this attack as being made by 10 Stukas and 18 Ju88's, attacks from heights varying from 2 to 10,000 feet. This lone Beaufighter had to return to base at 1623.

Lieutenant Church again:

The most severe attack, the worst I have ever experienced occurred at 1600, when between 12 and 18 Ju88's – opinions vary as to the number – attacked this ship. This was the most severe bombing I have so far experienced but apart from one small splinter hole in the Director the ship received no damage whatever and there were no casualties. During the afternoon, the RDF proved of great value, the 286 PQ set picking up large formations at seven miles so that we always had warning in reasonable time. Half the outfit of 4-inch was fired during the afternoon and the barrage put up was most effective, as were the Oerlikon guns. There were many near misses but much to my surprise we emerged unscathed, just in time to see the attack on the *Zulu*. She was hit in the engine room and stopped dead. At this juncture, I made a signal: 'C-in-C from *Hursley*. Bombed in position DJRP 3730. *Zulu* hit and stopped. T.O.O. 1615/14.'

This took place at 1602 and was described as 'a calculated and determined attempt to destroy *Zulu*'. Three formations of Junkers 87's and 88's came in from different bearings in quick succession. *Zulu* avoided the first two with great skill, but was inevitably hit by a plane in the third formation, by one delay action fused bomb which penetrated her side and burst in the Engine Room.

Commander White described this fatal attack like this:

At about 1600, a concentrated attack by about 6 Ju88's and 12 Ju87's was delivered on *Zulu* and the ship was surrounded by a hail of falling bombs. The last bomb to fall hit the ship's side, entered the engine room and burst. The engine room, No 3 boiler room and gear room were flooded and the ship settled down about two feet. I went aft and shut off the emergency steam valves to the engine room and when it had cooled down a little, looked down into the engine room. There was no sign of any bodies and the place was a mass of wrecked machinery.

She stopped, listing heavily, and *Hursley* closed to take her in tow while *Croome* went alongside to take off personnel. The Commanding Officer, two officers and nine ratings remained on board to pass the tow.

Now came a long and agonising fight to save the crippled ship.

Zulu's earlier attempts to save *Sikh* had left her with no towing wire of her own and *Hursley*'s was not yet ready so a large manilla was passed, but this only lasted for fifteen minutes before parting. Cable was ranged and very quickly *Hursley* got her wire ready and the tow recommenced. With her reduced complement, *Zulu*'s main armament of six 4.7-inch and two 4-inch HA guns were out of commission but the subsequent air attacks were met with two of the 20-mm Oerlikons and the multiple Pom-Pom.

At 1707, an attack was made by four Messerschmitt 109s at medium level and again at 1747 eight Stukas and Ju88's came in but accurate fire from the two Hunts forced several aircraft to jettison bombs and thus rendered the attack ineffective. Meanwhile, the RAF were doing what they could in the face of the difficulties, the split force, the inability to communicate and the fact that the warships fired at all aircraft regardless of type. (The Beaufighter might, just remotely, be confused at long range with a Junkers Ju88, both types being twin-engined, straight wing, single-tailed aircraft with the crew concentrated forward.) Having been bombed continuously all day, the ships' crews could perhaps be forgiven if they assumed that everything in the air was hostile!

The *Zulu*'s crippling had occurred in position 32 degrees 37 minutes North, 28 degrees 30 minutes East, and, on receipt of the news, Admiral Harwood ordered Force 'D' to close her, 'if fuel permits'. It did not and *Dulverton* was forced to signal that all the ships of her group were too low in fuel to comply with this order and were returning with all despatch to Alexandria. This was sent off at 1700 but, at 1723, second thoughts were had and the C-in-C was informed that *Hurworth*, the least affected, had been sent back to help the *Zulu* force.

Further aid was also in hand: Lieutenant H. A. Stuart-Menteth aboard the destroyer *Aldenham* was sailed from Alexandria in company with *Belvoir* and the tug *Brigand* while 252 Wing RAF was requested to provide further air cover until dark. The codeword assigned to this was 'Anger', no doubt reflecting Harwood's mood as the continuous stream of signals listing one disaster after another reached him throughout the day!

No progress had been made to get *Zulu* underway at 1749 and twenty minutes later *Croome* would not steer other than to the south-east, enemy-occupied territory. *Croome* and *Hursley* exchanged signals throughout the late afternoon as the struggle continued. The damaged destroyer had two degrees of port rudder on her and she could not be got out of it and the towing speed, only four knots, was further hindered by her constant yawing. It must be remembered that the 1,870-ton *Zulu* in normal conditions would have been quite a handful for the 1,400-ton *Hursley* even without the extra weight of shipped water.

At 1901, *Croome* asked *Hursley*, 'What wheel do you want *Zulu* to put on?', to which the reply was, 'Wheel amidships. Follow me.' Soon afterwards, *Hursley* informed her sister ship that she was going to try and tow to starboard and received the response, 'Try and get around to 120 degrees'. Then the Luftwaffe interrupted once more. Between 1915 and 1939, four Junkers Ju88's made two more attacks in pairs and one of these was shot down by accurate fire from *Croome*. Her report stated that these attacks,

'. . . were effectively countered by 4-inch gunfire, and a hail of short-range fire, substantially reinforced by Marines from *Zulu*'s assault party, with Bren guns. At 1930, 4-inch scored a direct hit on a retreating 88 at a range of about 4,000 yards, which was seen to blow up in the air. This plane had undoubtedly been severely damaged previously by short-range weapons.

At this time, two Beaufighters were patrolling at 14,000 feet and two more were at 1,500 feet. They saw two of the Ju88's after their attack and these were driven off into the clouds. This seems an appropriate moment to summarise the efforts of LG1 this day. Their sorties and their targets were as listed below:

CO Hakenbeck:

0813 departed Heraklion, Crete.

1127 arrived Quasaba (they claimed one direct hit and near-misses on several ships).

1403 departed Quasaba. (It was on this flight that the photos of *Coventry* being torpedoed were taken.)

1629 arrived Heraklion.

CO von Bergh:

0930 departed Heraklion.

1132 arrived Quasaba.

1405 departed Quasaba. (They attacked a force consisting of one cruiser and two destroyers, and claimed to have hit the cruiser.)

1605 arrived Heraklion.

CO Ilk:

1736 departed Heraklion.

1950 arrived back.

COs Leupert and Schaller:

1735 departed Heraklion. (Searched for British force north of Fuka, without success.)

1950 arrived back.

CO Schomann:

(Two machines departed Heraklion late afternoon. Attacked seven MTBs, leaving two burning.)

The Junkers Ju87 Stuka units had an equally busy day.

Proceeding as they were at such a slow speed, the little British flotilla also made a tempting target for any U-boats that might happen to be in the area, as Admiral Harwood appreciated. He informed them that 201 Group was to lay on an anti-submarine air patrol with two Fairey Swordfish biplanes, C5SY from 0001 to 0300/15 and C5SM from 0300 to 0630/15, respectively. This was to prove academic, however. More immediate problems beset the destroyers. *Hursley* informed *Croome* at 1943 that *Zulu* needed to straighten her rudder, 'otherwise I can't steer.' This message was passed on, to which Commander White replied, 'In about five minutes.' By 1949, *Hursley* was able to report that she thought she had her on the move a bit now, to which he got the reply, 'You must steer to the eastward, at all costs.'

Lieutenant Church describes the problems:

> The tow proved an exceptionally difficult one. *Zulu* appeared to be carrying a little port wheel so that she towed crab fashion on the port quarter with the result that she pulled me round to starboard until I was steady on 170 degrees, a most undesirable course in the circumstances. To try and improve matters, I asked *Zulu* to try and steer by hand and let out more cable, which he did. By 2000, by staggering the engines, and by first going to starboard and then to port, I managed to get her round to 100 degrees.

Within a short time they had managed to work up to six knots and by 2031, to nine. Both radar sets aboard *Croome*, the Type 285 and 286, were out of action due to the near-misses and, with night coming on, this was serious. Also, she only had 70 tons of fuel remaining. However, cheering word was received that *Dulverton*, *Beaufort* and *Exmoor*, having refuelled, were also being sailed back to join them under Operation Nation. But it was all in vain. By 2100, the long fight was clearly lost and *Zulu* was rapidly sinking. Lieutenant Church continued:

> My hopes of steering an easterly course were short lived for gradually she came round to port thereby pulling me round to starboard again. In trying to follow, she was using 15 degrees starboard wheel, but to no avail and I can only surmise that she was either being pulled round by the pressure of water going into the hole on the port side, or a plate was projecting out under water and acting as a rudder. By 2100, we were back to 170 degrees, in fact this time she tended to pull me round past south. She refused to come back to port so I tried towing her to starboard in the hopes that she would eventually come right round. I think there would have been a reasonable chance of this but at 2130 *Zulu* ordered me to stop.

Hursley was also instructed to signal *Croome* to stand by to take off the remaining crew but before this could be done the little ship rolled over to starboard and sank. The following signals tell the story:

Croome to *Hursley*: 'Has *Zulu* sunk?'
Hursley to *Croome*: 'Sinking and I can't slip the tow.'
Croome to *Hursley*: 'Can you cut it?'
Hursley to *Croome*: 'Am trying.'
Croome to *C-in-C*: '*Zulu* has sunk in position 32,20. 28.56.'
Croome to *Hursley*: 'Have you got rid of the tow?'
Hursley to *Croome*: 'Yes.'

As the *Hursley*'s commanding officer recalled, it all happened very quickly after such a long struggle:

> I was under the impression that it had been decided to scuttle her in view of her refusal to steer, so I asked for one more attempt but was told to stop immediately, which I did. Much to my astonishment, she rolled over. Great difficulty was experienced in slipping the tow for in trying to knock out the forelock of the slip it got bent and could not be moved. After some anxious moments, the tow was slipped just as she was sinking and the strain was coming on.

All the *Zulu*'s towing party took to the water and Lieutenant Dudley Burnley, an Australian officer, despite his own badly damaged arm, supported another man in the water for twenty minutes and kept him alive. Thankfully, these two, Commander White and the rest of the officers, 180 ratings and 60 Royal Marines, including ten wounded, four seriously who required immediate transfer to hospital, were all safely picked up by *Croome*. *Hursley* got one man aboard, Petty Officer Chillcock, and so did *Hurworth* which had just reappeared on the scene after steaming from Alexandria to assist.

Thus passed *Zulu*, after a gallant fight against ever-lengthening odds. She went down at 2154 in position 32 degrees 15 minutes north, 28 degrees 55 minutes east.

The news was passed to Alexandria, and *Aldenham*, *Belvoir* and *Brigand*, who were steering west at fourteen knots in position 32 degrees, 06 minutes north, 29 degrees 10 minutes east, reversed course. The RAF continued to tend over them. A special installation Beaufighter was despatched and remained over the other ships until 1½ hours after darkness had fallen but it made no contacts.

While these dramatic events were taking place, what remained of the Coastal Forces flotilla were making their own way back to base in two separate groups. In view of the ghastly carnage suffered

Overall view of Tobruk after the British raid.

A view of various sunken and beached vessels in Tobruk's inner harbour, 1942.

General Erwin Rommel (*left*) salutes Hauptmann Rippich, commander of 5./B.B.85 after the raid.

General Rommel shaking hands with the gunners of 5./B.B.85 and awarding decorations for their victory, 15th September 1942.

earlier in the day, it was perhaps fortunate that the bulk of the Luftwaffe's attentions were directed against the destroyers. Even so, the MTB's and Fairmiles did not escape the attentions of the Germans completely, air attacks being made by a minimum of eight Ju88 aircraft each time and were received at 1206 and 1430, when *MTB 266* suffered casualties from a near miss. It was reported that:

> Against bomber attacks, MTB's evasive tactics and heavy armament once again gave them immunity, and near misses at five yards did not affect their speed. MTB's in fact drew a number of bombers which might otherwise have found *Zulu* or Force 'D' and the day's experience confirmed previous and subsequent illustrations of the ability of these small craft, if well handled and kept in formation of 3 or 4, to look after themselves. The blind spot in 77 foot and 70 foot ELCO boats is ahead, Fairmiles are under-armed for Mediterranean conditions, and their slow speed is an added disadvantage.

There was a final air attack made on them at 1820 that evening. Each attack was met with all the fire these little ships could muster and no direct hits were received. Three of the MTB's with the CO aboard arrived at their base HMS *Mosquito*, at 2330 that night.

At 0705, on the following morning, the last of the surviving destroyers arrived at the Arsenal Mole to land survivors and wounded. Thus ended the disastrous naval side of Operation Agreement. Casualties had been heavy in the warships. *Coventry* lost 3 officers and 61 men; *Sikh* 2 officers and 20 men; *Zulu* 4 officers and 34 men; and the light craft between them 8 officers and 41 men.

In reply, the German bomber unit LG1 lost just two Junkers Ju88s, Karl-Heinz Bruns and his crew of three from the 5 Staffel and Alfred-Peter Auer and his three men from the 6 Staffel One of III/StG 3's Stukas was also reported destroyed in this operation.

Churchill was advised of the losses. It has been recorded that the premier, 'for all his admiration of offensive intentions, was gravely concerned.' Typically, he forgot his earlier petulant missives with which he had prodded Harwood into taking some sort of action and turned against him. 'I was not favourably impressed by Admiral Harwood's account of the Tobruk operation', he menacingly grumbled at the First Lord, Alexander, and the First Sea Lord, Dudley Pound. 'We certainly suffered very heavy losses for little or no result.'

Harwood, at the time of the River Plate the premier's blue-eyed boy, was soon to find out that politicians have highly selective memories and that in war they respect nothing but a success in which they could bask themselves with reflected glory. But the Admiral was not long to be disenchanted.

CHAPTER SEVEN

Agreement's Aftermath

All the bright hopes had been dashed. Many of the brave young men who had set off in such confident and determined fashion a few days before now either lay dashed to pieces on the rocky coast, face-up under the harsh desert sun or herded together in a dusty stinking prisoner-of-war camp. All told, British casualties amounted to 300 Royal Marines, 160 Army officers and soldiers and 280 naval officers and ratings. What is even more hard to take, but is almost certain, is that, even had the initial landings been successful instead of failures, the casualty list would have been much higher still, for there is little doubt that *all* the men put ashore would ultimately have been lost in the same manner. Their cause was a hopeless one.

It was the pity and the *waste* of it all that hurt, and still hurts, rather than the failure of the attack itself. Men in the prime of life, trained and fit, ready and able to give their lives if necessary, had just been wasted, by a combination of sloppy preparation, indifferent organisation and downright disgraceful security. The majority of casualties had been borne by the men of the 11th Battalion, Royal Marines. Many had died in heroic fashion facing hopeless odds storming a dug-in enemy. All death is waste, but if in war death has to be a price to be paid, then such a death may be a relatively more desirable one for a warrior. But the bulk of those men did not die thus; they were drowned within a few minutes of leaving the destroyers. They had no time even to glimpse their enemy, use their weapons, even fend for themselves. Jerry-built boats pulled apart and the packed men in them drowned in dozens. It was a bad death, a useless death, a wasted death and to a large part it was self-inflicted through haste, poor craftsmanship and the old British habit of trying to 'muddle-through' instead of doing the job properly. Just about the only lesson to be drawn from Operation Agreement's ghastly statistics was that 'muddling through' just didn't work, but the British were not a nation to take such lessons to heart.

Just one month before all these young men were sent to their pointless deaths at Tobruk, on 19th August, other young men in their prime, equally finely trained and eager to fight, were squandered at Dieppe, another muddle, another defeat, another example of sloppy thinking. It is not certain which was the worse, the attitudes that were bringing about such disasters even after three years of war or the hypocritical public image presented by the Government and the media that tried to turn such colossal blunders into victories. Almost all the same blunders and under-estimation of the enemy were made at Dieppe as were made a month later at Tobruk. Nobody learned anything or, if they did, they did not put it into practice. RAF bombing was said at Dieppe to have alerted the German garrison, yet exactly the same tactic was applied at Tobruk with exactly the same result. General Montgomery, then C-in-C South-Eastern Command, was against Dieppe; he was also against Tobruk. It still went ahead. About Dieppe, Churchill was to say:

It was a costly but not unfruitful reconnaissance in force. Tactically it was a mine of experience. It shed revealing light on many shortcomings in our outlook It taught us to build in good time various new types of craft and appliances for later use. We learnt again the value of powerful support by heavy naval guns in an opposed landing.

Yet none of these valuable lessons we were supposed to have absorbed were utilised in Agreement, indeed quite the opposite in almost every instance. About Agreement itself he said nothing at all.

From their lofty heights the 'Staff' could take the more academic and objective viewpoint. Thus, Rear-Admiral L. E. H. Maund, CBE, could write:

So ended a risky enterprise which might have achieved a great deal but might also have been tackled in an easier though less spectacular way. The lessons it rammed home were mostly familiar ones: the need for security, the importance of good intelligence (and exceptionally good intelligence about matters of vital importance to the success of the operation) and the need of first rate equipment. Perhaps the most important lesson was not so clearly seen as it should have been. The operation was handled throughout by the three Commanders-in-Chief of the Middle East in Alexandria. All three were concerned with a multitude of issues of which the raid was only one. The responsibility for cancelling the operation, should matters of security, information or equipment not be satisfactory, was shared by the three Commanders-in-Chief and by their administrative staffs. No one person was given executive control. When it was over there was no one to take the blame. After all, it is not the business of the highest authority to run battles. No one could ever have suggested that the Commander-in-Chief of the Middle East should conduct the campaign in the desert, yet it was the Commanders-in-Chief who were the joint commanders of the raid on Tobruk.

It should always be for the highest authority to indicate its wishes, and for the appointed commander or commanders of the expedition to prepare the plan and execute it. If the Commander, on examination of the details of the assault, finds it is an impracticable operation, as well it may be, he will soon say so, if only on account of his reputation. Or if he prepares a bad plan the higher authority may sack him and appoint someone else. But the preparation and execution of an operational plan is the concern of an operational commander and it is not the business of strategic planners or administrative authorities. It is strange that mistakes in connection with command and direction have been in connection with combined operations, as 'Command' was the one subject which had been so thoroughly thrashed out between the Staff Colleges during the sixteen years before the war.

Bruce Lockhart stated that the raid on Tobruk 'was one of those amphibious operations which prepared the way for the subsequent landings of the Allied armies in Europe.'

The sacrificial lambs themselves viewed the whole concept somewhat differently from their masters. Reflecting such viewpoints, the historian Connell was refreshingly blunt.

It was an operation, described by the lower-deck, as another senior officers' 'honour and glory, shit or bust' operation. It was another foreseeable failure of a kind that the naval staff seemed unable to resist or refuse.

I know from my own research that this is still how the bulk of the survivors feel about Agreement to this day. And justifiably so. Nor did it prevent similar blunders in the years that followed: Anzio, for example, or the disastrous Aegean operations a year after

Agreement when yet again troops and ships were sent in to islands dominated by the Stukas and were bombed off them with heavy losses. The lessons of Norway and Dunkirk in 1940, of Greece and Crete in 1941 and of Tobruk in 1942 had still not been taken on board in 1943! And here the premier, full of wise words and undisputed wisdom in 1942, was a year later urging his worried C-in-C in Cairo to 'Improvise and Dare'; never mind the careful preparations and suitable weapons and the rest then, and yet another tragedy followed.

The main causes of the failure were hotly debated immediately afterwards and caused vibrations in distant places. In his own summing-up, Admiral Sir Henry Harwood made the claim that:

> From a Naval point of view, the enemy's hold on the North African coast was intolerable. Convoys could not be run to Malta, and our few bases in the Eastern Mediterranean were exposed to short range bomber operations. Great risks were, therefore, justified when undertaking any operation which had a chance of relieving the situation.

This is not really so; the long-range Junkers Ju88 and Heinkel He111 bombers based in Greece and Crete had been there since May 1941, and they had frequently carried out long-range bombing missions against the Suez Canal. But Rommel's advance had not altered the situation with regard to these aircraft. The only short-range bombers available in North Africa were the Ju87 Stukas and similar, and these never made attacks on bases like Alexandria or Haifa, but were used in their normal close-range role.

Harwood made another claim that did not stand up to close scrutiny, stating that:

> Judged by direct results these operations failed to achieve their object, but indirect results are now known to have been considerable. Enemy forces were diverted from the El Alamein position to the coastal sectors, enemy reinforcements intended for Africa were diverted, and the enemy expended much valuable air effort and fuel in precautionary measures generally.

Again, as we have seen, the effects of the attack on the Germans at El Alamein were minimal, and the effects on back area organisation, other than a general tightening up and small reinforcements to select garrisons, were equally minute. Why should they be otherwise when even the immediate strategic reserve battalions, held in the event of such an attack, proved unnecessary to defeat the British attacks in all save one case? The attack was the most the British could do; the Germans and Italians were shown that they had an abundance of superiority in the back areas in the unlikely event that such an attempt be made again.

Harwood was on more certain ground in placing the blame for the actual failures to land the troops, either in the correct place or at all, on the 'failures in the Beach marking arrangments, from numerous causes.'

This indeed had been the key. When *Taku* had signalled the 'All Clear' to Force 'A', it had been before she had attempted to land her folbot and the blow-up punt. She based her estimate on the suitability of the sea conditions on a single run down-swell from the north-west. When it came to lower the canoe it was swept off her upper deck aft by a large wave which carried it forward. Then the folbot was again washed over the side by the high seas and completely wrecked. Such was the state of the water that it took her forty minutes to recover the unfortunate occupants. They tried to launch the blow-up dinghy but while transporting it aft along the submarine's decks it too was washed overboard and the blow-up fitting was torn out by the force of the waves. The captain of the *Taku* attempted to signal these facts to all concerned but it was by then too late and in any case his signals were not properly received by any of the listening stations.

This failure to mark the correct inlet meant that the destroyers sent in the first wave in weather conditions clearly unsuitable for the landing barges themselves, and also at the wrong spot, several miles further down the coast from the correct inlet. Even had more men survived the journey to the beach, then once ashore they would have had twice the distance to cover that they expected and their tight time-table would have immediately fallen down in any case.

A latter appraisal blamed 'The aftermath of the bad weather conditions, which were prevailing two days previously.'

Nor were the signalling arrangements at the southern side of the attack any better. Too much reliance had been placed on too few people. To give the man whose prime responsibility it was to guide in the MTB's another job to do when he already had little time to conduct an accurate marking, was as bad an order by Haselden as was the overall concept of expecting the young skippers of the

MTB's to make such sightings in the face of heavy seas, fierce opposition and pitch-blackness on an unknown shore. Admiral Harwood might complain in his report about these young captains being 'untrained and inexperienced', but even if it were the prime reason for their failure, which it demonstrably was *not*, then this condition was known to Admiral Harwood and his staff long before Agreement was planned or launched! No doubts on their abilities were expressed *prior* to the attack. The fact that some of these young officers had already distinguished themselves in action in the Channel, and others were to earn high decoration and praise for their subsequent MTB operations in the Mediterranean surely makes this excuse seem a pretty lame one.

Back in Whitehall, his report was not studied in any depth until February and lingered on going the rounds there until as late as May 1943, by which time of course the whole thing was pretty academic. This might account for the surprisingly light criticism that 'Their Lordships' gave it. The Director of Gunnery and AA Warfare noted that:

> The complexity of the operation orders and the large numbers of alternative plans to be adopted under varying circumstances is considered to have prejudiced the success of Operation Agreement from the outset.

Indeed, there seem to have been plans and codewords for every conceivable possibility, an enormous mass of documentation, but all of it so entwined and so utterly dependent on many different forces not in direct touch with each other, acting rigidly to a timetable, regardless of what steps the enemy might be taking.

No blame was attached to the RAF fighter patrols for the loss of *Coventry*. 'It appears evident that the Beaufighters did their best under difficult circumstances due to cloud conditions which favoured the enemy'. Improved methods of fighter direction and liaison had already been adopted, it was reported, which superseded the methods used during Agreement. This was certainly true but a satisfactory arrangement was never really achieved; American Spitfire fighter-bombers were bombing British destroyers during the evacuation of Tunisia even as these words were being written and later the Aegean fiasco already mentioned showed that long-range fighter protection from shore bases *never* worked, a lesson which subsequent British Governments shrugged off or ignored completely.

We have already touched on the adverse effects of the bombing attack. The Director of Training noted this also. 'In Operation Chariot – the raid on San Nazaire in March, 1942, an abnormally heavy bombing attack just before the raid was found to have the effect of generally waking up the defences and putting them on the *qui vive*.' He could have cited numerous other examples, the attack on *Scharnhorst* in June, 1940, for example, when Royal Navy Skua dive bombers were massacred by German fighters brought up from their airfields by a 'pre-emptive' RAF strike designed to keep them on the ground.

Another comment was on the very practicality of the plan to retain the destroyers in Tobruk harbour during the hours of daylight.

They were therefore for at least six daylight hours, to remain 270 miles beyond our own front line outside range of even Beaufighter protection and within 25 miles of at least eight enemy aerodromes or landing grounds, depending largely on captured enemy AA guns for their defence. It is considered most doubtful that the methods which the destroyers were instructed to appear as sinking Italians could have fooled the Germans. Moreover the AA guns crews would have been severely hampered in their own defences as a result of these measures.

This didn't sink in either. Almost exactly a year later, on 23rd September 1943, while at anchor off the disputed Aegean island of Leros, the destroyers *Intrepid* and *Queen Olga* were sunk by Junkers Ju88's while carrying out the same suicidal policy of relying on Italian AA gunners to protect them. In the Falklands campaign of 1982, the landing ships *Sir Galahad* and *Sir Tristram* were sent forward with no AA protection, other than Army Rapier close-range missiles which they were themselves to land. This presented the Argentinian pilots with a similar opportunity and resulted in similar losses.

No doubt the same conclusions could be reached for all these examples; the one given for Agreement could be equally applied: 'Desperate causes require desperate remedies.'

This is true and in war such risks must always be taken; if they succeed the results are often highly beneficial and can save lives, when they fail, as they did with Agreement, or partly fail as in history they did at the blocking of Zeebrugge in the Great War, then a grim payment has to be exacted from the men on the spot. The peculiar tragedy of the raid on Tobruk is that, even had the operation succeeded, it was hardly worth the effort or such a risk. Their Lordships concluded:

> The prize to be gained was largely moral. The physical disablement of a port is never very effective for long and it is considered that the risks outweighed the prize.

There is little doubt that the outcome of Agreement ultimately contributed to the fall of Admiral Harwood from grace even if it was not the immediate cause of his going.

Although the First Sea Lord, Admiral Sir Dudley Pound, adopted his usual tactic of stalling a reply until the issue died a natural death, the premier never forgot this débâcle. Montgomery himself developed an intense personal dislike for Harwood, and the fact that Agreement's failure somehow rubbed off on the publicity-conscious general, despite his careful distancing of himself from it, and spoilt the new ever-victorious image he was trying to impart on his new command, may have contributed to this feeling. Harwood himself certainly thought so and said as much to Pound on 12th March 1943. But Pound refuted this in his reply.

Sir Henry Harwood's rise to the top of the Naval tree had been meteoric and his fall was to be equally so. But of his downfall his biographer, Commander Kenneth Edwards, says only:

> In February, 1943, it became necessary to regroup the high command under the Supreme Commander in North Africa. The Naval Command in the central basin of the Mediterranean then passed to Admiral of the Fleet Sir Andrew Cunningham, and Admiral Harwood became Commander-in-Chief, Levant. As such he retained the responsibility of supplying Malta from the east and of supplying the Army as far as Sousse, in Tunisia.
>
> Harwood held this command for only a short time, however, as his health broke down and he was invalided home.

Again not a single, solitary word about Agreement. However, the late Captain S. W. Roskill was more forthcoming about both Harwood's dismissal and the reasons behind it. This he first was in an article in the *Royal United Service Institute Journal* entitled 'Marder, Churchill and the Admiralty 1939 – 42'. In it he claimed that 'the

relief of Admiral Sir Henry Harwood as C-in-C, Mediterranean in
March 1943 was instigated by General Montgomery who worked on
Churchill through General Sir Alan Brooke, and R. G. Casey, the
Resident Minister in the Middle East, when the Prime Minister was
in Cairo.'

It is certainly the case that, in spite of the sacrifices the Navy had
made on this operation, Richard Casey was soon telling Churchill
that 'the Navy had not done enough during the advance of the
Eighth Army.'

Roskill concluded after examining all the evidence that
Montgomery, for his own personal reasons, used the accusation that
the port of Tripoli was not cleared quickly enough, 'as a pretext for
getting rid of an officer from another service – whose position in
the command hierarchy was moreover superior to his own.'

That Harwood's health broke down in the trying circumstances
in which he found his command in the desperate days of 1942 is
hardly surprising; to have to fight a vastly superior enemy fleet and
air force with a steadily dwindling fleet was bad enough, to have a
deputy whose own health was poor to help him was another, and to
have earned the premier's displeasure as well was well-nigh fatal.
But, in addition to these hurdles, to have unwittingly found enemies
in the highest echelons of Middle East Command who were after his
scalp, despite his best efforts with what he had, was the last straw,
especially when his own superiors in London failed to see what was
afoot. He was to die shortly after the war. Fortunately, he had
achieved lasting fame and a more durable monument to his memory
than Agreement and he will always be associated with the burning
wreck of the *Admiral Graf Spee* in Montevideo harbour, Nazi
Germany's first defeat in World War II.

*

While such weighty matters were being discussed and conclusions
drawn behind locked doors in high places, for many of the victims
of the débâcle the agony was only just beginning. Of the many small
parties trapped far behind enemy lines, their own survival was all
that concerned them and the need to reach safety. Sadly, very few
of them ever made it. For others, those few brief hours were but a
prelude for long and tedious months or years of captivity and
despair. These were the majority.

One can imagine the agony of spirit of David Lloyd Owen at
having to pull his LRDG patrols out and leave the others to their

fate, but there is no doubt he took a correct and courageous step in so doing. They could have done nothing to save the disaster and would have only joined the rest dead or 'in the bag' had they attempted otherwise. He decided to pull back to Sidi Rezegh and set up his wireless and contact someone in order to ascertain the true position but repeated attempts throughout the day were without success. It was not until much later in the day, from still further south, that they discovered the full extent of the disaster.

Jim Patch gave me a very moving account of those terrible hours and decisions when the patrol found themselves alone in the midst of the enemy hosts knowing that all their companions were either dead or captured.

We kept going all day, stopping or deviating whenever aircraft were seen or heard. We stopped after dark by a lone hill. When I made my cross on the map after plotting my dead reckoning I found it was adjacent to a trig point. There were not too many of these on the Italian maps but they could be relied upon, having been fixed and plotted by competent surveyors. I, like everyone else, was very tired and I asked David Lloyd Owen whether, if I could find the trig point on top of the lone hill, I could be excused from taking a star shot just for that once. I climbed the hill and, on top, found the trig point. I have always considered that day's dead reckoning to be the peak of my navigating career.

The next day we arrived back at Hatiet Etla and laid up there awaiting further orders. Soon we were ordered to Landing Ground 125 to pick up survivors from the Barce raid. Arriving there at dusk, we could see nothing and settled down to prepare an evening meal. Then a shadowy figure was seen moving about beyond our laager. It was Jack Davis, the New Zealand navigator who had stayed with Doc Lawson and the party of wounded men in the hope that he might be able to guide them, somehow, back to Kufra. The forlorn party were camped about a mile away from where we had stopped, the wounded men lying under a tarpaulin supported by 40 gallon drums.

No time was lost in calling up airborne help. It came next day in the form of a Bombay bomber. It had flown 450 miles from Kufra straight to LG125. As Bill Kennedy Shaw says in his book, it was like finding a cricket field in Inverness-shire from Croydon, with one check, if visibility was good, on the way. The pilot was Bill Coles of 216 Squadron. . . .

You have to remember [Jim concludes] in all this that, although navigating, I was only a private soldier and had nothing to do with the decision making which had to take place in the course of the operation. I am also aware that my account of events after we left Tobruk are at variance with what David Lloyd Owen has written in his books. I am sure we went more than 20 miles south of Sidi Rezegh, which is what he says. It is one of my most vivid memories that I climbed the hill as I describe in the dark looking for that trig point and it was after a long day's drive.

Only six of Haselden's party ever got out of that trap. One of them was Lieutenant D. Russell whose account was one of the first to reach the outside world and gives some indication of what had taken place. It is representative of many others. 'We left him with Lieutenant Barlow of the Light AA detachment and Lieutenant Langton of the SBS and eight other ranks after the main party had split in two.' Russell recounts that after that his party walked in a south-easterly direction and then lay up in a small wadi during the daylight hours to avoid detection. That night, having decided their party was still too large, they had divided the food and water and had then drawn lots and each officer set off with two or three soldiers to make their best attempts to get away. Russell's companions were Privates Opprower and Watler.

I then started the parties at ten minute intervals. My party left first, the second proceeded five degrees south of me and the third one five degrees south of that. I managed to get my party as far as the Bardia area by walking at night and laying up by day. We arrived just before dawn on the day of D + 7. We were handicapped by the inadequate food and water which the commandos had with them. For the walk to Bardia we started with one and a half bottles of water and enough for one small meal a day for two days. We found a quarter of a tin of jam and some water by Gambut aerodrome. On D + 7 we were fed by an Arab in the Marsa Lukk area and that night set out to look for the bay where we had been told a MTB would come in on D + 8 to pick up stragglers.

Unknown to Russell and other like-minded survivors, this plan had been scrapped. It was thought that the enemy had got wind

of the whole operation and would have set an ambush for the MTB
so none was ever sent out from Alexandria. A cruel decision but no
doubt the right one. It was at this time also that Russell first learnt
from Opprower that he had seen Colonel Haselden killed.

We searched the whole coast and at dawn ran into Italian
coastguards, who fired on us. We ran as fast as we could . . .
Private Watler . . . had proved himself to be extremely plucky,
as he suffered from a bad cough and had almost suffocated
himself in his efforts to control it when we were within hearing
distance of the enemy. As soon as I noticed Watler was not with
us I made Opprower sit down and ran back to where I had last
seen Watler. I made a circular cast and called him, but could find
no trace of him. He was very deaf and when I had previously
asked him about this he told me his deafness was permanent as
he had previously worked in a riveter's yard.

It now being almost light I made off with Opprower to find a
wadi to lay up in that day. The next night we reconnoitred that
area and then moved southwards to the part of the coast which
we had not reconnoitred the night before, in an attempt to find
Watler and possibly the MTB. Shortly after dawn, on finding
neither, I made for the Tobruk – Bardia road and lay up for two
or three days in a wadi with Private Opprower. Each night we
reconnoitred the Tobruk – Bardia road trying to find a truck
which we could snatch in order to drive back. On the third
morning we met an Arab shepherd who gave us some bread and
showed us a pool of water. I asked him if it was possible to walk
to Alamein but he said that there was no water, so I decided to
walk to the Jebel and contact our agents there.

They set out but on the morning of the second day Private
Opprower was taken ill and could go no further.

At this point we were about ten miles south of the Bardia road.
He said he would walk there next morning and stop the first
enemy truck he saw. I left him one water bottle and a piece of the
Arab bread we had. I walked westwards and when unable to go
any further was fortunate enough to meet Senussi (tribesmen),
who looked after me.

Having lost my compass when falling down a wadi in the
perimeter of Tobruk, I went off my course one starless night and

found myself at Gazala at daybreak one morning, but the Italians took no notice of me and I walked through two battalions who were doing some form of battle drill. I was forced to leave my hosts about the end of October and as I was not able to walk very far, I stopped just west of Mechili, with an Arab who happened to be in British employ. On 18th November, I sent out Arabs to look for armoured cars which I had seen the day before and was picked up by 4/6 SAAC, who took me to Benghazi.

His erstwhile companion, Tommy Langton, had a similar tale to tell when he eventually stumbled back into Allied lines. After the splitting of the small party into three he had led his own men out and made for the perimeter.

Later in the night – after avoiding two enemy posts, I joined up again with Lieutenant Barlow's party. Soon after we met, we bumped into another enemy post and had to take hurriedly to the nearest wadi. When we regathered, Lieutenant Barlow was nowhere to be found, and I have not seen or heard of him since. After 'bumping' several more posts we eventually got through the perimeter wire and lay up next day in a cave in a wadi. My party now consisted of Sergeant Evans of the Welsh Guards; Corporal Wilson and Fusiliers Macdonald and A. and G. Leslie of the Royal Northumberland Fusiliers and Private Hillman of the SIG. The last-named had no boot to one foot and a very lacerated heel as well. He also had the added burden of knowing he would be shot if caught. He changed his name there and then to Kennedy and he was known thus until we were safe.

We had two nights of dodging camps, etc, during part of which we walked on the road. On the fifth night, just as we were desperate for food and water we found the first Arab village where we were taken in, fed and given water. Private Hillman acted as interpreter. The Arabs knew all about the Tobruk raid. They also said they could not understand how the English managed to come all the way from Kufra.

Going from village to village, we eventually reached the Wadi Am Reisa. There was a large Carbineri post at the shore end of this Wadi, the strength of which had recently been doubled, according to the Arabs. They also told us of boats cruising up and down at night – they said they thought they were British. One had landed a party one night and someone had shouted 'Any British here?'

The Arabs then showed us to the Wadi Kattara about five miles north of Bardia. Here we found an Indian soldier of the 3/18th Garwhal Rifles, who had escaped three times from Tobruk and had been living there for two months. We also found Private Watler.

We lived in the Wadi Kattara for four weeks being fed by the Arabs as best they could. We tried making fires by night to attract the attention of aircraft, but only got a stick of bombs extremely close. The only news or information we got was obtained from Italian or German soldiers via the Arabs who sold eggs, etc, on the road and engaged the soldiers in conversation. It was apparent that the enemy was very low in morale and very short of food. We had to take great care not to get caught because the Italians would undoubtedly have 'wiped out' the village. As it was, we saw no one during our four weeks there.

After three weeks Sergeant Evans unfortunately got dysentery, and later we had to help him to the road by night and leave him to be picked up next morning. The same happened a few days later to one of the Leslie twins and his brother went with him. The rains had come down heavily and it was very cold and damp. I decided to move. The Indian stayed behind, and so the party consisted of Corporal Wilson, Private Watler, Private Hillman and myself. I was lucky to have a German compass and a small German map, though the latter was not much use, being 1:5,000,000. We had some tins of bully-beef, some goat meat and bread and ten water-bottles. We started on October 26th.

Apart from getting fired on on the second night, our journey was uneventful. We did not see anyone from the day after we climbed through the frontier wire until we were picked up at Himeimat on Friday, November 13th, with the exception of one convoy which looked very like an SAS patrol, near the Siwa – Mersa Matruh track on November 5th. We walked south of the Qattara depression for the last four days and thereby missed the German retreat.

This is how it was for the few. What was it like for the many, for the Royal Marines that survived the fighting on the beaches, for the seamen who struggled ashore from the sunken *Sikh*, for the soldiers forced to raise their hands after desperate resistance? Here are a few answers.

Royal Marine Con Mahoney was in one of the power landing craft that tried to make a run for it.

While *Zulu* was trying to take *Sikh* in tow, we 'paddled' around them like youngsters on Highgate pond ready to pick up survivors from the latter when she was finally abandoned. Soon it was daylight and air activity so our plan was to make a landing to the east of Tobruk with El Alamein our ultimate haven if there were no other alternatives. But enemy coastal patrols were under way and they were soon seen approaching us from the east while enemy aircraft swooped overhead to guide them to us. No Allied aircraft were to be seen of course and soon a vessel came alongside and we were all ordered aboard and then below their deck. Within an hour or so we were taken into Tobruk harbour itself. The wounded from *Sikh* were already there when we finally arrived. After a night's rest we suffered interrogation and were then taken in lorries to Derna for a flight to southern Italy. Fighters from Malta made our Savoia bomber pilot jumpy and we took cover by flying almost at sea level for one part of the journey. Finally we reached Bari POW camp where Captain Micklethwaite became Senior British Officer and I his Adjutant for six months before going to our permanent camps.

Photographer Earl Graham's experiences were typical of the officers.

After giving us something to eat and drink, the Germans loaded the officers into trucks and took us to Derna. Here we spent the night, and the next day we were flown to Bari in southern Italy. We spent the winter there; it was very cold and having only tropical clothing we all felt it keenly. Cigarettes were in short supply and it was then that I saw a rather uncommon sight: a naval captain and a lieutenant-colonel of the Marines scrambling on the floor after a lecture in one of the huts looking for fag-ends. Early in 1943 we were transferred to northern Italy, first to a castle at Retzinello in the foothills of the Apennines, and then to a newly-built unused orphanage in a small town called Fontelalato, near Parma. We all got out at the Italian armistice and split up into small parties. Most of us headed for the mountains and tried to make our way south to join the Allies. I and two others kept going for about six weeks and then unfortunately we ran into a German convoy in a narrow pass north-east of Florence. I spent the remainder of the war in Germany, ending up in a camp just outside Brunswick. The last months were very hard but at last on 14th April 1945 we were released by the Americans. A few days later we were brought home; so it happened that on VE Day I found myself somewhere I would have never expected to be – Piccadilly Circus!

For the ratings that survived the sinking of *Sikh*, it was much the same. Tug Wilson recalls that they were eventually shipped out to Taranto.

There we went into two camps, firstly a temporary camp composed of just tents, Campo 70, then to a second, permanent one, Campo 51 at Brindisi. And there we stayed until repatriation came up. The first we knew of this scheme were rumours flying about, as they always will. The Red Cross people kept coming round taking our names and details, but nobody could tell us what was happening. Then, all of a sudden, they cleared everyone into the compound one day and we were told we were going back to the UK.

They gave no reasons at all, of course, not at the time. We did eventually find out the reasons but I cannot recall when we were finally told. It appears that the Shah of Iran had about one thousand Italian seamen interned in his country; their ships were interned there from time to time when they called in, but by 1942 Iran was in a bad way and he couldn't afford to feed them any more, or keep them and they were an embarrassment to him. So he apparently appealed to the Red Cross to see if some sort of exchange could take place. I suppose it must have gone on for weeks and weeks and in the end they estimated that about 700 of us, from various ships, submarines, pilots, etc, in Italy would make a fair exchange if we did not participate in the war any more. Turkey acted as the neutral country where the actual exchange took place; I think it was at the port of Merzin. Our liner came in and anchored one side of the bay and we came from Italy on an Italian hospital ship. Then, at a given sign from the Red Cross the transfer of prisoners from one ship to the other began.

After that we stayed about three weeks in Egypt, then came home on the *Ile de France*. This was a ghastly ship, the food was terrible and aboard her there were all sorts of weird women, WRNS who had got pregnant, Polish evacuees, all manner of strange women. They were eager for male company and we had to have shipboard patrols in an attempt to stop temptation, both sides were queuing up for it! Anyway, we had to have patrols for the whole journey. We sailed to Cape Town, then across the South Atlantic to Rio de Janeiro, then back again to Freetown and from Freetown, finally, all the way back up to Greenock; the whole nightmare journey took about seven weeks. From Greenock in Scotland they then had to tranship us all the way back down to Chatham barracks and then we had leave. We could not fight and I spent the rest of the war as a fireman at Coventry Ordnance Depot.

Able Seaman Collins from the same ship actually got back into the fight, and somewhat sooner than expected. After being given First Aid treatment by the Germans, he and the other wounded were handed over to the tender mercies of the Italians who took them away in lorries, Collins being taken to a tent hospital. He described this as 'disgustingly dirty' and the Italians staffing it as 'completely negligent regarding the prisoners'. He did not even get his wounds dressed for more than 36 hours after his arrival and although he only had light wounds so was not much concerned for himself, he stated that many of the more seriously hurt sailors died at this time, in his opinion, 'entirely due to lack of any reasonable attention'. He stayed here for two days and then was moved to Derna where he met Lieutenant Sharp of the *Sikh*. 'Conditions here were equally bad and Lieutenant Sharp spent his time in making tremendous rows about it and was threatened with being placed in a concentration camp if he did not desist.' Happily, Lieutenant Sharp survived to become Rear Admiral P. G. Sharp, CB, DSC, now retired from the Royal Navy and living at Hove in Sussex. Indeed, his stand produced results for soon afterward there was a visit from an important official and thereafter conditions improved, if only slightly.

After a few weeks here, Collins was moved on again this time to a transit camp where he remained for about a week. There were only three other inmates at this time and he had to wait until the camp filled up before a lorry load of fifty prisoners was taken to a prison camp in Benghazi where about 6,000 British POW's were herded in a pen. Ten yards way was a second pen with about 5,000 white South Africans, the former garrison of Tobruk when it had fallen in June. 'There was a lot of ill feeling between the South Africans and the British as the latter considered that the South Africans had "sold the pass" at Tobruk.'

Collins was ten days in this camp and recorded they 'had much joy in watching the RAF raids on the harbour and had a front seat view of ships burning and blowing up'. When a particularly good fire or explosion was started, the prisoners used to cheer and the Italian sentries then fired over their heads. While there, Collins witnessed a prisoner being shot when three men tried an escape. 'Two got away but a third apparently lost his head and tried to get back through the wire. The sentry shot him in four places and finally bayoneted him through the stomach and his body was left where it lay for 48 hours.' The black South Africans were used as labourers in the docks but not the whites. When asked why, Collins stated:

Oh no, all the British prisoners were much too weak from starvation and dysentery to do anything of that sort, and most of them could hardly walk.

He was then taken to Tripoli by lorry in a journey which took four days. Here the prison camp was largely run by a South African Captain, 'who was well in with the Italians and got plenty to eat himself but did little to help the British. In fact he seemed to be much more pro-Italian than pro-British. Captain Gilbert, RAMC, however, did good work.' The food here was lightly better and they got one hot meal per day which consisted of beans and rice. There were only about 1,000 men in this camp.

Then, at very short notice, they were all told to embark aboard the freighter *Scillian* but only 830 of them could be crammed aboard her, the rest being sent back to the camp. Those on board were all in her upper hold standing without any room to sit and the hatches were battened down leaving but a small strip. The latrines were on the upper deck and only five men at a time were allowed up. Collins bribed an Italian cook with his ring to let him stay in the ship's galley rather than go below there again, and it was fortunate for him that he did so for on the second night out of Tripoli the British submarine *Sahib* first shelled and then torpedoed her. Collins was not sure of how he got into the water 'but thinks he did an assisted dive, the ship lifting under him to the force of the explosion as he took off.' By the time he had come to the surface and pulled himself together the ship had practically disappeared. He knew of only one man – another British sailor – who by a superhuman effort got himself out of the hold but he did not believe that anyone else could have possibly survived. He could see no more than 100 men in the water after the ship went down. The two British sailors were eventually picked up by a British ship.

Surviving such ghastly experiences on top of Agreement, men such as Able Seaman Collins are as deserving of praise as any 'Boys Own Paper' heroes of famous victories. And, of course, we must remember the ordeals of those aboard the *Zulu* and *Coventry* when they went down; their tales could be harrowing ones also, as the cruiser's chaplain, Donald L. Peyton Jones, DSC, recalled to me. When his ship was crippled he estimated that:

All below must have been killed by bombs, flames and water rushing in. 'Abandon ship' was exercised without rush or panic as the hull was still afloat though now a stationary target billowing smoke.

We helped our wounded on to life rafts and float nets (for twenty years afterward I had the HMS *Coventry* lifebuoy I placed around a young seaman which he later returned to me and I later presented it to the city of Coventry Sea Cadet HQ).

The sun was out and the sea was warm, our survivors were everywhere but tried to keep together. Nightmares for several weeks remembering the sad sight of non-swimmers, too frightened to jump. (We taught all our youngsters to swim but if you were a senior rating you didn't have to admit you couldn't.)

How lucky to be picked up (after what seemed like hours) by several destroyers diverted to rescue our ships' companies. A healthy feeling to lose everything you possess (no need to remember where you put your toothbrush!). So shorts and toothbrushes issued on landing, a good meal and a long sleep.

For young Midshipman Geoffrey David, too, a harsh introduction to the war at sea.

Looking across the water, I saw one of the Hunts, *Dulverton* as I later discovered, only a few hundred yards away on the starboard beam, and steering towards us, so I resolved to make for her. I stepped across to the guard rail, blew up my lifebelt, took off my shoes, and – still wearing my tin hat – jumped over the side. The water was a bit choppy, but not so cold as I had expected, and supported by my lifebelt I made reasonable progress. About halfway across to *Dulverton*, I was hailed by some men pushing a Carley Float with wounded aboard, to come and give them a hand. So I swam over to them and joined in the pushing party. In this way we reached the side of *Dulverton* in about 15 minutes or so, and after waiting in the water while the wounded men in the Carley Float were hoisted aboard, I then climbed up the scrambling net to safety. Somebody in *Dulverton*'s company took my name and rank, and then directed me down to the wardroom. There I stayed until we got back to Alex some time that evening. I think I spent most of the time sleeping, or attempting to sleep, so I saw nothing of the attempts to sink *Coventry* by gunfire nor her final sinking by *Zulu*, nor of *Zulu*'s final destruction by air attack. For me Operation Agreement was over.

And so now it was for all of them.

*

To the victor – the Spoils! If Operation Agreement was, in the words of Jim Patch, 'a most inglorious episode', as far as the British were concerned, then to the Italians, to whom such victories were so rare as to be treasured novelties, it was heady stuff. Indeed, it was the very stuff from which legends were made and, as we have seen, have been. The repulse of the sea-borne landings by the Italians' Coastal Defence gunners and the makeshift army of cooks and clerks, the gallantry of the San Marco Marines, the false claim of the destruction of the *Zulu*, all have been mixed up into a cocktail of fact, fantasy and fiction and served to the world as a great Italian victory, like similar claims made in connection with Operation Pedestal the month before. And, like that Malta Convoy battle, enough 'neutral' historians have swallowed it hook, line and sinker to ensure the endurance of the legend for ever.

That it *was* an Axis victory is clearly beyond dispute; that it was more a German than an Italian victory, is debatable; but that it was a *great* victory is hardly credible. The British almost defeated themselves with the numerous errors we have already enumerated, and all the courage and fighting ability of their young men was not enough to nullify those mistakes. Equally, there is no doubt the German and Italian defenders reacted with both speed and bravery. Certainly then the Axis were right to celebrate; after all, as far as North Africa was concerned, apart from the bloody nose they were to give the Americans in Tunisia, it was to be the last time they were to have the opportunity of claiming *any* sort of victory on that continent.

That the landing was *not* expected has received several
confirmations. Nigel West wrote that he had no relevant
information about a possible British leakage at the time and did not
recall hearing of any subsequent British security investigation.
'However, our own signals security in the desert was appallingly
lax, and this may have alerted the Afrika Korps B-Dienst.'

But a member of that organisation who was actually on the spot
firmly squashes all such speculations. Hans-Otto Behrendt told me
that:

> After the loss of our own Intercept Company 621 on 10th July
> 1942, with all their documents which alarmed the British side as
> they learned to their horror how much we knew – I exclude the
> possibility of any code-cracking on our side. You had learned a
> lot more about security! To my belief the fact that your fleet was
> not attacked *before* the raid took place instead of on its return is
> the best proof there is for us not having been warned beforehand.

Rommel's diary recorded events as he saw them:

> In the early hours of the 14th September, after relay bombing
> attacks by a hundred and eight aircraft on the port and
> surroundings of Tobruk, the British attempted to land strong
> forces in the fortress area. According to documents which fell into
> our hands, their mission was to destroy the dock installations and
> sink the ships in the harbour.
>
> The AA batteries on the peninsula immediately opened a
> furious fire on the British. German and Italian assault groups
> which were quickly formed up succeeded in enveloping the
> landed enemy troops. Fearing that the British were planning to
> capture Tobruk, we immediately set a number of motorised units
> in march for the fortress. But the local forces soon succeeded in
> restoring the situation. The British suffered considerable losses in
> killed and prisoners, and – according to reports from the AA
> batteries – three destroyers and three landing or escort vessels
> were sunk. Next day our Air Force caught the British again and
> reported the sinking of one cruiser, one more destroyer and
> several small war vessels. A number of British ships were
> damaged by bombs.
>
> On the 15th September I flew over to Tobruk myself and
> expressed my appreciation to the troops of the well-conducted

defensive action they had fought. The reports of the British attack had actually caused us no little alarm, for Tobruk was one of our most vulnerable points.*

Apart from the glow of satisfaction of a job well done, and the securing of their lines of communication at a critical time, the Axis forces had gained one more item from the abortive raid. If their Intelligence had failed to capitalise on the loose talk in Egypt before the attack, they had superb chance to gain substantially after it. For not only did they obtain full and complete copies of the whole Operational orders for Agreement, but, when some time later their divers went down to the sunken wreck of the destroyer *Sikh* in the shallow waters off Tobruk, they found an even more important find, nothing less than the Royal Navy's Top Secret codebooks!

These were in the hands of the cryptographic experts of the famed B-Dienst by 29th October and they called the code 'Munich Blue'. By as early as 1015 the next day, the brilliant German code-breaking team under William Tranow had cracked it and were able to plot the current daily locations of all the major warships of the Royal Navy. This was potential dynamite; it was a *coup* which should have given the B-Dienst team, and therefore Germany, an edge in all the subsequent major landing operations during the invasion of French North Africa and later, even Normandy itself, for whenever there were major landings they were always covered by the battleships and aircraft carriers of the Royal Navy. Thus, any new heavy ship concentrations were almost bound to mean a new assault was being readied.

And yet this biggest prize from Agreement never seems to have been grasped by the land-thinking Germans. Tranow himself certainly grasped its potential, reducing work on other systems to concentrate on 'Munich Blue'. Even the introduction of a new variant of the code by the British on 13th December was quickly solved and the movements of most British battleships and aircraft-carriers continued to be logged up until 19th April 1943, when a new code was introduced. B-Dienst were able to break this new code after seven months' effort and thereafter continued logging all heavy ship movements in the British fleet. Many Germans seemed unable to grasp its usefulness, 'in a war without any major fleet actions.' Well, of course, there *were* in truth many fleet actions, but the main point is that the big ships went where the main battles, land and sea,

* Quoted in *With Rommel in the Desert* by Heinz W. Schmidt.

were expected to be fought, and they went in advance of those battles. A clever reading of their dispositions should therefore have enabled the Germans to predict each major landing.

Perhaps the lack of exploitation of this windfall was to prove a much greater defeat for the German nation in the long term than the brief, bloody and tragic setback the British suffered at Tobruk on 14th September 1942.

Codenames

AGENT	Fighter protection code for Force 'D'
AGREEMENT	Attack on Tobruk
ARCTIC	Destroyers can enter harbour
BIGAMY	Attack on Benghazi
BUNGHOLE	Alternate plan 'Z'
BUTTON	Guns at Lighthouse Point not captured
CABBAGE	Guns at Lighthouse Point captured
CANNON	Fighter protection code for Force 'C'
CIGAR	Have reached R/V (Oil Tanks at west end of Tobruk harbour)
COASTGUARD	Demonstration at Siwa
COFFEE	GHQ
CONSTANT	Normal withdrawal plan 'W'
CUPBOARD	Force 'A'
EYEGLASS	Harbour area under control
GEORGE ROBEY	Password for forces ashore at Tobruk
GINGER	Withdrawal begins at . . .
HELMET	Have Reached . . .
HIGHLIFE	Agreement on, Bigamy off
HOOPOE	Occupation of Siwa
HOUSEBOAT	LRDG patrols to release POWs now
INDEX	AA guns along North Shore of harbour captured
INKPOT	LRDG patrols proceed to R/V at Axis Monument
JACKDAW	Held up at . . .
JUSTICE	Alternate plan 'X'
MELON	D22 (*Sikh*)
MOTOR	Force 'C'
MUSIC	Alternate plan 'Y'
NICETY	Occupation of Gialo Oasis
NIGGER	CD guns at Mersa Sciusc captured, MTBs can enter bay

PICTURE	Force 'B'
RABBIT	Forces 'B' and 'C' come under command of Force 'A'
RIBBON	C-in-C Med. (Control)
RIVAL	Spare Fighter protection code
SENTIMENT	Agreement, Bigamy and Nicety cancelled
SHOVEL	CP Mersa Sciusc
STAPLE	SO MTBs
TABLE	Fighter protection code for Force 'A'
WAYLAY	Original code for Agreement
WINDOW	Unable capture guns at Mersa Sciusc
WOODBINE	Enemy approaching Tobruk

Abbreviations

AA	Anti-Aircraft
AFV	Armoured Fighting Vehicle
AOC	Air Officer Commanding
AOK	Army High Command
ASH	Argyll and Sutherland Highlanders
C-in-C	Commander-in-Chief
CD	Coastal Defence
CO	Commanding Officer
COS	Chiefs of Staff
CTC	Combined Training Centre
CC RR.	*Carabiniera Riservare*
cm	centimetre
Coy	Company
Cwt	Hundredweight
(D)	Senior Officer, Destroyers
DCO	Director Control Officer
DDMI	Deputy Director Military Intelligence
DMO	Director of Military Operations
DSC	Distinguished Service Cross
DSO	Distinguished Service Order
D1, D2, etc	Day One, Day Two
F-lighter	Self-propelled barge
FDO	Fighter Direction Officer
GHQ	General Headquarters
HA	High Altitude
HAA	Heavy Anti-Aircraft
HE	High Explosive
HF	High Frequency
HMS	His Majesty's Ship
HO	Hostilities Only
ID	Identification
IFF	Identification Friend or Foe
JPS	Joint Planning Staff

Ju	Junkers
LA	Low Angle
LAA	Light Anti-aircraft
LRDG	Long Range Desert Group
LG	Lehgeschwader
MEF	Middle East Forces
ML	Motor Launch
mm	millimetre
MNBDO	Mobile Naval Base Defence Organisation
MO	Medical Officer
MT	Motor Transport
MTB	Motor Torpedo Boat
Me	Messerschmitt
Mg	Machine Gun
NCO	Non Commissioned Officer
OCTU	Operational Commands Training Unit
pdr	pounder
POW	Prisoner of War
PRU	Photo Reconnaissance Unit
RA	Royal Artillery
RAF	Royal Air Force
RAMC	Royal Army Medical Corps
RASC	Royal Army Service Corps
RCO	Range Control Officer
RCS	Royal Corps of Signals
RDF	Radio Direction Finding (Radar)
RE	Royal Engineers
RM	Royal Marines
RN	Royal Navy
RNF	Royal Northumberland Fusiliers
RNR	Royal Naval Reserve
RNVR	Royal Naval Volunteer Reserve
RSM	Regimental Sergeant Major
RT	Radio Telephone
SAAC	South African Army Corps
SAP	Semi-Armour Piercing
SAS	Special Air Service
SBS	Special Boat Squadron
SDF	Sudanese Defence Force
SIG	Special Intelligence Group
SS	Special Services

StG	*Stukagruppen*
TOO	Time of Origin
T/G	Telegraph
Trop	Tropicalised
VHF	Very High Frequency
WSW	West-South-West
W/T	Wireless Telegaphy

Bibliography

(This reference includes only relevant books which are generally
available to the public)

Bragadin, Marc, *The Italian Navy in World War II* (United States
Naval Institute Press).

Cacchia-Dominioni, Paolo, *Alamein 1933 – 1962* (Jonathan Cape,
London).

Churchill, Winston S., *The Second World War* (Cassell, London).

Cocchia, Admiral Aldo, *Submarines Attacking* (Kimber, London).

Connell, G. G., *Jack's War* (Kimber, London).

Cowles, Virginia, *The Phantom Major* (Cassell, London).

Cunningham of Hyndhope, Viscount, *A Sailor's Odyssey*
(Hutchinson, London).

Davies, John, *Lower Deck* (Fiction) (Macmillan, London).

Edwards, Commander Kenneth, *Men of Action* (Hutchinson,
London).

Kahn, David, *Hitler's Spies* (Hodder & Stoughton, London).

Kennedy Shaw, W. B., *Long Range Desert Group* (Collins, London).

Ladd, James, *Commandos and Rangers of World War II* (Macdonald,
London).

Lansborough, Gordon, *Tobruk Commando* (Cassell, London).

Lloyd Owen, David, *Providence Their Guide* (Cassell, London).

Lloyd Owen, David, *The Desert My Dwelling Place* (Cassell, London).

Lockhart, Sir Robert Bruce, *The Marines Were There* (Putnam,
London).

Maclean, Fitzroy, *Eastern Approaches* (Cape, London).

Maund, Rear-Admiral L. E. H., *Assault From the Sea* (Cassell,
London).

Peniakoff, Vladimir, *Popski's Private Army* (Cape, London).

Pope, Dudley, *Flag 4* (Kimber, London).

Roskill, Stephen W., *Churchill and the Admirals* (Collins, London).

Roskill, Captain S. W., *The War at Sea* (Vol. 1) (HMSO, London).

Saunders, Hilary St. George, *The Green Beret* (Michael Joseph,
London).

Schmidt, Heinz W., *With Rommel in the Desert* (Arms & Armour Press, London).

Sims, George, *H.M.S. Coventry* (Privately Published).

West, Nigel, *Unreliable Witness* (Weidenfeld & Nicolson, London).

Index